D0922785

SLEEP

SLEEP

BY

GAY GAER LUCE

AND

JULIUS SEGAL

COWARD-McCANN, INC.
NEW YORK

Copyright © 1966 by
Gay Gaer Luce and Julius Segal

All rights reserved. This book, or parts thereof, may not be reproduced in any form without permission in writing from the Publisher. Published on the same day in the Dominion of Canada by Longmans Canada Limited, Toronto.

Library of Congress Catalog
Card Number: 66-13124

Third Impression

PRINTED IN THE UNITED STATES OF AMERICA

To the scientists whose work is the backbone of this book, and to the many others who enriched it with their generous personal and professional contributions.

Contents

PREFACE

PRESUMABLY a book has a definite point of origin, and this one might be traced back to an article I wrote for the Philadelphia *Bulletin* in 1960. In candor I must confess it was a case of growing affection for the subject matter, owing to fortuitous and prolonged contact—for in 1960 I was quite unaware of the scope and importance of sleep research. A small circle of scientists and clinicians of disparate background had already formed an unlikely brotherhood, the Association for the Psychophysiological Study of Sleep. They met annually to exchange research results and ideas with a forthright vigor rarely possible in gigantic professional meetings. The very existence of APSS symbolized a convergence of disciplines and headlong progress in this area, but the association was inconspicuous in the yearly roster of conferences, almost private, and like most of the public I was unaware of it or its import.

In 1963 I was engaged as a special report writer by the National Institute of Mental Health, the agency through which our government assists scientific explorations and a variety of services and activities designed to improve the mental health of the nation. My task involved visiting laboratories, speaking with scientists, reading and describing their work in nontechnical language, thus helping with the Institute's effort to communicate the substance of its massive programs to the scientific community and the public. I began by visiting a few of the scientists whose work was clearly demarked in the area of sleep. At the time it seemed feasible to cover the major projects within a few months and summarize them in a modest paper. At each laboratory, however, I learned of other studies germane to sleep, some of them studies that might have seemed to fall in unrelated categories such as endocrinology or data processing. The task of summarizing work in sleep continued for almost two years, and the modest review originally intended turned into a sizable monograph that was completed in the spring of 1965.

People were already beginning to appreciate the relevance of this research for life beyond the laboratory. Unrelated segments of the information were finding their way into the popular media and the public began to share in the excitement of the new doors opening in the study of human consciousness. Some of the undercurrents of any live and swiftly moving science could not be conveyed in all of these accounts, among them some of the imaginative and informal backroom speculations and extrapolations that may eventually turn out to be wrong, but which often provide an impetus for fruitful research. The convergence of data about sleep and its real and potential impact upon everyday life seemed to call for integration in a book. I decided to write it, with some trepidation, for it required a compilation of new material, much of which lay outside the domain of the earlier and more technical review.

Such a project could be accomplished within a short time only by collaborative effort. During the summer of 1965, Dr. Julius Segal—on leave from his duties at the Institute—devoted his talents as a clinical psychologist and writer to amassing this new research. He collected some of the more recent data confirming earlier findings, but primarily concentrated his exploration on the implications of sleep in everyday life and the potential importance of the new body of research. He was thus led to probe the meanings of sleep in many settings—gleaning information in baseball dugouts, in the consultation rooms of psychiatrists and marriage counselors, in the frantic offices of newspapermen and government officials, and even, on one sultry summer night, beside the cages of the nocturnal animals in the National Zoological Park.

While I wrote, and occasionally refreshed my notes at nearby sleep laboratories, he sent a continuous flow of information—unexpected observations from scientists returning from Europe or Russia, from doctors, hospitals, or the aftermath of manned space flights. During the course of writing, parts of the book were being reshaped and refined by the scientific community, whose generosity and graciousness would require an entire chapter for adequate acknowledgment. Even while the manuscript was being revised, scientists sent new papers and data that might enrich the story, and suggestions that might give it balance. Scientists and other consultants interviewed by Dr. Segal were advising and helping, indeed, until the day the book went to press.

Many of the hypotheses and implications that thematically bond this book together evolved from informal discussions with scientists, but should not be misinterpreted as representing therefore the view of the very heterogeneous scientific community. With the usual reluctance and regret, the size of this book had to be restricted by excluding quantities of interesting and pertinent information, and by adherence, for better or worse, to a plan that was conceived at its beginning. In a field whose pace has so quickened that information multiplies each month, a totally comprehensive review could become a lifelong venture. There can only be installments of this story, for there is no ending.

GAY GAER LUCE

INTRODUCTION

ALL men sleep. Between the darkness out of which we are born and that in which we end, there is a tide of darkness that ebbs and flows each day of our lives. A third of life is spent in sleep, that profoundly mysterious sovereign to which we irresistibly submit, lying almost immobile for hours, removed from the waking world. It is surprising that men succumb to this daily plunge from consciousness with so little curiosity. During the brief span of life each person tries to find out who he is, taking pride in the acts and thoughts that are peculiarly his own and seeking command over his inner forces. The search for identity is never finished, nor the self-command complete, and at the end of a lifetime a man is still more of a stranger to himself than he thinks. He has led two lives, but has known only one of them. By age seventy he has been almost a total stranger to the twenty years of his sleep.

During the day he acts, observes, experiences, and reflects. But by night, what is happening within his own body and mind? He falls asleep and a curtain drops. Through the looking glass in some mirror image of his being, his unknown identities rise up to stalk the night. They are part of him, but he does not know them. When asleep he cannot consciously pry into his own mental activity. Within sleep lie buried the deeply personal unfathomed secrets of us all. They have more than a personal importance, however. They contain the motive forces of waking action, the riddles of personality. Ultimately the fate of mankind may hang upon the degree to which we solve these riddles and face the realities of human psychology, the extent to which man can understand and control himself. In the larger social view the study of sleep has contributed a new dimension by adding to the self-awareness of each individual and, more important, by shedding light upon the kind of creature that man is.

Whatever any man does he first must do in his mind, whose machinery is the brain. The mind can do only what the brain is equipped to do, and so man must find out what kind of brain he has before he can understand his own behavior. During the last two decades, as scientists have begun to unravel some of the enigmatic natural laws of sleep, they have instigated what is perhaps the most active single approach to the exploration of the brain itself.

The scientists have converged from extremely different backgrounds, sharing information that might once have seemed unrelated. Many were experimental psychologists. Some were men working on problems of fertility, others on anesthesia, drugs, or pain. Among them are mathematicians concerned with computers, scientists trying to foresee problems of man in space. They found themselves in correspondence with neurologists treating epilepsy and psychiatrists attempting to understand and cure the insane, with psychologists who were exploring the incongruous world of dreams, doctors with bed-wetting patients, biochemists, physiologists and the trainers of astronauts. As they converged upon the universe of night they found they were working on related events, fundamental mechanisms involved in mood and memory, in learning and personality, psychosis and sanity, physical illness and health. Sleep, far from being separate from man's waking life, was an integral part of its rhythm and relevant to every aspect of it. The new research into the brain mechanisms regulating sleep and wakefulness brought vital information. For the first time we have begun to gain a glimmer of the astonishing machinery of the mind during periods when it is speaking to itself.

Sleep and wakefulness were once conceived to be the light and dark of human consciousness, but now we have learned that there are many shades in between. Sleep, itself, is not all unconscious, and the forgotten darkness of each night contains intervals of intense inward experience—resembling waking. There are dreams and many kinds of thought. Sleep, indeed, is usually composed of two alternating states, states so utterly different that some scientists have argued they should not both be called sleep. One phase, accompanied by vivid dreaming, is a paradoxical state of deep slumber that is impenetrable to irrelevant distractions at a time of heightened mental responsiveness. It appears in the newborn infant and persists throughout life. Much of the current study has focused upon this phase, for herein may lie fundamental keys to man's nature, to the development of his psyche, his waking insanities. Scientists are puzzled by the purpose of this state. Is sleep merely a vehicle for the recurrent dream state, or is the dream state simply a side product of a rhythmic lightening and deepening of sleep?

There are questions yet more difficult. The most difficult and basic questions are asked innocently by children, ignored as obvious by most adults, and considered with trepidation by scientists. As the animal world plunges into its periods of stillness each day, the courageous and innocent wonder: Why all of this sleep?

Sleep would seem to be one of the most essential needs of higher mammals. A man can survive starvation for over three weeks, but three weeks' loss of sleep will make him act like a psychotic. We still do not understand the mental illness that attends severe sleep loss. Nor, indeed, do we know what lies behind our basic requirement for sleep. We have only begun to track some of the unseen forces that govern the rhythm of our lives, the clocks within our flesh that strike the tempo by which we wake or dream, by which we feel strong or vulnerable, mentally acute or befogged, exhilarated or woebegone. We have only just begun to reckon with a fundamental fact of life—that our experience and behavior are the consequence of natural laws, that our minds are part of the matter we are made of. The importance of that reckoning has come clear in the studies of sleep now gathering momentum in Europe, Russia, Japan, the United States, and many other parts of the world.

In their pursuit of scientific answers the researchers have contributed discoveries of considerable practical importance to us all, particularly to medicine, as a few examples will indicate. Sleep disorders are the precursors of many mental illnesses, often the prelude to acute attacks of depression, and the harbinger of suicide attempts. There are also illnesses such as epilepsy whose nighttime symptoms are revealing something of their nature and origins in the brain. It now seems possible that studies of a person's sleep patterns may help doctors to foresee imminent personality disorders. Studies of drugs and sleep are beginning to clarify the specific effects of different drugs, which will enable us to use them more sensitively than we now do, and with greater caution.

Not all people sleep alike. An individual's personality often seems to be reflected in his sleep patterns, his habits, and behavior during sleep, for sleep is not a temporary death but is punctuated with movements, talking, snoring, smiling, waking. The sleeping person makes subtle discriminations, and may slumber through a thunderstorm yet awaken to a baby's whimper. In future decades studies of sleep may become an enormous asset, for we may learn how some people fall asleep at will and awaken to a mental alarm clock. Each person has an inner timing throughout the day and night. We may learn to sense this rhythm in ourselves and schedule our activities for greater productivity and pleasure. We may also learn to gain control over body functions and feelings and exploit our full powers of concentration. Aided by sleep studies that treat the mind and body as a single entity, man may at last gain command over his mind.

Sleep has generously poured out revelations about man's waking nature, his mysterious capacities, his nightly edge of madness and remarkable daytime talents. Yet many people think sleep is their enemy. Some consider sleep dull. Most of us think that all sleep resembles our own. For every person who finds in sleep a blissful refreshment, there seems to be another who fears its approach as though it were a sea serpent rising to consume him. Some both fear sleep and lapse into panic when they cannot fall asleep. The meanings of sleep are as varied as the human personality, and even when they are denied outright by the conscious person they seep into the habits and rituals of his everyday life.

SLEEP

I

THE MEANINGS OF SLEEP

IN the middle of the last century the great English writer Charles Dickens toured the United States, leaving behind him a trail of bewildered hotelkeepers. Dickens was an odd guest. When he departed the furniture of his room was entirely rearranged. Whenever he moved into a new room the first thing he did was march to the bed, draw out his pocket compass, and shove the bed around until its head was pointing due north. According to a theory of the time, magnetic currents streamed north and south between the poles and the sleeping person was thought to reap innumerable benefits if he allowed these currents to flow in a straight line through his body.

Dickens, with his compass, epitomized the presleep ritualist. Although his ceremony was unusual and supported by a scientific rationale it was no more elaborate than the rituals many of us perform before we can go to sleep. By adulthood these nightly acts seem so inconsequential and so difficult to explain that most people don't consider them rituals at all. Still, in children one can see how strong emotions and symbolic acts, devoid of their realistic meaning, begin to acquire a soothing witchcraft.

An eminent Latin scholar at the University of Pennsylvania recalls a time during his boyhood when he absorbed his family's fundamental religion and his grandmother's patriotic spirit as distilled powers. On vacations in the Sierra Mountains of California he could go to sleep only if he had placed the Bible under his pillow and folded the American flag across the foot of his bed—to protect him from the mountain lions.

Most primitive people and almost all children create rituals and amulets—whether of blankets or stones—whose special and secret meanings help them to fall asleep. Parents are usually unaware of these rituals because they do not watch for them. An observant parent may be surprised to discover even a two- or three-year-old follows an intricate soporific performance. One infant, so observed, carefully wraps four fingers in the sheet, wets it with her mouth, then sticks her thumb in her mouth and continuously rubs the damp mitt over her nose as she sucks. At this point, her eyes begin rolling in the first descent into sleep. Another youngster picks off pieces of fluff from his blanket and rubs them between his palms repeatedly and automatically as his eyes begin to roll. Still another little girl rolls her blanket into a ball and, using it as a pillow, carefully makes a nipple of the satin corner, and after the blanket corner is thoroughly wet shifts and sucks her thumb noisily. These curious and animalistic habits have indeed been observed in puppies, who may similarly lull themselves to sleep by chewing on a blanket or piece of cloth, not randomly, but in a ritualized style.

The roots of our sleep rituals are usually obscure, yet our practices do not stop after childhood. There are people who say they have no problems with sleep and no feelings about it, who nevertheless take a sleeping pill every night. Somewhere, locked away in the brain, sleep must have meaning and inescapable feeling for each man. However we prepare for sleep each night our acts betray attitudes we may never acknowledge, meanings woven of the fabric of our lives that have long slipped away from conscious memory. Sleep, the ultimate privacy, is overlaid with intense emotional connotations.

The very environment for sleep, the bedroom and bed, provides the setting for many of life's major personal dramas. Most of humanity is born in bed and there in bed die. Bed is the place of illness, but also of pleasure. To go to bed is to make love. Children play in bed, opening to each other their most guarded confessions in the whisperings after dark. The pillow is the confidante of sobs and is hugged by the irrepressible or the lovesick. Emotions well hidden by day find their release in the bedroom. There discontented husbands and wives are unmasked, and there perform the marital circle of fighting, bitterness, and reconciliation. The bedroom is a chamber of anguish for the insomniac, of surcease for the weary, of night terrors and also glory-filled dreams.

Attitudes toward sleep begin in infancy and almost every adult has watched them form, becoming self-conscious about sleep when a newborn baby enters the household. It is surprising that so small a creature can so thoroughly disrupt the sleep of his parents. At first he will not sleep through the night, taking intermittent naps instead. The young mother, formerly a deep sleeper, now awakens to the slightest cough or whimper. After some harassing weeks the infant finally adapts to the nightlong sleep that his parents consider a necessity. His sleep education has already begun. His family's idiosyncrasies and his own constitution will begin to fashion the habits and feelings he evolves for sleep.

Before he is three years old, sleep may become a major issue in this child's daily life. He may fight the hour of darkness, and even though he is exhausted and cranky, he may invent the most diabolical strategies to postpone bedtime. Yet he may fall asleep informally almost anywhere, on his parents' laps, in buses, cars, on doorsteps, in gardens, at concerts, in church. Children probably do not hate sleep itself but rather what it portends.

Sometimes the fear emanates from within, for dreams are reality to children. As a sympathetic child psychiatrist puts it, "If you went to sleep one night and found a tiger in your bed, would you want to go back?" True, the tiger is not in the bed before sleep, yet the child knows that when he closes his eyes it may return to pounce upon him. A child is inarticulate and cannot explain such dreams, and his feelings toward sleep will be colored by the response of his family and the quality of their own bedtime ritual.

Pediatricians have noticed that there is a new trend in the most recurrent problems of parents with their children. Twenty years ago it was eating. Family meals were often explosive, with forced feedings: cajoling and bribery were employed to get children to eat their meals. Today the problem is sleep, especially among very young children, and bedtime has become the focus of family strife in many homes. This shift probably reflects no profound change in children. Thirty-odd years ago food was a tense issue among millions of American families afflicted by the depression, and even when hunger became a distant memory, and food no daily worry, the residual tensions in parents caused them to force their children to be well fed. Pediatric research instigated the development of palatable baby foods and parental tactics that forestall feeding crises. As these problems declined, sleep problems had mounted. Nobody had studied the child who refused to sleep, whose ruses to avoid bed would cause a veritable battlegame.

No child has a vocabulary to express the terrors that make him cling to his father's hand and irritatingly awaken whenever his parent tries to slip away. He cannot explain why he needs to hear the same story, droned over and over ad nauseam. Until recently there had been no serious attempt to explore the reasons, although psychiatrists had some wise conjectures. Psychiatrists today describe a child's reluctance to allow the bedroom door to be shut as a basic "separation anxiety."

Nighttime separation from parents begins at a very early age in the United States. It is, in fact, a kind of subtle training in our own peculiar national character. No other society quite prepares its children for independence as we do, and many people feel that this bedtime separation of a child from his parents is the first step in building the independent American character. Many babies and children find this a harsh lesson and, acking words to express their fright and loneliness, they cry.

Throughout the world, wherever there is poverty and little iving space, indeed throughout man's history, it has been comnon for the family to sleep in one room, children snuggled next o their parents. The cave was the first communal bedroom and lthough it may seem an anthropological curiosity to the affluent modern man, the custom still provides comfort and warmth. African Bushmen, who often sleep on the icy ground around a ire, keep their children cuddled close. It is not only primitive ribesmen who enjoy family sleep, warmth and protection gainst the animals and spirits of night, but millions of crowded lum dwellers in modern cities. In large families, children often leep together, in the same room and the same bed. The huddling of family sleep may extend back into man's prehistory, for nan's furred ancestors, the large apes, the gorillas and monkeys, leep close together at night.

The private bedroom was an invention of about the fifteenth entury, and is still not the norm for mankind. A child who is eluctant to be left alone for sleep, who insists on leaving his loor open and having light, may be showing an impulse for rotection and comfort that was more readily satisfied during ast eras, and today among the less privileged.

The comfort may have to be taken from a soothing bedtime itual. Benjamin Spock, our most widely read pediatric authority, has suggested that bedtime rituals can be cultivated deliberately until they become soothing habits. Nobody knows how rofoundly a child's emotions about bedtime and his presleep ituals may influence him as an adult. It is reasonable to guess nat they leave deep impressions, but psychiatric case histories arely mention sleep habits, and child therapists do not generlly bother to obtain the sleep history of their patients, even nough sleep patterns often reveal valuable information about athology. Nighttime behavior is an unexplored territory.

Reginald S. Lourie, of Children's Hospital in Washington,

D. C., has noted that the young children in the slum neighbor hood of the hospital will rush howling to bed if they get hurt or the streets. Bed is their substitute for a mother who is rarel available. In this region, which is predominantly Negro, the un asked questions about nighttime behavior are particularly per tinent. A psychiatrist might want to know who sleeps with whom in his patient's family. Which adult is sleeping with the chil merely to protect him from another adult in the house? A Lourie indicates, the night experiences of a person in thi neighborhood might offer crucial information about his menta disturbances.

If sleep now seems highly relevant to medicine and psychia try, until recently very few people thought it worth observing Our knowledge of sleep customs in cultures around the world i limited for this reason. Anthropologists did not stay up night watching how people prepared for sleep and slept. What w know derives mainly from spoken attitudes. Among primitiv cultures fear was dominant—fear of the night and its perils, bu also fear of sleep itself.

Sir James Frazer, in *The Golden Bough,* has theorized tha the common fear of sleep evolved from a belief that animals an men lived and functioned only because each was inhabited by little man or animal inside. This little man inside the ma became known as the soul. Life depended upon the existence c the soul, and death was its absence. Sleep appeared to be temporary absence of the soul. In the Fiji Islands of the Sout west Pacific, as among other tribes, people took great care neve to awaken a sleeping man, for his soul was out wandering an might not have time to get back. In Burma, for the same reasor awakening a sleeper is a discourtesy tantamount to pushing person in front of a truck. The association between sleep an death, enhanced by the immobility and remove of the sleepin person, did not always encourage a protection of sleep. Ther are parts of Tibet where a sick person, invalid, or woman wh had given birth to a child was carefully prevented from sleep ing. The main duty of the nurse was to sprinkle the patient

ace with water if necessary; and some doctors made their pa-
ients stand or lean against supports lest they lie down and sleep.
This unkind therapy probably arose from a local disease with
symptoms resembling dropsy, and people feared sleep because
leep or coma often preceded death.

The primitive association between sleep and death, a view of
leep as departure from life and a severing of body and soul, is
not really extinct. It is inherent in many of our bedtime rituals
and quite explicit in bedtime prayers. "In your hands I entrust
ny spirit," intones the Orthodox Jew before sleep. When he
awakens in the morning he feels delivered, and thanks God for
he new day. "I thank you for the soul you have returned to
ne."

Millions of children and adults say even more familiar words
as they kneel by their beds before sleep.

Now I lay me down to sleep
I pray the Lord my soul to keep,
If I should die before I wake,
I pray the Lord my soul to take

Throughout the world religious people have devoted the last
ninutes of the day to prayer and meditation. With the burdens
of the day shouldered to the best of their abilities, presidents,
tatesmen, and kings have placed their souls in trust and ac-
epted oblivion. Only God never sleeps. As the ancient rabbis
xplained, the angels had mistaken man for a deity—until
he slept. When God put man to sleep they realized man was
nortal.

It is hard to say how deeply the words of the bedtime prayer,
he lingering sense of morality, may influence a person's ac-
eptance of sleep. Surely there are many people who lie down in
bed only to find their hearts pounding, suddenly alert. This is a
elatively common experience, but most people would not as-
ociate it with fear of sleep.

There are many people who do fear sleep and anesthesia be-

cause they cannot bear to relinquish control over themselve
and the world around them. Anesthesiologists in hospitals an
dental clinics notice this fright in business executives and chil
dren alike. Reluctantly, doctors and dentists have been force
to perform painful operations without giving anesthesia becaus
their patients so preferred pain to unconsciousness. To som
extent this is merely an exaggeration of the prospect of slee
and the difficulty of letting go.

Freud believed that anxiety toward sleep and compulsiv
bedtime rituals were universal. The man who likes a glass o
milk or a Scotch before bed would probably say that this wa
stretching a point, for he may feel no anxiety. Bedtime snack
are very common. Among some obese people nightly snack
become compulsive and gargantuan orgies, a pattern know
among psychiatrists as a "night-eating syndrome," for which un
derlying anxieties do seem to be the cause. Frequently the bed
time feast consists of ice cream and milk products reminiscent o
the soft foods of infancy. It resembles the last meal of a con
demned man. For many other people the ritual does not involv
food or drink but lights. They must leave lights on when the
go to sleep. Others require recorded music or the radio. Onc
again, we are reminded that man is a social animal with a lon
history of company during sleep.

During crisis the desire for company often becomes explici
The hospitalized child wants his parents at his bedside as he i
falling asleep. Even the most powerful man in the world ma
need company in order to sleep after crisis—and in Novembe
1963, the new President, Lyndon B. Johnson, kept his clos
friend Horace Busby at his bedside until two in the mornin
after his first grueling day in office, following the shock an
tragedy of President Kennedy's assassination. It has been sai
that trauma evokes the feelings and needs of childhood, bu
anxiety about sleep is so widespread that its manifestations ar
accepted throughout our society. When a famous MIT scienti
turns up at a meeting looking haggard, nobody will call hi
childish as he explains that his wife is away with her family an

e cannot sleep without her. Many people, indeed, cannot sleep nywhere but in their own beds.

However inconspicuous, almost everybody performs some rit-als embodying unspoken and perhaps unrecognized feelings, ıd without these rituals it is hard to sleep. It may be the eremony of bedtime ablutions, washing, bathing, brushing eeth. It may be the dog's walk, locking the house, turning on ight lights—or something more bizarre. Perhaps no custom is bizarre as the habit of a San Francisco gentleman who would end a half hour in his wife's room each night, but could only ll asleep when resting comfortably in an open coffin. In parts f Polynesia there are people who always sleep with their heads ırned toward the east, never their feet. To the east lies an noccupied portion of the house used only for funerals. Super-ition is often combined with hygiene. Many Iranians sleep cing Mecca, and their elaborate rituals stress cleanliness, the rinking of curdled milk, and falling asleep on the left side to revent indigestion.

Benjamin Franklin, whose bedroom was often aired to the eezing point, believed that a cool skin was essential to pleasant eep. He advised an air bath to anyone unable to sleep. Better t, he suggested two beds, so that a person could always move to a cool bed when his bed grew warm. Winston Churchill emed to share this penchant. During a Big Three conference 1953 he insisted on having twin beds. He slept in one until e sheets got wrinkled and in the middle of the night would imb into a fresh bed. Perhaps out of a desire for both freedom ıd coolness, about one person in three sleeps nude.

The neat bedclothing and nightdress of today are recent in-ovations. In the ninth century, during the reign of Char-magne when the bed was coming into use throughout Europe, e sleeper still wound himself into a shroud of linen rather an using sheets. It is easy to see why this sleeping shroud olved. The first beds were earth, straw, and skins. Although e Bible comments about Queen Esther's luxurious bed of shions, it really consisted of a few pillows on the floor. The

early Egyptians, Babylonians, and Assyrians had put up wit
greater discomfort, sleeping on narrow pallets like low table
with a wooden headrest. The metal and jewel-encrusted palle
of the wealthy were even harder. Perhaps the first sign of luxur
arrived with the cradle-shaped pensile beds of the Romans. On
was filled with warm water, the other with a mattress. First
person relaxed in the warm water, rocked by a servant, and the
was rocked to sleep on the mattress.

Beds took on a public character in the seventeenth centur
during the reign of Louis XIV. The king commonly use
his enormous bed as a throne from which he overlooked sta
proceedings and parliament, his favorite place for holding aud
ences. This started a fad among the elite, who also began ente
taining from bed. The beds were built high and overhung wit
canopies. It became essential to have steps in order to climb in
bed, bed warmers, and a growing mass of accouterments th
vanished with central heating.

The bed is still an important piece of furniture. America
beds are several feet longer than the beds of George Washin
ton's day, and each year they seem to be wider, accommodatir
generations that are much taller and more generously propo
tioned than their forebears. If anything, the modern bed
showing an automated approach to Roman luxury. Some m
torized beds incline for sitting, others deliver a vibration ma
sage. One experimental model consists of a fiberglass tub. Th
sleeper, fully immersed in a chemical bath, will be weightless
relaxed, relieved of gravity and by theory, at least, should r
quire little sleep because his rest will become so efficient.

Beds and bedding have generated their own rituals over th
centuries. Although people express a variety of idiosyncrasies-
such as sleeping only on white sheets—the most commonly a
cepted fetish is a refusal to sleep with one's feet at the head
the bed. Today, particularly in industrialized societies whe
life and lovemaking are routinized, many people consider th
bed the only proper place for making love, and the appropria
time, before sleep. The association between bed, sex, and slee

, so strong that it has created yet another idiosyncrasy: some dults believe they cannot fall asleep without sexual satisfac- on. Marriage counselors hear complaints on this score from ouples who do not agree that nightly sexual activity is crucial or sleep. Perhaps because males tend to fall asleep more rapidly an women after intercourse, this is more apt to be a male equirement. One psychotherapist was struck with the power of is relief when a patient came to his office looking unusually eary and drawn. He asked the man why he was so exhausted, nd was startled by the reply. The man had suddenly decided at masturbation was a poor idea and had given up his usual ractice for several nights. He had been totally unable to sleep.

Under normal circumstances people comfortably follow the tuals and habits that permit them to sleep, however fussy the rangements. Under conditions of stress, pain, horror, and ex- austion these all vanish, for sleep is a resistless master. Unlike e basic biological drives of hunger and sex, the power of sleep n suddenly overtake a driver on the road, a soldier on sentry ity or in a slit trench. People have slept in mine shafts and ogs, on rafts and in space capsules, and in the unimaginable arters provided by the Nazis to their concentration camp ctims. At Auschwitz, men accustomed to comfort huddled on ank tiers, nine of them in a seven-foot shelf, sharing two blan- ets in the bitter cold, using their mud-caked shoes as pillows. ramped, cold, and afraid, they still slept and for a few hours caped, oblivious to their pain. When life becomes unendur- le sleep is the escape possible for all men. Before an unpleas- t day, most people find it hard to wake up in the morning, d those who are in the throes of deep depression often sleep d doze to great excess. When sleep is impossible in a situation duress, many people will panic because they cannot sleep.

People often behave as if there were a rigid prescription that ctates how much sleep individuals must have each night. If ey sleep an hour less, they worry about it, and search them- ves for signs of fatigue and low resistance. The magic number, ght hours, was decided long before modern medical science.

Centuries ago, Maimonedes decreed, "The day and night is 2 hours. It is enough for a man to sleep one third of them." H was probably not the first to divide the day into thirds. Th doctrine of eight hours' sleep has been propounded ever sinc on the basis of no particular scientific information since almo none exists, and despite the variance exhibited by the sleepin populace. The prescription, to which mothers are devoted, ma be more than a matter of faith or a length of time that satisfi some median group. Among athletes, for example, there is r peated emphasis upon the need for eight hours of sleep.

If many athletes require eight hours sleep at night, and also pregame nap in order to feel fit, there are professionals wh have gone to the other extreme, sleeping very little. Many st dents have preferred two long naps of about three hours to solid night's sleep. One writer functioned best when he napp two hours out of every six. A Baltimore printer-salesman-edit has supposedly managed his triple career by subsisting on a hour's sleep a day. There have been no large-scale and system tic sleep studies comparing different professionals and so we not know whether intellectuals need less sleep than athlete and whether physical exertion, as contrasted to mental exertio influences the amount a person sleeps. Personal anecdotes ca not decide this question. Even when they are not deliberate falsified they are unreliable, for people are not accurate abo their sleep habits.

Every child has heard that Thomas Alva Edison slept on two hours a night. This popular lie serves several purposes; suggests that by discipline and strong will anybody might shri his sleep requirement and thus gain time in which to inve and grow rich. This was exactly Edison's point of view althou he never claimed to have whittled his sleep to two hours. "F myself," he bragged, "I never found need of more than four five hours' sleep in the twenty-four." Edison was an inveter napper, however, and there is no way of knowing how mu daily sleep he failed to count. He considered sleep a waste time, a sign of weak will and stupidity. Although he train himself to awaken early, he would often drift back to sleep for another hour, and his obsession against sleep was so intense that he actually recorded these instances of weakness in his diary. "Most people overeat one hundred percent and oversleep one hundred percent because they like it," he wrote. "That extra hundred percent makes them unhealthy and inefficient. The person who sleeps eight or ten hours a night is never fully asleep and never fully awake . . ." Edison saw the long night's slumber as a damnable heritage from our caveman days, and fondly hoped that electric light would change all that.

Scanty sleep was Edison's prescription for a productive life, but it has not been the rule of other great men. Sir Winston Churchill held the opposite opinion of sleep. In *The Gathering Storm* he said, "I always went to bed at least for one hour as early as possible in the afternoon. By this means I was able to press a day and a half's work into one. Nature had not intended mankind to work from eight in the morning to midnight without the refreshment of blessed oblivion which, even it it lasts only twenty minutes, is sufficient to renew all vital forces." President Truman, at age seventy, was asked where he obtained his unflagging energy. "If I feel tired," he said, "even while in a meeting, I excuse myself, go into a nearby room, take off my shoes, and take a nap, if only for five minutes." The ability to nap and to be revived by a brief rest has been cultivated by many presidents and statesmen who live under pressure.

Some people with arduous schedules need no spare room and no couch. In Madison Square Garden, as thousands assembled to hold a meeting on Sane Nuclear Policy, Norman Thomas electrified the audience with a thundrous introduction of Mrs. Eleanor Roosevelt. When he stepped back to present her, however, he found that she was sound asleep in her chair and had to be awakened to begin her speech. As she had told friends, she had developed an ability to nap under any conditions, and this was essential to preserve her strength.

It is still a moot question whether the capacity to fall asleep easily and at will can be acquired by anyone, or whether it requires a special genetic endowment. Some Russian cosmonauts and American astronauts have given superlative demonstrations of the ability to sleep on command, although it should be added that these people have exhibited other proficiencies in self-command. Perhaps the most interesting aspect of the 1965 heavyweight fight between Sonny Liston and Cassius Clay was that Clay went to his hotel, willed himself to sleep, and after several hours of afternoon sleep arrived in the ring refreshed and in top form. Many great athletes, among them the baseball champion Gil Hodges, admit that they cannot perform this trick. Nor can many important men. Scientists are interested in this difference among people. They wonder how attitudes toward sleep may bear on a person's capacity to sleep away from home and without his cherished rituals. They wonder how childhood bedtime feelings and training may affect the ability to sleep on command. The anecdotal evidence merely indicates that human beings express a richer diversity of feelings and sleep habits than an imaginative storyteller could invent.

One descriptive report from the southernmost tip of South America suggests that constitution and culture go hand in hand, generating special sleep abilities. In the rough Andean territory several hundred miles north of the continent's tip, a relatively primitive tribe of Indians, the Yahgans, all show a talent for falling asleep effortlessly, remaining observant while asleep, and yet ignoring distractions. They sleep lightly, awakening rapidly and easily, at once alert and fresh. Even during sleep every member of the tribe seems to know what is going on, and on awakening shows a remarkable understanding of what has happened during his sleep. Curiously, these people do not seem to be annoyed or fatigued by repeated awakenings, for they fall back asleep as easily as they awaken. Each member of this tribe seems able to lie down and sleep no matter what the time of day, and no matter how much commotion is going on around him.

Our own culture displays as much diversity in genetic composition and sleep habits as the Yahgan tribe shows uniformity.

Many of our idiosyncrasies, our special demands for earplugs or sleep masks, our need for company in sleep, our unverbalized anxieties, may have their roots in early childhood training and the institution of the separate bedroom. At the same time, however, people are physiologically different even within a single family, sleeping at different depths, some lightly and others deeply cut off from their surroundings. For some the night is punctuated with awakenings, and morning finds some beds thrashed like the wake of a hurricane. Others arise after hours of immobility and are no more traced with memory than a stone that has been passed by the shadow of a cloud. To each, in his behavior, sleep has a special meaning, but questions about sleep habits, attitudes, and constitutional propensities had to await our era to be answered, and they have not yet been answered. It is misleading to speak of sleep in general. Gigantic population studies are needed before we can describe the habits, attitudes, and qualities of all mankind's sleep.

II

THE CLOCKS OF LIFE

IN past millennia, man lived by the tempo of the turning earth. Dominated by the alternation of sunlight and darkness, he worked by day and slept by night. He was restricted to the speed of animal feet, unaware and unaffected by humanity beyond his small province. In his adjustment to a pace that seemed natural and eternal, he could not have envisaged in his wildest dreams that men would disrupt the stately order, to create day out of night, and trespass into the zone beyond the sky, there to traverse many days and nights within twenty-four hours. For most of history man lived by the the clocks of nature and drew from them his philosophy. Then, overnight in human history, society developed a new sense of timing. Electric daylight, jet travel and worldwide communications created the irregular schedules and swift changes of an urban pace that soon will encompass the world.

The regular routine of nightly sleep, man's historic rhythm of sleep and waking, was quick to suffer. Now there are small signs—such as symptoms among travelers and airline crews of "jet exhaustion"—that raise questions about the necessity for nightly sleep. Is nightly sleep merely a habit? Insofar as we know, people the world over sleep five to eight hours in every 24 hours, generally at night. If this were sheer habit one might expect to hear about groups that subsist on short naps. So far, no such cultures have been reported. In Latin countries, even after a long afternoon siesta, people again sleep at night. If sleep were controlled by light and darkness, one might expect the inhabitants of the Arctic Circle to show very different customs. There, in northernmost regions of Canada, Norway, and Russia, winter brings on months of night, and summer unending daylight. At one time, rumors circulated that Arctic people hardly slept during the summer. Tourists cruising around the complicated coast of northern Norway were surprised to see townspeople assembled on the docks at all times, around the clock. Their descriptions aroused the curiosity of Nathaniel Kleitman, a physiologist renowned for his study of sleep. He and his daughter went to Tromsö in northern Norway and systematically interviewed the townspeople. What they found was no exception to the human rule. The townspeople slept about seven hours a day in summer and perhaps an hour longer during the winter months. When members of a more recent Arctic expedition could sleep as much as they pleased, each man averaged about 7.9 hours a day—emphasizing that human sleep is not determined by light and dark.

Although not everyone does his sleeping at night almost everyone sleeps for a long interval every 24 hours. We do not know whether there is an intrinsic need to sleep for a long stretch, or whether we require some absolute amount of sleep that could be distributed differently. Our sleep schedule seems to be interknit with body clocks that revolve around an axis of roughly 24 hours. Like any intricate machine, man's body will function smoothly only when its billions of components intermesh with proper timing. Clocks within our cells pace out the meter, and sleep is generated, in part, by these tempos within. These biological clocks are geared to the rhythmic changes of nature, and are found in all life.

The long history of mankind's habit of nightly sleep seems clear after a look at the natural world, for it is immediately plain that there is something special about a period of rest every

24 hours, the solar day caused by one revolution of our tilted planet in its yearly spin around the sun. Plants and flowers move their leaves in a daily rhythm, which will persist even when they are transplanted into deep caves of unchanging darkness and temperature. It is almost impossible to find a living creature whose activity does not subside for at least one period a day. Lobsters become immobile. Clams breathe less vigorously. Butterflies fold their wings at night, attach themselves firmly to a blade of grass and refuse to budge until a civilized hour in the morning. Insects do not sleep as we do, but according to Julian Huxley, the repose of ants has certain characteristics that are all too human in appearance:

> They may choose a depression in the soil as a bed, and there lay themselves down, with legs drawn close to the body. When waking (after some three hours rest) they behave in a way startlingly like that of our proud human selves. The head and then the six legs are stretched to their fullest extent, and then often shaken; the jaws are strained open in a way remarkably reminiscent of a yawn.

At night, some fish lie on their sides at the bottom of their aquarium. Others float on the surface of the sea. The coastal puffer will "sleep" in shallow water in the sand, often in groups, lying close together. Frogs, lizards, turtles, grow still for long periods. Birds and mammals sleep. Every creature seems to reflect in its alternation between activity and rest the biological heritage of the earth's revolution—and the tides of the moon.

In the beginning, life emerged from the sea, whose tides follow a lunar day of about 25 hours. Although we are generally insensitive to the rhythms within us, we do recognize the lunar month in the 28-day menstrual cycle. In historic Southern Rhodesia, the king regulated his public appearances by the phases of the moon, Egyptian pharaohs thus timed the rites of planting and harvest, and the moon cults of prehistory celebrated with erotic festivals and orgies. Ignorant of evolutionary origins, these people sensed a link between the moon and reproduction. It can be seen directly among fish.

Something of a modern folk festival has evolved in Los Angeles on nights when small fish, the grunion, pour out of the waves into the shallows to spawn. They arrive in the spring tides on nights just following the full moon. At this time the eggs they lay in the sand will not be washed away by the next high tide, but some parent grunion are temporarily stranded between waves where waders catch them. Los Angelenos arrive in crowds and their bonfires dot the shore. To many of them this is merely another of the Californian's God-given rights—that a fish fry should swim directly into his hands. Few would imagine in themselves and their own reproduction some ancient trace of this seaside spectacle. Sea creatures are highly geared to the changes of the moon, whose monthly waxing and waning pulls on the waters, creates atmospheric tides and regular changes in barometric pressure. Were fish not timed to act on a particular signal, they might appear to spawn a few at a time and would not reproduce sufficiently to survive.

Biological clocks enhance the possibility of survival by putting a creature in tune with the regular changes of nature. The simplest creature without a brain is already pre-set to anticipate approximately the next shift of the outside environment. One California scientist has recorded the spontaneous firing of a single nerve cell in a giant mollusk that is found in tidal pools along the coast. Although the mollusk had been residing in an unchanging tank of seawater in the laboratory, it continued to beat with the tides. The precision of the "clocks" we have found in simple creatures begins to lend some insight into talents they possess, talents once viewed as miraculous.

The uncanny time sense of the honeybee may in a general way indicate how people may set mental clocks to wake themselves, to check on dinner in the oven, or make a phone call. The great Austrian naturalist Karl von Frisch found he could train bees to come for food at a particular hour each day. Did they tell the time by the light of the sun, geography, the earth's turning? Von Frisch designed a simple test. Paris-trained bees were flown to New York. If they relied on outside cues for time, they would have been fooled, but they came to the assigned feeding place on Paris time, exactly 24 hours later. Several hives of trained bees have since been flown between New York, California, and Paris with the same results—showing that they contain a day clock within them. Left in a new place, however, they will slowly adjust to the local time, as will man.

Visible light from the sun appears to keep the rhythms of the body in phase with the daily rhythm of the environment. Colin Pittendrigh of Princeton, along with several other workers, has demonstrated that the environmental light cycle is of primary importance in regulating the precision and phase of internal daily rhythms in organisms. These rhythms may function almost as alarm clocks, timing various aspects of metabolism to specific times of day, and thus modulating critical life processes in a wide range of living things, from plants to man.

Man is a light-loving animal. His nearest animal kin, the apes and monkeys, are also diurnal. One might say that light alerts them even more than food, in the sense that a laboratory monkey will shift his activity cycle for an hour of light in the darkness, but will not similarly change for a shifting feeding schedule. Not all creatures are diurnal. Moths, bats, owls, rats, cats, and many others come alert when darkness falls. A cat's nocturnal proclivity is partly understood. Cells in the retina of the cat's eye dispatch signals to an "arousal" portion of its brain the moment the lights go off. If this "dark discharge" mechanism is surgically eliminated the cat no longer shows his intense alertness in the dark. For man the opposite seems to be true, although we don't know why. Light awakens him and dawn was his alarm clock throughout most of history, presumably because his built-in clocks made him physiologically ready to get up.

The cycle of sleep and waking probably results from a myriad biological rhythms that revolve around an interval of roughly 24 hours. It is not precisely a day but about a day—*circa dies,* in

Latin, and is known as the circadian rhythm. Although most people do not sense this rhythm in themselves, it is one of their most important attributes. It can influence a person's competence at work, a patient's response to surgery, judgment, stamina under duress. It will influence man's ability to explore and survive in space. The circadian rhythm might be called a man's inner timing.

A man at 10 A.M. is not the same man at 4 P.M, or midnight. Indeed, the same individual is radically different at 2 A.M. One of the obvious signs of this daily rhythm is the body temperature. It varies about two degrees each 24 hours. With great regularity the body temperature rises during the day and falls at night, dropping to its lowest point between about 2 and 5 A.M. Ordinarily a person will feel at his best during the hours when his temperature is high, and if he is awake when it falls to its low point, he will feel frankly terrible. As body temperature drops one may feel chilled, sleepy, and dull-witted. Most people are in bed asleep at this time, although a stewardess may be serving a meal over the Atlantic, a pilot flying, an intern performing surgery. This is the time when night workers and railroad people have most accidents, the time when a doctor will receive the most calls reporting night coronaries. Even the seasoned newscaster who can, so to speak, live on adrenalin for 36 hours while covering a crisis, may begin to slur words at this time of morning and have difficulty ad-libbing.

Efficiency declines as the temperature begins to drop before one's normal bedtime. Nathaniel Kleitman and his associates at the University of Chicago conducted mental and physical tests on people before retiring and just after awakening. Performance was poor at both times, and people did not give their best performance until the middle of their waking period; which is not to say that man cannot rise to the challenge of a crisis if he must, nor that all people reach their apex of efficiency at the same hour.

If one were to draw out a graph of body temperature for every person, there would be some notable differences in the time of the peaks and lows. There are quick risers who love the early morning and who wake up whistling and charged with vitality—the so-called larks. Their keenest moments come early, and their body temperature starts rising early during sleep. Owls are very different. They begin slowly and only hit their stride in afternoon. The Hungarian playwright, Ferenc Molnár, who wrote *Liliom,* was such a night owl that he saw daylight only when he was forced to appear in court. Riding through the springtime streets of Budapest to get to court, he remarked in surprise about the number of people on the streets at that hour. "Are they *all* witnesses?" he asked.

When people work at night, their temperature shifts around so that the high point comes during waking, the nadir at their time of sleep. Unfortunately, the shift does not occur at once. It may take three to ten days or much longer. The rise and fall of temperature is merely one gauge of the many body cycles that follow a 24-hour period. The heart rate, blood pressure, metabolism, blood cell count, the number of cells dividing in tissue, the volume and chemistry of the urine, kidney function and many others follow a roughly 24-hour cycle of peaks and lows, many of them in parallel with the temperature. The body chemistry, the composition of blood, the activity of the brain, are different at the time of the bottom temperature than they are during the temperature high.

Man's body clings very stubbornly to this circadian rhythm, even when he is taken away from day and night, away from clocks and all social activity that remind him of time. How flexible is the 24-hour rhythm? How much can it be altered? These questions are particularly urgent for the plans of manned space flight.

Some initial answers were provided in 1938 when Nathaniel Kleitman and a student descended into Monmouth Cave, Kentucky. There in a deep cool cavern once traversed by tourists, they set up living quarters in unchanging temperature and absolute darkness, excepting for their electric lights. For over a month they tried living a short day of 21 hours, which was not very difficult. Then they tried a long day of 28 hours. The young man managed to adapt to the lengthened day, but Kleitman, then in his forties, found that his body obdurately followed a 24-hour day and a seven-day week. Trying to live a six-day week forced him to be awake when his body wanted to rest and to sleep when his body was awake. The wretched sensation of being out of kilter is familiar to many travelers who take long jet flights across time zones.

Kleitman and his student created their artificial days and nights by electric light, which did not answer the possibility that constant light might affect the nervous system, perhaps making it easier to stretch the daily rhythm. Since then a related experiment has been conducted in Spitsbergen, Norway, during the summer season of unremitting daylight. Mary Lobban of the London Medical Research Council took groups of students there, placing some on a 21-hour day and others on a 28-hour day by a clever device. Upon arrival their own wristwatches were taken away, and the students were given "cheating" watches that looked ordinary, but actually compressed or lengthened the day.

By no means all of the students adapted, but a few began to show a 21-hour or 28-hour body temperature cycle. The research team was also observing what happened to cycles of body chemistry, and since urine excretion is easy to track, they measured the concentrations of sodium, potassium and calcium. These ions are critical to body function, determining how the kidney membranes shall pass substances in purifying the blood and maintaining the excitability of heart muscle and electric balance of brain cells. The normal 24-hour pattern of their concentration in urine was well known, but not whether they would shift to a new schedule. Among the students who adapted best to their new schedule and who stopped urinating at inappropriate times of "day" and "night," the sodium and calcium excretion showed adaptation, too. But potassium did not. It stuck with the 24-hour pattern, and was now out of phase with the other chemicals of the urine. In itself this is not an alarming fact, for the amount of potassium excreted is small, and an enormous change would have to occur before potassium balance would be destroyed in the body and would begin to cause symptoms of nervousness or muscular debility. Nevertheless, this stubborn 24-hour cycle raised an important question: How many other chemical cycles, unseen and untested, remained out of phase with this artificial day? Does cycle disruption have serious consequences in the long run?

Insect and animal researches provide our only answers at present. Jane Harker of Cambridge University has discovered that the daily activity cycle of the lowly cockroach is directly controlled by secretions from a secondary brain behind its mouth. When that is removed, the creature shows no daily rhythm of activity. If given a transplant from another roach, it would resume its rhythm of rest and action. However, if that donor roach happened to follow a daily rhythm that was 12 hours out of phase with the recipient, the recipient cockroach would develop malignant tumors. Nobody knows what this may mean about body-timing mechanisms and cancer, but it suggests that there may be serious reason to understand what happens when body cycles are thrown out of phase.

Russian scientists, who have long considered the understanding of diurnal rhythms an essential step in manned space exploration, have poured resources into this field of study. They have generated neuroses in animals by disrupting diurnal cycles. In 1959, G. M. Cherkovich reported that a disruption of the diurnal rhythm had caused coronary insufficiency in monkeys.

A person can feel whether or not his body functions are in phase. A group of German students were recently tested for the persistence of their circadian rhythm when they were left to follow whatever schedule they pleased in a luxurious, but timeless subterranean apartment. Jurgen Aschoff, Director of the Max-Planck Institute, wanted to see what might happen to man removed from all earthly time. Most of the students were cramming for exams, and their body functions showed cycles that drifted between a 23- and 25-hour day. However, there was one dramatic exception, a fellow whose day progressively lengthened until he was living a 32-hour cycle. Nevertheless, his body temperature and excretion of water and potassium stayed on about a 24-hour cycle, and calcium excretion was totally out of phase with these. Every third or fourth day the young man's body cycles would come back into phase. His diary notes revealed that he felt the difference, for these were the precise days when he mentioned feeling well and alive.

Aschoff himself tried the underground bunker for ten days. One morning he forced himself to get up when he thought he should, but felt so rotten that he went right back to bed after breakfast. A later look at the records showed that he had forced himself to get up at the lowest point of his temperature cycle on that day. Jet travelers, airline flying crews, night workers on rotating shifts, Navy men on rotating watches, newscasters, interns, and many others are familiar with these feelings. The fatigue is not merely loss of sleep. They also suffer from disrupted cycles, and if the irregular schedule is prolonged, they may have a hard time getting back in phase with themselves.

The implications for passenger safety and crew health are serious enough so that several major airlines have begun to study their personnel. One pilot phrased it succinctly in an article for an airline magazine when he said that landing a jet through clouds was analogous to performing a surgical operation—but with over a hundred lives at stake. "How many people would like their surgeon to have been on duty 18 hours and have crossed five time zones just prior to taking out their tonsils or appendix?" An Air France survey has shown that experienced pilots and stewardesses minimize their diurnal disruption by exercizing a difficult self-constraint. Parisians stay on Paris time. If it is 6 P.M. when they land in New York they go to bed, for in Paris and their bodies it is midnight. Unfortunately they are likely to awaken at 3 A.M. in New York—and some flight schedules cross so many time zones east or west that disruption is inevitable, even when the stopovers are long enough to allow for "plenty of rest."

In nine days, a stewardess may fly from New York to London, Beirut, Bangkok and return. Just serving the evening meal during the Atlantic crossing, as a pedometer has shown, she walks about nine miles. When she arrives in London in the early morning, she may want to sleep all day, but will force herself to get up after a few hours so that she can sleep that night before the next hop to Beirut. After nine days of crossing time zones her body will be out of phase with her environment. The girls' irregular eating habits often produce stomach disorders, diarrhea, and constipation. The medical director of one airline has noticed that young stewardesses have menstrual irregularities, sometimes missing a period or suffering unusual cramps and flow. They are girls who lack seniority and therefore work the toughest schedules. A European survey of flight personnel indicated that professional fatigue and the crossing of time zones were usually blamed for their depressions. Psychologically and socially many stewardesses found themselves out of phase with their communities, their dates, unable to join clubs or take classes. As one former stewardess said: "It was like being on the fringe of life looking in."

Some people withstand jet life better than others. Still, cases of "jet exhaustion" are becoming more common. A Norwalk, Connecticut, doctor has been treating a young airline pilot for symptoms of fatigue and irritability, but most annoying, the man also has a hard time keeping his eyes focused. The doctor says it is "plain fatigue," but this is hardly reassuring for the pilot. A medical examiner for the FAA takes a gloomy view of the long-term consequences, and has mentioned signs of premature aging among pilots who often lengthen their day by flying from east to west. He told the Flying Physicians' Association that people who constantly travel by jet may find that the time saved on trips comes off their life-span.

The issue of diurnal disruption is becoming germane to a

great many modern institutions. More than four million Americans work at night, and not just in heavy industry, but in insurance companies and other white-collar jobs, transportation, communications, businesses. The computer has aided and abetted this trend. Data-processing centers operate around the clock, and because of the overload and costliness of computer time, many businesses must use them at night. Increasing automation looks likely to enhance the trend toward night work. Yet few people are truly night people.

Night workers have been found to be less efficient than day workers, in general, and to have more psychological problems. Their sleep patterns are usually disturbed, and they are cut off from normal social life. For many people the prospect of months of night work is so unpleasant they would rather alternate between two weeks of day work and two weeks of night duty. For some of them, as a British survey tells, this rapid adjustment is impossible. Indeed, out of a large group of workers only 25 percent adapted from day to night schedules within five days, many taking as long as two weeks, and some never adapting at all. Two-week rotations seem unwise in the light of this evidence, yet the natural sociability of men has prevailed.

Nowhere, perhaps is the sharing of night duty scheduled in a more stressful and absurd manner than medical schools. Instead of shouldering night duty for a month and then resuming normal social life, the young interns and residents follow a routine that savagely disrupts their diurnal rhythm and duties that sometimes last 36 hours. During a month of his internship when he was working on the accident ward, Elliot D. Weitzman, a neurologist at Albert Einstein College of Medicine, recalls that he had been on duty 24 hours, and was given a few hours to sleep in the morning before afternoon rounds with patients. "The intern is inexperienced to begin with. When he is on duty he is busy, sometimes with life and death situations—often during hours when there may be nobody around to call for help. I knew my decision-making abilities were diminished and by 3 A.M. I hoped nobody would come into the emergency room."

When older doctors are told that this routine is as unfair to patients as it is hard on interns, they take the attitude that everyone in medicine must go through this endurance test. Architecture schools also create three and four-day drafting marathons, known as charettes, in a similar tradition of mock heroism.

If medical schools and hospitals have paid little attention to the effects of disrupted cycles on their staffs, the concept is rather new in medicine, and doctors have paid even less attention to the importance of body timing in treatment. The man who is less efficient at certain times of day and night is also physiologically different and may respond differentially to drugs, to X rays, and to surgery at different points on his circadian rhythm.

Man's days, his nights, his disease symptoms, his time of trouble, hours of confusion, moments of clarity, his weakness and strength may well be determined and balanced by the complex gearing of his body clocks. Little is known about cyclic variations in man, but their potential importance to medicine, to understanding behavior, has been underscored by biologists. Within the biology laboratory it has been demonstrated that animals react to specific drugs, to extreme temperatures, to ultraviolet light, and to X rays differentially—depending upon what time of day they are presented.

Rats, nocturnal animals, are often used in these experiments. Daytime is their inactive period. If they are injected with sodium pentobarbital at the end of their day they will fall unconscious rapidly and for a long time. They are not so responsive if injection comes at night. Botulinus bacillus, notorious for causing food poisoning, will kill a rat if injected by day. By night the same injection will make him sick, but he will survive. Most injuries hurt the rodent less during the night, his active period, but X ray is the opposite. Laboratory mice would die from nighttime doses of X ray that, if delivered in daytime, would merely make them sick. Even malignant tumors have a rhythm of cell division, and periods at which they may be more vulnerable to irradiation than others.

Our own language is filled with phrases that imply we can sense in ourselves the waxing and waning of strength, of mental alertness, of moods. Oddly enough we have paid little attention to these cues and have never explored the timing of medical treatment. One of the rare instances in which a body cycle dictates the timing of surgery is glaucoma, a painful disease in which the sufferer experiences a cyclic rising and falling of pressure in his eyeballs. In general, however, hospital routines are devilishly calculated to create maximum discomfort, from the patient's point of view. The owl is treated like a lark, awakened early with pills, thermometers, breakfast, and rolled off to surgery in hours that may seem to him the dead of night.

At this point there is no organized information on the relative merits of rescheduling hospital procedures, and nobody obtains the patient's temperature curve. Until recently there was no way of obtaining a severely ill patient's temperature continuously without disturbing him, but small thermistors have been developed that could do this job. Many doctors and surgeons have not thought about the timing of X-ray treatments or surgery, but a few strongly feel that proper timing may be critical for the patient.

Morton H. Rose, a Washington, D. C., physician who has specialized in circulatory problems, has noticed that his patients vary in their speed of awakening in the morning. Some are slow, and while mentally awake, their bodies do not gather vitality for a half hour to an hour after awakening. Others get up like a jack-in-the-box. Rose speculates that the slow starter may have sufficient brain circulation, but that blood circulation may be lagging in the remainder of his body, and not enough blood is circulating to the cortex of the adrenal glands which secrete the stimulating hormones that ready the body for stress. Early in the morning, the slow starter may not have enough cortisone to withstand the shock of anesthesia, surgery, and subsequent bleeding. "I feel this group of patients may suffer some real dangers from early morning surgery. For them, perhaps, surgery should come later in the day."

The idea of timing surgery and drugs according to body rhythms is new and relatively unexplored in medicine, yet substantial scientific research suggests that timing can sometimes mean life or death. The future medical world will owe a singular debt to one man, Franz Halberg of the University of Minnesota Medical School, who has studied the circadian fluctuations in special body cells, the blood, glands, and organs in animals, and has pulled into focus the timing of disease symptoms and well-known statistics showing that births and deaths tend to cluster around certain hours. Halberg has emphasized a new dimension in our view of the human body—for it must not only supply the correct amount of the right materials to the right place, but also at the right time.

Biological cycles exert their power upon us from birth until we die, although most of us take little note of them, remaining ignorant of regular periodicities in our moods, strength, days of efficiency, days of sluggishness. Most women do not even notice that they are emotionally changed each month, just before and at the onset of their menstrual period. Studies of sleep, keenly attuned to the temperature cycle and all the known subcycles of the body, are beginning to boost our self-knowledge, and suggest research into the timing of medical therapy. Many cycles do not fall within the daily unit, however, and one of the problems we confront in trying to understand ourselves, and diseases, is learning how to recognize a regular cycle when we see one.

Curt Richter of Johns Hopkins University has described many disorders with odd cycles of symptoms in his book *Biological Clocks in Medicine and Psychiatry*. To a patient or his doctor the symptoms might seem random. Some recur every 48 hours, others every seven days or seventeen months, and in some cases, every ten years. There are epileptics who regularly have seizures every two weeks. One star athlete at Cambridge University suffered a painful swelling of the knee every nine days, so predictably that his team scheduled games in advance so they never coincided with his attacks. One outstanding salesman suffered immobilizing attacks of depression every other day, and on those days had no appointments, but on alternate days he was outgoing, persuasive and outdid any other representative of his company. Manic depressive symptoms are often cyclical, and many psychoses are intermittent, leaving the person quite normal for long periods between attacks. Mary Lamb, the sister of the great English essayist Charles Lamb, lived with a cyclical psychosis for fifty years. It was severe, and during her second attack she killed her mother, whom she dearly loved. Fortunately she was left in her brother's custody, and since the attacks were regular and both knew the first hints, she would quickly get into a straitjacket at the first sign of irritability. She had 38 attacks and lived until eighty-three, most of this time as a normal person.

Richter has speculated on a link between some of these illnesses and normal body rhythm. He hypothesizes that the body's many metabolisms all have particular rhythms or cycles of activity. Usually many of these are out of phase and the body as a whole remains relatively constant. A shock, an accident, emotional or even allergic trauma might jar the system so that some of these subcycles fall into synchrony, exaggerating their effects and causing a waxing and waning we know as symptoms.

A vast amount of research must be done upon biological clocks in man before we can confirm such an hypothesis, but we have compelling need to do this research in any event. We need to know how irregular schedules and disrupted diurnal cycles may play out their effects on people. We need to know more about the timing of medical therapy. It is, indeed, a crucial issue for an age of jet travel and for manned space flight.

Using biotelemetry—small instruments that can detect brain waves, pulse, temperature, skin resistance, respiration, muscular tension and other changes from an active person or animal and radio these messages to a distant receiver—the Soviets have taken one major step in assessing circadian rhythms. If we are to evaluate the effects of space flight on a person, we must know the variations that make up his normal background. Recently, the Russians have managed to sample brain waves in several people for as long as a month, taking readings at certain hours around the clock. Until this study was performed the only knowledge we had about these rhythms of consciousness came from psychiatric patients, or people asleep. Round-the-clock recordings from healthy young men, for intervals of ten days to a month, give a first look at the changing background rhythm of the brain, as recorded by the electroencephalograph or EEG. It is a surprising picture. Throughout waking the Russians found wave forms—known as theta and delta—that were believed to occur only in sleep and pathological states. No particular rhythm characterized a time of day, but the total bioelectric intensity of the several combined wave forms gave a distinct daily pattern, falling lowest at night and around 5 A.M. and reaching a peak around 5 P.M. The individuals also showed characteristic shifts in the frequencies and amplitudes of certain rhythms at points along their own circadian cycle. It is not clear what this pattern may say about fluctuations in consciousness, or about man's mental abilities. Its importance is in giving some picture of a man's normal variations, before trying to measure the effects of stress or space upon him.

The Russians appear to be well ahead of us in the exploitation of biotelemetry, and according to reports they have used long-distance recordings to get a physiological picture of men and animals under a variety of circumstances. They have clocked the physiological changes in athletes training for the Olympics, obtained 24-hour recordings from animals in space, and from their cosmonauts. During one of their preflight tests, cosmonauts P. R. Popovich and A. G. Nikolayev each spent three days in isolation in a mock-up of the Vostok capsule. There, scientists noticed a difference in the diurnal variations of the two men. During periods assigned for wakefulness, for instance, Nikolayev would show brain waves of drowsiness, a tendency related to his particular sleep patterns. On tests, he characteristically made more errors in the evening than in the morning. Soviet physiologists and engineering psychologists were meanwhile studying athletes in action, pilots, fishermen, and train dispatchers to find out how body and mind reacted to long hours of exacting jobs, and at what hours stress or solitude took their toll. Biologists were looking for rhythmicity in brain chemistry, cardiovascular function, the components of the blood, and for changes induced by cycle disruption. These provided the ground work for the first team space flight, a four-day flight of Popovich and Nikolayev, in August of 1962.

The goals of the flight were to assess the major features of diurnal rhythm in man and the effects of weightlessness, and so the spacemen's schedule was kept as earthlike as possible, not to confuse the medical records. Work, sleep, and eating approximated the cosmonauts' usual routine. Only by doing things this way could they study the natural periodicity of human physiological functions as affected by space flight. There were indeed changes that showed up. Both cosmonauts, for instance, had usually shown a higher pulse rate toward the end of the day, but in space flight they either showed no variation or a decline in the afternoon. Although their EEGs suggested a predominance of excitation, both cosmonauts managed to get long and restful sleep.

The Russians continue to expend a great scientific effort in exploring the rhythms of insects, animals, and man on earth and in space. Insidious effects of cycle disruption might cause no problems on short space trips, yet devastate a costly long mission. Without knowing more about our basic daily rhythms, it is hard to tell how people will react when they must live in an artificial day and night, work and rest on unusual schedules. Basic understanding of the circadian cycle might eventually allow us to "kick the cycle," making it fit the demands of the situation. The Russians are reported to be working on a method of doing just that, by mild electrical stimulation to the brain. If it can be done, keeping the entire body complex in its usual phase relationship, it is a major breakthrough indeed.

In our manned space effort we too have begun to pay attention to the issue of physiological rhythms, although we started with an empirical approach. Our first space team, the Gemini IV flight of June, 1965, originally scheduled the astronauts to exchange work shifts every four hours, each man alternating four hours' duty with four hours of sleep. It did not work out quite that way, in actuality, and the men could have used more rest than they got. Presumably there were good reasons for the plan, among them the fact that the Americans were flying their own capsule.

For many years researchers have been trying to discover the most efficient schedules of work and rest. Earl Alluisi and his colleagues at the University of Kentucky and elsewhere have tested many groups of Air Force cadets, who would live in enclosed chambers for a month at a time, performing assigned tasks and following a specific routine. How could a man's duty time be maximized without diminishing his performance? It was found that ambitious young cadets could work a 16-hour day, if they worked four hours and rested two hours. But this was a vulnerable schedule if they lost sleep. A more stable schedule seemed to be a 12-hour workday—four hours on duty alternated with four hours of rest.

This latter schedule was, at least on paper, the plan of astronauts Edward H. White and James A. McDivitt. Still after circling the earth for four days in a cramped capsule with the constant noise of ground communications, they returned tired. They had not slept well, and Major McDivitt suggested a more earthlike schedule for future ventures, permitting a long stretch of sleep each day. Was this the urging of biological necessity or merely the whispering of habit?

A lifelong habit of sleeping eight hours a night would take on profound physical meaning as it became embedded in the nervous system and biochemical timing of the body, and so, if the inflexibility of the circadian rhythm seems to stem from habit, that word does not imply that it can be changed easily—if at all. A number of scientists have speculated that our sleep habits could be radically changed by training in infancy and have proposed animal experiments to test this hypothesis. Still, the mounting evidence suggests that the 24-hour rhythm is a reality, ticked off by the central nervous system, and that a baby begins to sleep through the night, not because his parents train him, but because his brain has sufficiently matured.

Again and again, adults have departed from time, and gone into deep caves. Michel Siffré, a spunky cave explorer, lived 390 feet belowground in the Carcassonne chasm, and although he lost grip on time and emerged on September 17, 1962, thinking it was August 20, the records of his sleep and waking showed that his body had continued to revolve around a 24-hour day. The clocks within our flesh appear to be quite real. Grandmother's injunction to keep regular hours may sound old-fashioned, but in final analysis it may be the best way to maintain body harmony and health. Irregular hours of sleep and eating have physical and perhaps mental consequences whose extent we simply do not know.

Now that the circadian rhythm in man has begun to grow into a national issue via our space effort, new research may begin to reveal the nature of its subcycles. These shorter rhythms within the day appear to influence our efficiency, our strength or weakness, and the symptoms of our illness. The one third of the day to which American scientists have devoted concentrated attention is the inactive period of sleep, and there, nightlong studies have begun to track the subcycles of the biological fluctuations that may influence our bodies and minds during waking.

III

THE TIDES OF NIGHT

ON any night when the quiet of sleep invades the household and a veil falls over the consciousness of each person, an extraordinarily patient and sensitive observer might see the subtle signs of the night's journey. From outside, the body may look motionless excepting for a shallow and even breathing, an occasional snore. Sporadically a twisting, a groan, a murmur or phrase, a fluttering of eyelids, may break the stillness. The relaxed sleeping face has a peculiar beauty, yet it may suddenly grow tense and the person may grind his teeth as if in a frustrated rage. Something is happening inside, which the sleeper will not remember, for in the morning all sleep seems to have been the same, a darkness that has settled over mind and body. We think of the mind as having slept. Nothing could be less true.

Sleep, as we now know it, is not a unitary state but a progression of repeated cycles, representing different phases of brain and body activity. By watching a person sleep, the untrained observer may sense that there is change, but he will not see that the sleeper rises and falls on waves of a recurrent tide, and at regular intervals enters a state that, in many respects, resembles his most alert moment during the day. The place to watch a night's sleep is not the dim bedroom of a home but through the continuous recordings of brain waves, of pulse rate, muscle tension, temperature, blood pressure and biochemical change that are taken within the laboratory.

Within a single decade of laboratory study we have evolved a totally new picture of the normal night of slumber. It is a picture pieced together by numerous researchers from more than 12,000 nightlong vigils involving over 4,000 sleeping individuals. Even a description of a typical night in a sleep laboratory will hardly convey the horrendous amount of work implied by those figures, the exertion and personal sacrifice exacted of each contributing scientist.

While most Americans are eating a leisurely dinner or watching television, sleep researchers will have gulped down a hasty meal and be filtering back to their control rooms. There are by now more than two dozen sleep laboratories in the United States, located in university buildings, hospitals and old residences. They vary in size and newness and the complexity of their equipment, but they are basically similar. Before a night watch, the atmosphere of the laboratory resembles the cockpit of a jet in a preflight instrument checkout. Like any pilot, the experimenter himself must see that the machinery shows exactly the responsiveness he needs. He may already have spent half the day testing connections, soldering wires and troubleshooting. Most sleep researchers were not trained in electronics but in psychology, psychiatry, physiology. Still, this new breed of scientist has acquired the deftness of an electrician or engineer, and many have had to learn surgery and biochemistry as well.

As any visitor would notice during these evening hours, attention centers around a large polygraph machine widely known as the electroencephalograph. Basically it is a huge amplifier system. It is sensitive enough to receive very tiny shifts of electric potential that occur within the brain and are detected by metal contacts on the surface of the head. By amplifying these shifts, the EEG machine makes brain rhythms visible. In general the machine is also used to amplify other oscillations, changes in blood pressure, pulse, respiration, body temperature, skin resistance, muscle tone. Although certain body changes could be detected by patiently and intently watching the sleeping person, precise measures of body changes require sensing devices that produce signals to be amplified in the manner of brain waves.

With a container of coffee beside him, the scientist will sit down at the big EEG panel and begin turning knobs and dial switches, so that the potential shifts from different parts of the head and body will be amplified precisely the right amount. The natural beat of a brain region comes from continuous shifts from positive to negative charge, fundamental changes within the living brain cells. The machine will transmit these changes to magnetic tape, and will also drive a row of ink-pens that sit on the desklike surface. Each pen, moved by a signal from a part of the brain, will swing upward when the charge is negative and downward when it is positive. As a continuous sheet of graph paper slides forward under a roller, beneath the oscillating pens, the up-and-down movements of the pens are traced out as waves —brain waves. The experimenter must check that the paper always moves at a constant speed. The amplitude, or height, of the waves will indicate how much voltage emanates from the brain area. The shape of the script, the closeness of the waves to each other, will indicate how rapidly the electrical shifts are occurring in the brain. At a glance, this inked record will tell whether the brain potentials are shifting in a regular and synchronous fashion, with high voltages, or whether the shifts are irregular and swiftly changing. This record of a night's sleep has value only if the machine works properly.

The researcher, joined by an associate and perhaps a graduate student, will busily clean the pens, fill the inkwells, and move through a jungle of wires, testing leads for insulation and possible breaks. A thousand-foot sheet of folded EEG paper is inserted in place beneath the rollers, and reels of magnetic tape are pushed onto their spindles. Watches and clocks are checked.

At midwinter, at the University of Chicago it is ten below zero on the snowbound campus. A solitary row of lights marks the brownstone annex containing the sleep laboratory, but few people venture by on such a night. Around the gigantic modern hospital at the University of California Health Sciences Center, a balmy Los Angeles wind rustles the palms. The parking lots, jammed with cars by day, are almost empty. It is silent around the sleep laboratory. These are lonely hours and will become lonelier as the night wears on. While others sleep the scientists maintain a strenuous vigil. Sometimes their purpose will force them to keep watch for nights on end, weeks, occasionally a month or more, monitoring sleep of others by night, yet fulfilling academic and administrative duties and analyzing data by day. The pursuit of the sleeping mind is a harrowing as well as a seductive chase. The public and volunteers rarely know about this side of it. When a volunteer rises from his laboratory bed in the morning he is, at the very least, somewhat refreshed, but the scientist may have just a few hours to nap—and then on with the duties of the day.

Over ten thousand such nights have produced our current picture of a night of sleep, a composite portrait drawn from a variety of volunteers. The majority have been young men in their twenties, students or professionals. Often they were paid to sleep in the laboratory and abide by the rules of the study, which may prohibit napping in daytime, drinking coffee or alcohol and taking drugs. Some of the volunteers have been women, some laborers, some patients in hospitals, some children and even newborn infants.

Typically, the volunteer will arrive before 10 P.M. He will wash, change into pajamas and robe, and seat himself in an anteroom to be decorated for the night. People speak softly. The air may be permeated with odors reminiscent of a photographic darkroom—acetone, collodion, solder. They are part of the painstaking process. With the meticulousness of a surgeon, the experimenter will mark the right points around the head and face, wash each with icy acetone, touch them with gel, and firmly affix the small metal disc electrodes, pasting them with tape at the eyes, temples, on top of the head. Each electrode is attached to a brightly colored wire, following a color code designating its place on the head and connection to the EEG machine. The array of multicolored wires is finally drawn through a ring at the top of the head like a brilliant ponytail.

By the time this strangely hypnotic procedure is finished, a person is usually drowsy and happy to settle down in the laboratory bedroom, sink into the bedclothes and adjust his head on the pillow. Now the wire leads from his head will be plugged into a jackboard at the head of the bed, a board whose cables attach to the EEG machine in the control room. The laboratory bedroom is usually ordinary, and pleasant. It is soundproof. There is an intercom system by the bed and often a tape-recorder microphone within easy reach. The person can move freely in bed; however, if he decides to make a trip to the bathroom, he will have to call the experimenter on the intercom system to come and unplug him. Some of the newer laboratories have, mounted in a corner near the ceiling, a closed-circuit television camera and quite a few have a mirror on one wall that is, in reality, an observation window through which monitors can check the sleeping person.

When the bedroom door is closed people tend to fall asleep surprisingly fast. A few novices may have difficulty on their first night. One World War II veteran was reminded of the Pacific: "The quieter it got, the more I waited for ambush." A few confess to feeling trapped by the wires holding them to bed and surveillance beyond the door, but the discomfort of electrodes, electrocardiograph contacts, even a blood-pressure cuff usually turns out to be trivial. "I kept wondering if I could sleep in all these attachments—and what would happen if I had to go to the john in a hurry," said one man, "but it didn't turn out to bother me any." The preparation for bed is generally all too lulling. Frederick Snyder of the National Institutes of Health has remarked, "The subjects often fall asleep before we want them to." He himself had anticipated difficulty falling asleep when he was a subject in his laboratory, for at home and on trips it frequently took him some time. The laboratory experience was a revelation. "I not only fell asleep at once, I could hardly stay awake enough to get the preparation done." People usually fall asleep within 10 to 15 minutes in his laboratory. However, even if feelings of anxiety do not keep a person awake, they do show up in sleep.

The laboratory bedroom is private and pleasant. Most people know that their brain waves cannot reveal anything more than a tempo, surely not their thoughts, yet this is a strange situation at first—monitored sleep. In all human studies an unpredictable emotional element, an elusive interplay of feelings, may cast their mark upon the outcome. On their first night in the laboratory, most individuals do not exhibit the patterns that subsequent nights will reveal to be their personal signatures. For some purposes a scientist may record sleep on five consecutive nights, even ten nights, to obtain the base line that is the person's normal pattern of sleep. Only then will he begin to collect the information he is after. Despite these and other precautions, there is a so-called "laboratory effect." It has been relatively rare, for instance, to find a violent nightmare or nocturnal emission in the laboratory over the thousands of nights of recording. Thus, we should keep in mind that the typical night of sleep as we now see it is a night spent in a laboratory, and therefore subject to subtle modifications.

When the volunteer begins relaxing in bed and the experiment is ready to roll, everything should follow smoothly. This is one of the points at which a minor flaw in the equipment could alarm the volunteer and ruin hours and days of preparation. During the early 1950's, when Eugene Aserinsky was a graduate student at the University of Chicago, he recalls that he could not afford to pay subjects and spent considerable effort persuading his friends to sleep in his laboratory. One temperamental classmate finally assented, after weeks of cajoling. "I rejoiced," Aserinsky said. "I got him to sleep and went back to the EEG, and he was up screaming. He accused me of electrocuting him. I told him that was impossible, but he wasn't having any more of it. He got up and went home in a huff." On the following night,

Aserinsky wired himself up as his own subject. Indeed, as he lay in bed, he could feel a mild but unpleasant tingle. Nobody could have been electrocuted, but there was a mysterious flaw in the equipment—and one volunteer who would never again return. Experimenters have worried about this kind of accident. It has bad psychological ramifications, for it reinforces a popular misconception of the EEG. It is not intended to send current into the brain as some people think, but to pick up the electric changes emanating from the brain.

Aimless thoughts about the EEG laboratory, about a girl friend, or an exam are likely to sift through the mind of the person in the bedroom as he relaxes. Although he doesn't real-

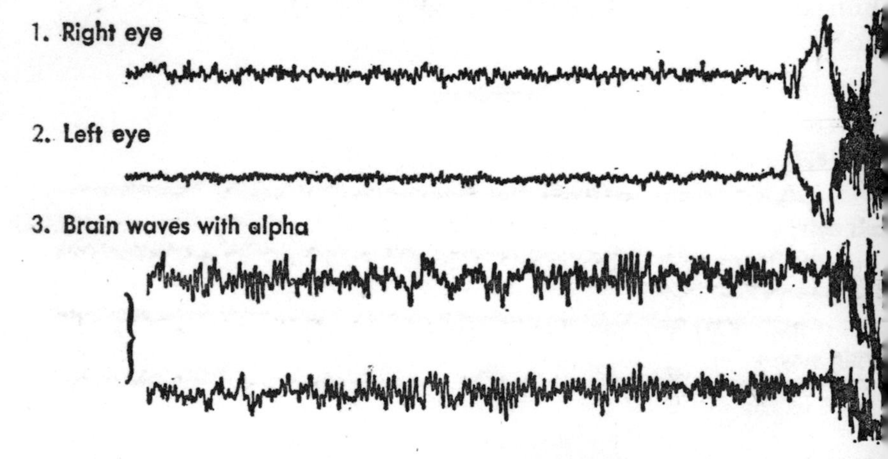

ize it, even as he drowses in a transition into sleep, the EEG begins to unfold a score that is uniquely his. His general progression throughout the night will be that of all normal adults, but the tempo of changes, the subtle inflections, will convey his individuality, like a signature written in brain-wave changes.

In the control room, now, the experimenters glance expectantly at the graph paper as it rolls from the oscillating pens. Widely spaced, there are eight lines that look like pure scrawl. From a glance at this illegible penmanship the experimenters know that their subject has just closed his eyes. The EEG is small, irregular, and rapidly changing. Pulse is growing even, and breathing becoming regular. The subject is wearing a thermistor, a miniature device no bigger than the head of a pin, which tells that his rectal temperature is slowly declining.

Even if the experimenters have been old hands in "the sleep business," they have an air of anticipation now. Out of the scribble on the topmost channels, the brain waves are showing a new pattern. It is known as alpha rhythm, an even rhythm of about 9 to 12 cycles per second. This is a state of serene and pleasant relaxation, devoid of concentrated thought. A moment of tension, a loud noise, an attempt to solve a problem, and the alpha rhythm may vanish. The experimenter knows the subject is on the crest, about to begin a swift descent into sleep. "I give him ten minutes," says one. "I give him two." "There he goes. . . ."

Drowsiness

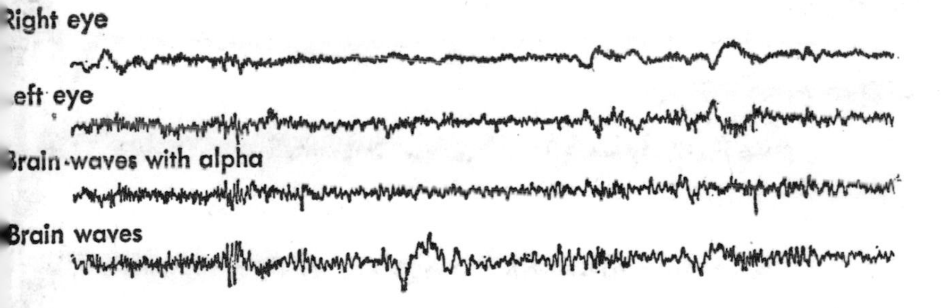

The alpha waves have grown smaller as the young man has relaxed and this heralds a real change in the brain. He is approaching the borderland. He does not know it but his time perception has changed. If two quick flashes of light were aimed at his eyelids now, he would see only a single flash. Something is slowing his perceptions. He is on the border between waking and early sleep. As the alpha rhythm diminishes, the experimenters may lay their bets as to how many seconds his descent will take.

The man in the bedroom is unaware of these changes. The world is easing away. Images, bizarre thoughts, fragments like dreams or reverie may drift into his inward screen. Were he sitting in a dull meeting, class, or at church, his heavy eyelids would have dropped, and perhaps a strange vision of chicks in a barnyard might make him shake his head and open his eyes. He was drifting off, but was he asleep? When has he passed the border?

The experimenters are standing around the EEG, carefully watching the top four channels. A buzzer sounds every few seconds, and a pen at the bottom marks the interval. This timer is set at one-minute intervals. Before it buzzes again, the alpha rhythm will become even smaller, and perhaps a new script will emerge. The young man could be awakened very easily now, but left alone in this strange process he has moved farther inside himself. He is passing through the gates of the unconscious. His eyes are very slowly rolling.

For a moment, he may wake up during this early part of the descent, alerted by a sudden spasm that causes his body to jerk. This, too, is a sign of the neural changes within. It is known as the myoclonic jerk, resulting from a tiny burst of activity in the brain related to the epileptic seizure. The myoclonic jerk, however, is normal in all human sleep. It is gone in a fraction of a second and descent continues. The young man did not feel the peculiar transformation, but now he is blind.

Anyone sitting in his own living room, watching a sleeping pet, might have observed the functional blindness of sleep. It happens under our very noses. Indeed, many people sleep with their eyes half open, unaffected by movements around them. Several years ago, at the University of Chicago, Allan Rechtschaffen and David Foulkes discovered that this blindness might be one of the first marks of sleep. They began testing volunteers who learned to sleep with their eyelids taped half open. There was no danger of harming the eyes. As two ophthalmologists had long ago discovered, a surprising number of Chinese students often slept with their eyes open. The laboratory volunteers did not seem to mind, and fell asleep with astonishing ease.

The Chicago laboratory is cramped in an old brownstone, and its offices have served as bedrooms by night. The control room wears a homemade appearance, thick black cables poke through the ceilings, run down the hall and into the bedrooms, giving a visual map of the connections between monitor and subjects. Despite the appearance of a crash military installation, and bedrooms on two floors, it is a comfortable research place. On a typical night, Rechtschaffen, wearing headphones and a microphone, would monitor the EEG. Psychiatrist Gerald Vogel would man the tape recorder. Upstairs, in the bedroom, Foulkes would station himself. He received his instructions through earphones from the control room downstairs. His colleague watched the EEG—the subject's eyes rolled and his alpha rhythm diminished. "Go ahead." Foulkes then held an illuminated object, a sign, a coffeepot, a comb, directly before the open eyes of the subject. His flashlight operated an automatic marker on the EEG below, and his colleague saw when the light turned on and off. Foulkes would hold the illuminated object right in front of the subject's nose for several seconds. He could see the pupils of the eyes.

After a few seconds, the monitor would awaken the sleeper by using the loudspeaker system from the control room. Their conversation over the intercom went something like this:

> "Mr. Axelrod."
>
> "Mn."
>
> "Mr. Axelrod, was anything going through your mind just before I called?"
>
> "I was picturing decorations on State Street . . . the Christmas decorations, you know. The candy canes and the whole works . . ."
>
> "Can you describe them a little bit?"
>
> "I saw the tops of the light poles, candy canes and wreaths and—uh—the miniature Christmas trees. That's about all I can say about it."

This gives the gist of what happened on many nights in the laboratory, as volunteers whose eyes were taped open were shown lighted objects during their descent into sleep. They were unaware that a lighted sign or key or some other object had been held sometimes six inches from their noses, and yet they were often cocksure they had been awake the whole time. As the Chicago team probed beyond this pilot study, they found that there was functional blindness in the various stages of sleep.

David Foulkes and Gerald Vogel demonstrated that the threshold of sleep meant more than functional blindness. On rare occasions, there were sensations of falling or bodily weightlessness, possibly related to momentary startle, but the general pattern was one of visual imagery, dreamlets, and even vivid dreams. With descent into the stages of sleep came a progressive removal from reality. Awakened later on, the volunteer might not remember where he was.

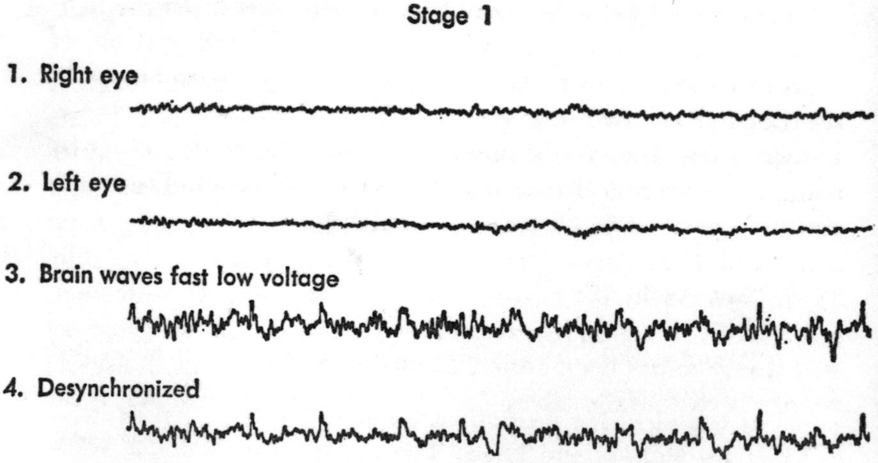

Stage 1

1. Right eye
2. Left eye
3. Brain waves fast low voltage
4. Desynchronized

The threshold of sleep merges into Stage I. The pens write out a scribble that is small and pinched, low in voltage, irregular, and rapidly changing. Occasionally the regular waves of the alpha rhythm break through. The person may be enjoying a floating sensation, or drifting with idle thoughts and dreams. His muscles are relaxing, his heart rate slowing down. Although he could be awakened easily, he might insist that he was not asleep but wide awake. After a few minutes at this port of entry, if not disturbed, he will descend again to another level, another step removed from the world.

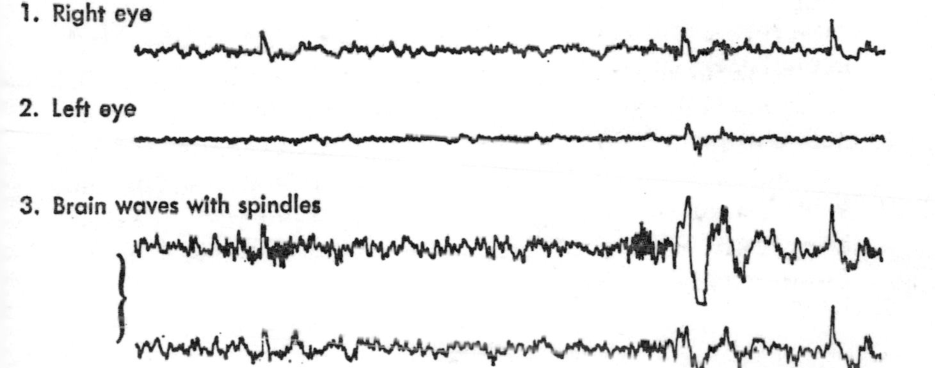

As the EEG script begins to exhibit the pattern of Stage II the pens may chatter slightly. They trace out quick bursts known as spindles. The waves form a rapid crescendo and decrescendo, resembling a wire spindle, and they are unmistakable on the record. The channels representing the eyes now show shallow undulations as the eyes roll slowly from side to side. With eyes open, the young man will not see. If awakened, which can be accomplished easily with a modest sound, he may still think he has been awake all along. At this point, however, he has been soundly asleep for perhaps ten minutes. Whatever happens now in his imagination is beyond his conscious grasp unless the experimenter chooses to awaken him.

Level by level he descends into deeper sleep. He becomes harder to awaken. The experimenter, who has spent the last half hour or forty minutes watching the EEG record like a hawk, is waiting for particular signals to appear. If nothing goes wrong with the equipment and nothing awakens the volunteer, then the interminable scratching of the pens should take on the rhythm he expects within another half hour. But the unexpected can happen. An experimenter in any laboratory may turn his head to talk shop with his colleagues. A friend may drop by after a concert or his wife may come by to bring him a sandwich and coffee. He could turn back only to discover that a lead has come loose and things have gone haywire. If the atmosphere in the control room seems casual—a sharing of jokes, desultory stories during the long wait—there is an undercurrent of tension, of vigilance.

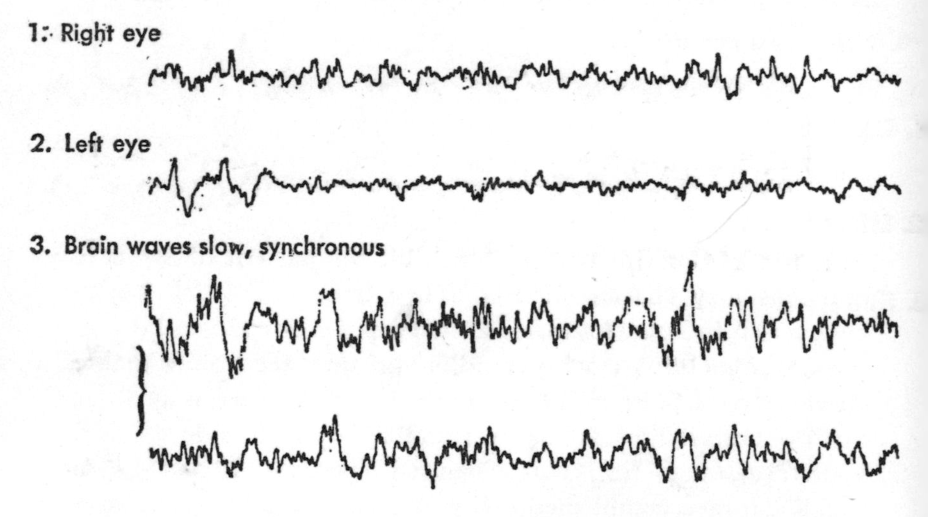

Now the spindle bursts and irregular small script is interspersed with large, slow waves. Stage III is beginning. It is characterized by large slow waves that occur about one a second. Sometimes they are about five times the amplitude of the waking alpha rhythm. The EEG now receives an electrical input as high as 300 microvolts on occasion. The waking alpha rhythm generated only about 60 microvolts. It will take a louder noise to awaken the volunteer, perhaps a repetition of his name. His muscles are very relaxed and he breathes evenly. His heart rate slows. His temperature is declining. His blood pressure is continuing its drop.

The experimenter may shake his head as he glances through the one-way mirror. People sleep through almost anything. We know this from casual observation, from episodes of battle. Even so, it is surprising to confront the power of sleep in the laboratory. A young medical student, sleeping in the National Institutes of Health Laboratory, wears a pressure cuff around his ankle. It has just been inflated. Frederick Snyder at the control panel knows how this feels. "The inflated cuff makes you feel as if a shark just grabbed you by the leg and were pulling you under water." Despite the tight grip of the ankle cuff measuring his blood pressure, the young subject sleeps on, sinking deeper.

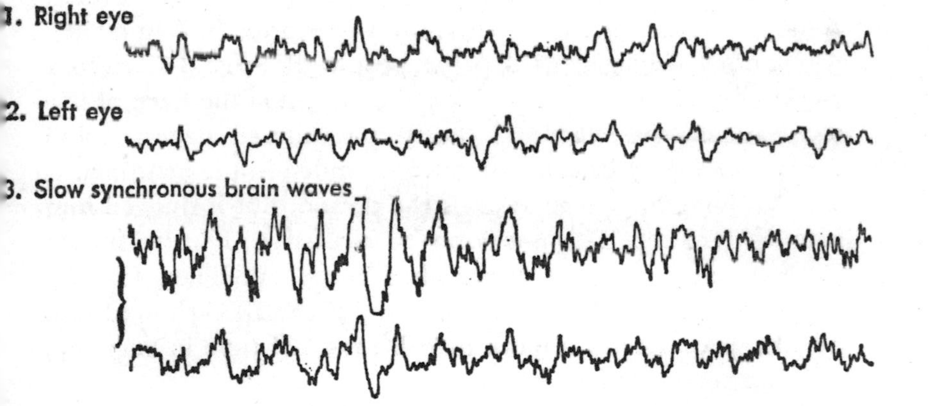

Now, he has really entered oblivion as he passes into Stage IV. It is often known as "delta sleep," for it is spelled out by large synchronous waves known as delta waves. The sleeper is almost immobile, and sounds that might have awakened him ten minutes ago will have no effect. Shake him, ring a bell, call his name and he may take a few seconds to come to the surface. Most likely he will say his mind was blank, remembering nothing. Throughout his sleep and even now he may have been mumbling slurred and indecipherable phrases, but he won't remember. If he has a tendency to wet his bed or sleepwalk, he is likely to do it in this deep sleep.

This might be called the sleep of the weary. Ordinarily a person devotes a large portion of his sleep time in the first half of the night to Stage IV, especially if he is tired or has lost sleep on previous nights. Everyone has heard Grandma say that the best sleep comes before midnight. Many grandmothers probably used to go to sleep around eight or nine o'clock and were probably referring to delta sleep. We don't know what restorative, revitalizing functions this stage of sleep may have, but we know that we need it.

If for some reason Stage IV sleep were removed on several nights, leaving all the other stages of sleep, the person would later compensate, devoting more of his sleep to the delta phase. This has been demonstrated by Wilse B. Webb and Harmon Agnew, psychologists at the University of Florida in Gainesville, where they managed to deprive people of Stage IV without awakening them. For forty nights they watched the sleep of five medical students. Whenever the sleeper entered Stage III, and before delta sleep began, a tone was sounded in the bedroom. It was not loud enough to awaken the person, but it nudged him into lighter sleep. This was done for successive nights with each student, every time he approached Stage IV. Then for two nights he was left alone. On these nights the EEG showed that he was spending much more than his normal time in Stage IV, as if compensating for his loss.

A person may not hear sounds during Stage IV, but EEG studies have shown that the brain has a large reaction to sounds or external sensations at this time. However, the brain systems that convert a stimulation into what we know as conscious perception or experience appear not to be working in their usual way. The brain receives the sound, but there is no conscious awareness.

If this seems to be the depths of oblivion, a person can become even more remote in another phase of sleep. About an hour or 90 minutes from the time he fell asleep, a person will have started drifting up from Stage IV into III, and the lighter sleep of Stage II. Now, when he emerges into Stage I, he will not be back where he started as he first went to sleep, but so removed from the world that it may take a horrendous noise to perturb him. Paradoxically, a meaningful whisper will also get through. This is the time of mounting tension in the control room. It may be closing in on 12:30 or 1:00 A.M. before the subject has been asleep for 90 minutes. The EEG shows that he has drifted into Stage II—there are spindles. All eyes focus on the unfolding script, for if everything goes well, the most spectacular change of the night is about to occur. If the volunteer is an old customer in the laboratory whose sleep pattern is known, the experimenters may predict his timing within a minute or two. No matter how many years they have been monitoring sleep, the script holds them enthralled.

The pens jabber and slash the page with huge oscillations. The sleeper has turned over. They hope he will not awaken. If he does, they have to wait over an hour, while he descends through the four stages of sleep again and reascends to this point. Again the pens scratch out wild excursions. "Now—he's coming in," an experimenter will bet. As the oscillations die away the record shows an irregular small script, of low voltage, rapidly changing and reminiscent of waking. Until the 1950's, encephalographers often mistook this script for an interval of waking. Now, instead they know it is a special variety of Stage I sleep.

The experimenter pencils the time—12:40—on the EEG record. It is some 90 minutes since sleep began. Now everyone watches another pair of channels on the script. One researcher holds a stopwatch. Suddenly the two pens driven by electrodes at the eyes make rapid darts. Both eyes have moved in the same direction as if to look at something. These are different from the slow rolling eye movements of earlier sleep. They could be following a movie. When there are rapid eye movements in this stage of sleep (abbreviated as REMs) the odds are 99 in 100 that the person is having a vivid dream. This first dream period is usually short, lasting no more than ten minutes. Unless awakened, the sleeper would not remember he had this dream. The experimenters will let him dream for about five minutes before waking him, and meanwhile they follow the polygraph recording with the intensity of brokers following a

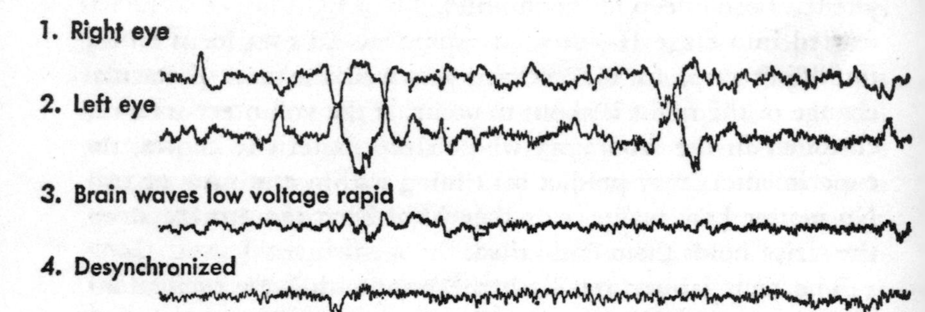

stock market surge on the board. From their many nights of watching they have an almost uncanny instinct about the private world inside as reflected by the script. Something of the intensity of the experience is told by sparse or furious eye movements, by irregularities of respiration.

Whatever the person is experiencing during these minutes, his body has begun to show remarkable changes. Early in the 1920's, a doctor who was searching for the cause of nighttime heart attacks and medical crises observed sleeping patients pass through intervals of disturbance, and inferred they were dreams. A few encephalographers, noticing the similarity with waking brain waves during these intervals of sleep, actually awakened people and discovered they were dreaming. Despite clues and correct guesses, the importance and regularity of the dream cycle was not intensively explored until the 1950's. Eugene Aserinsky, then a graduate student of Nathaniel Kleitman at the University of Chicago, had been clocking patterns of restless and peaceful sleep in infants. After many tedious cribside vigils he noticed that quiet slumber and rolling eyes were regularly followed by periods of body activity. When Aserinsky began watching adults, he saw with startling regularity periods of rapid eye movements in sleep—REMs. As he and Kleitman applied EEGs and other measures, they found the REMs accompanied by a brain-wave pattern resembling waking, and when they woke people at this time they almost always reported dreaming, although they rarely had dream memories when aroused from the other phases of sleep.

At the time, the discovery was incredible to most people, and set ablaze the imaginations of psychologists and psychiatrists, but the work that followed showed that Stage I-REM was even stranger than anybody suspected. Some people said it was not sleep at all but a unique state of consciousness. As experimenters wait to awaken a dreamer, watching the polygraph record, they know a good deal that is happening inside him. Gone is the even pulse and respiration. Were he awake one might say he showed signs of agitation or fright. During the oblivion of delta sleep the heart rate and blood pressure fall to the lowest levels of the day, heart rate reaching its nadir about two and a half hours after sleep begins, blood pressure continuing to fall until about an hour before waking. Now, however, the steady decline is interrupted. Heart rate and blood pressure grow irregular, sometimes showing the wild fluctuations seen during intense emotion or exertion. Oxygen consumption increases, but occasionally a person is as depleted as if he held his breath for several minutes. Perhaps this is a factor in nighttime asthma attacks. Throughout the circadian cycle, the adrenal glands pour stimulating hormones into the system, alerting the body for action and supplying energy, and some of these steroids jump to their highest daily concentrations at the time when REMs dominate sleep, the early morning hours.

Despite the storm of activity in body and mind, the dreamer may seem unusually still. His body muscles have slowly lost the tone they had during waking, and now they are quite flaccid.

His head and neck muscles have gone slack, and would not support the chin and head. They turn off like a switch at the beginning of REM sleep, yet occasional contractions of the masseters that control the jaws may now cause tooth grinding, which generally occurs at this time, particularly in tense people. Otherwise the body seems limp as silk, and a person suddenly awakened in the midst of this might think himself paralyzed.

Even with his eyes open, the dreamer is blind to the outside world. Shine a light in his eyes and they react in an unusual way, slowly diverging, drifting out and then back together. Were it to happen in waking, the person would have double vision. Indeed, narcoleptics, people who lapse directly from waking into a REM state, frequently suffer from double vision, as if walking around in a partial dream state. The brain of the dreamer is anomalous. By contrast with Stage IV sleep, its EEG reactions resemble those of waking, in moments of intense concentration. Deep within the brain the temperature rises, as in waking. It is easy to understand why this particular interval in sleep has drawn more study than any other. Its peculiar attributes seem relevant to nighttime medical symptoms, to emotional states and insanity. It has been thought that we need a regular amount of this sleep; thus the REM state has become an index in observing people with many mental and physical illnesses.

As experimenters count the minutes and watch the EEG they are aware of all these myriad transformations within the immobile person in the bedroom. This internally active sleeper is impervious to habitual noises, and totally engrossed, immersed in himself, he does not hear the door open nor sense that he is about to be awakened. The bell rings. "Are you awake?" the experimenter asks.

> "Yes. I was just dreaming—about two characters, cowboy types . . . like you see on television . . . facing each other, and one is holding a gun on the other one. Maybe there were two people around. This fellow who was holding the gun, he wasn't talking at all. He was just pointing it at him. All I

> could see was the gun—the barrel of the gun, you know, pointing directly at me, and I could see the sight, the big gunsight on top of two winglike projections on either side of it, with the center post in the middle, if you know what a gunsight looks like . . ."

This is merely the beginning. As night wears on there will be several more, longer and perhaps more extravagant. We spend a total of about six years of our life in this remarkable condition. Left alone for the rest of the night, the volunteer would sink back into sleep and begin the entire process again, drifting down again into Stage IV, and in another hour or 90 minutes, re-emerging in the charged excitement of another REM state, this time for about 20 minutes. Four or five times he would repeat the cycle of sleep stages, and each time, toward morning, the dream would be longer and more vivid.

Each individual will show his distinctive variations, for nobody is as regular as a mechanical clock. Nevertheless, normal adults will exhibit roughly four or five complete turns on the wheel of sleep. At about 3 to 5 A.M. body temperature will hit its lowest point and start to rise. This is the richest time for the researchers tracking dreams, but the hour is taxing, and they themselves may be hitting their daily nadir and beginning to feel that the night is interminable. As they watch the EEG on this last round, forcing themselves to be alert, drinking coffee, they may begin to envy the fellow in the bed.

The gray light of dawn falls upon cartons of coffee, full ashtrays, coats and sweaters draped over chairs, scattered notes made during the night. The sleeper's temperature is rising, and something has gone wrong with an eye lead. A doctor in the adjacent laboratory has come in early, and sticks his head in the door with a cheerful greeting. He looks disgustingly fresh. The experimenter runs his hand over a growth of beard. At seven he will be able to awaken the volunteer. In the remaining time, the researchers think of problems—of analyzing this mass of scribbles and tape.

Some of their problems are judgmental. The EEGs will not tell them everything. For example, during the third REM period, which looked so active on paper, they awakened their man and he denied that he was dreaming. They would have laid bets that it was a whopper, perhaps sexual, perhaps violent, but the young man firmly denied dreaming. At the National Institutes of Health, Frederick Snyder recalls an incident like this. He and his associates puzzled over it. "Later we understood. Our subject told his friend that he'd be damned if he'd tell those people his dreams." Defiance is rare, but subjects can cause as much trouble when they are too eager to please. During an equipment failure, one hospital patient endured a whole night of intense discomfort, but kept firmly insisting he was comfortable. Later he admitted his discomfort to friends and said he would not go to the laboratory again.

Patients from psychiatric wards present special problems. One scientist recalls walking into the bedroom to find that his subject, a brain-damaged patient, had systematically unscrewed all the wire leads, one by one. More often the agitated patient will tear off the electrodes. Mental patients have special anxieties and fears, but more than that, as one former patient of St. Elizabeth's Hospital in Washington, D. C., succinctly said, "Sleep is the only privacy in the hospital." To her, as to many patients, the impersonality of the experimenters may seen inhumane. A detached relationship with subjects is carefully maintained, lest volunteers, and particularly women, interpret night awakenings and repair of equipment as a personal assault. All of these hidden factors enter into the analysis of transcripts and polygraph records. The experimenter knows that his data hides many subtle attitudes, meanings of sleep, and idiosyncrasies that may cast doubt on the volunteer's verbal statements, or suggest some new puzzle.

Heated but sotto voce discussions will be held on these points of judgment. The researchers will have to decide when data is invalid and should be cast out, and whether a particular subject ought to quit the study. If anything perplexing or dubious happens during this night it may rekindle the weary men at the controls even in the last hour before unplugging the volunteer. Once again, as he sits perhaps stuporously on a stool while the electrodes are removed, the subject will be greeted by almost standard questions: "How did you sleep this time?"

When the young man has dressed and departed he leaves behind him a manuscript that covers almost 2,000 feet of graph paper. At the end of a long study, his sleep record extends for several miles. Hundreds of miles of EEGs have been painstakingly studied to derive our first description of a normal night of sleep. Now we need normative studies, encompassing people of all age groups—thousands of miles of EEG tracings—so that we can clearly outline the protocols of the nighttime nervous system and obtain a yardstick against which to pinpoint disorders.

For the person who donated his sleep to science, the night was brief and is now over. The end of the long night is merely the beginning for the scientists. They must discover what the brain has been saying. The task of interpreting these body changes and brain waves from half a mile of what looks like illegible penmanship is an interesting story in itself.

Anybody who thinks twice about the constant changes of sleep realizes that there are not just four distinct EEG states. It is a convenient taxonomy, and these approximate categories have been as useful as national boundaries. Where sleep once seemed all the same, a closer look revealed gross subdivisions, and now we are aware that there are finer subdivisions within each state of sleep. Indeed the same rhythms can be detected throughout waking, but not by looking at an inked record. The subtleties of sleep have begun to emerge only as magnetic tapes and computers have become available.

For many purposes, visual analysis of the record is sufficient, for others impossible. Any wave, including brain waves, has several important aspects that define it. Frequency—how fast the waves are coming—requires a count of the number of waves in a specified time. To do this by eye means literally counting the number of waves in each second on the graph paper. Amplitude, or height, tells about the extent of electrical shift in the brain, the voltage. To measure amplitudes of brain waves with a ruler, one would need huge enlargements so big that a few minutes of the record would cover the walls of a large laboratory. Although many questions can be answered by a visual comparison of EEGs and body changes and behavior, one could not answer many simple questions. Are brain waves during a dream alike? If one were to sample five seconds from the beginning, five seconds from the middle, and the end, would they be the same? Answers to such questions reveal a great deal about the way our brains work. Fortunately, they can be supplied by computer analysis.

When brain waves are recorded on multichannel magnetic tape, the computer fed this tape can be asked to count how many waves occur each second, or to screen for waves of a certain voltage. Each few seconds of sleep contains a whole spectrum of frequencies. How are they distributed? Do high frequencies occur only in waking and dreaming? The computer can be programmed to do a spectral analysis, showing up frequency changes that would be imperceptible to the naked eye. Similarly one can examine the voltages to show the distribution of energy, or power, in different stages of sleep. This has been done. W. Ross Adey and his colleagues at the University of California in Los Angeles have pioneered in developing techniques that enable detailed pictures of energy changes in the human brain during waking and the different phases of sleep. During waking, for example, the energy may be spread among the high frequencies—the fast waves are biggest in amplitude. But as drowsiness begins, there is a shift, and a gradual increase of energy among the low frequencies—the slow waves, which are growing larger. Adey's group has also looked at the relative timing of brain waves—for phase shifts. Small segments of the EEG record that look coherent to the eye contain many variations within, upon analysis. Moments of sleep that looked alike visually have proven to be far from identical.

These methods can now be combined so that the night's sleep is automatically recorded on tape and fed to a computer. A scientist can look at the computer's summary and know precisely how the night went, and whether the individual enjoyed a sleep that was normal for his age or showed deviations that invite medical investigation. Adey's laboratory has analyzed, in this manner, 24-hour records from monkeys destined for space flight. Such a baseline is considered essential by many scientists for determining how space affects the sleep-waking cycle, and while we have performed such EEG studies on animals, ironically we have not done so for human beings in the course of our manned space flight program.

One might wonder how brain waves detected from the scalp, and therefore the outermost layer of the cortex, can tell us what is happening deep within the brain. A good deal of what we know is, of course, based on inference, after repeatedly comparing surface EEGs with brain waves obtained from sites deep within. Data of this sort comes from animals with implanted electrodes and also a few human patients, whose deep electrode placements may guide a neurosurgeon before he operates. Some implants have been so microscopic as to give readings from single brain cells.

One very important technique is known as the averaged EEG response. Every time our senses are stimulated by light or sound or touch, whether we are aware of it or not, our brain reacts. The EEG reaction is infinitesimal, but if the stimulus is repeated, and the EEG responses superimposed upon one another, the shape of the response shows up clearly. It may sound like a tedious process, but the results are magical for, like reading the Bible from the head of a pin, a scientist can scan a few squiggles that last only five-thousandths of a second and learn something about the way in which a sound signal travels through the brain, and how different parts of the brain are processing it. By this method we have found that the waking and dreaming brain react in a similar manner to a sound, and that the deeply sleeping brain responds quite differently. The shape of the EEG responses have been analyzed to reveal this information.

By these new methods of treating the EEG, it has become possible to detect the points of neural damage from which epileptic seizures emanate, to locate tumors, to track the mind of a sleeping person, and to use the EEG as a sensitive radar into the behavior of the brain—as a striking example will indicate.

Manfred Clynes and his associates at Rockland State Hospital have been averaging the EEG responses of a person who sits in a dark room, looking at colors projecting upon a screen. Without being in the room, the scientists can look at the averaged brain-wave responses and tell what color—indeed, what shade—the person was seeing. Different colors appear to excite different portions of the brain and so the location of the electrodes and shape of the response disclose the color. With this kind of sensitivity, and the speed of computer analyses, we can hope to clarify the picture of normal nightly sleep, and use sleep patterns for diagnosing disorders. Today, the combination of many kinds of animal and human research, and new methods of EEG analysis are allowing us to track the activity inside the brain without neurosurgery, which was necessary in years past.

With these new instruments we are rapidly refining our picture of nightly sleep, and beginning to discover what hidden transitions occur in the body and brain during the various EEG stages. If it was once surprising to imagine that a person at an EEG machine could follow, and even predict the course of a sleeping man, the implications of this mapping are more surprising yet. We are likely to map out the normal range of sleep progressions for people of a certain age, and to discover what biological rhythms these rising and falling tides appear to represent, what changes in metabolism, and brain function. Already, a person's sleep patterns tell quite a bit about him. If he suffers from a nervous disorder such as epilepsy, he may have sleep seizures during particular phases and at no other times. If he is anxious or has taken certain drugs, his sleep picture will reveal characteristic deviations from his normal pattern. Some individuals have shown bizarre sleep patterns, such as an oscillation all night between the two lightest stages, a clue that their trouble may be pinpointed within a particular region of the brain. Sleep, with its hours of stillness, is a convenient time to study a person, and its orderly changes are part of the rhythms that influence his normal or abnormal waking life.

IV

MAN WITHOUT SLEEP

IN 1959, New York City beheld one of the most disturbing ordeals a man can undergo. Day and night, while the public gathered in a spirit of carnival curiosity around a Times Square recruiting booth, a well-known disc jockey was staying awake for 200 hours to benefit the Polio Fund of the National Foundation. He looked weary, but no radio listener or casual onlooker could have imagined the truth of his experience. It resembled a medieval torture.

Peter Tripp was neither the first nor the last to volunteer for a state so grueling within, yet so invisible to the public. In Detroit a couple of years later another disc jockey stayed awake longer, and yet another achieved 230 sleepless hours for the Muscular Dystrophy Fund. A San Diego high school student outdid them all and remained awake for eleven days and nights.

Everyone has heard anecdotal "proof" that man can manage well without sleep, and it has never seemed so essential to us as food, air, and water. But is sleep a necessity? Scientists who supervised, at least in part, several of the famous wakathons have found in them—as in their laboratory studies—disheartening evidence about the psychological effects of sleep loss, raising serious questions about aftereffects. One disc jockey with a record of some mental instability went seven days without sleep, suffered persistent symptoms, and ended in a mental institution, although a high school student recovered without noticeable traces after a much longer vigil. One way of finding out about the necessity for sleep is to take it away and see what happens. This method is age-old, but it has not always been used for disinterested or scientific purposes.

During the Inquisition one of the most diabolical tortures inflicted on people accused of witchcraft was the *tortura insomnia,* enforced sleeplessness. Many supposed witches were in fact mentally ill, and after being prevented from sleep or even from resting day after day, they were plummeted into deeper insanity, growing more deluded, even violent, until ultimately they found peace only in death.

From the beginning, interrogators seem to have known about the weakening impact of sleep loss. It is a method of torment that can break the will without leaving scars, a cheap and humiliating way of eliciting confessions. It is still used by police departments, and was used on American POWs during the Korean war. Louis Jolyon West, Director of the Psychiatry Department at the University of Oklahoma, observed some of the returning Air Force prisoners who had given false confessions of germ warfare. He found they had been awakened at irregular intervals and only allowed to sleep in snatches. It was not long before they began to suffer the chronic symptoms of sleep loss. They were confused about time, disoriented, and had a hard time distinguishing between reverie and reality. Many became suggestible and some temporarily psychotic. A few began to believe they *had* been dropping germ bombs on Korea. Throughout, and above all, they wanted sleep—and those who complied were rewarded with sleep. Interminable questioning, indoctrination, and sleep loss were mistakenly known as "brainwashing"—as if the method were new and secret.

A glance at history shows innumerable battles lost, major accidents, diplomatic misjudgments, ruined careers and "inexplicable" episodes of mental illness that can be traced to lack of sleep. It has been written, indeed, that Perseus, the last of the

Macedonian kings, was totally prevented from sleeping by the Roman conquerors and thus put to death. Certainly, shrewd military tacticians guessed the importance of sleep. In a manner of speaking, it is to this that Haiti owes its independence. In 1802, when Napoleon sent a huge army to quell disorder in the rebellious little colony, the guerrilla fighters were far outnumbered. Through the nights, however, they feinted attacks that prevented the French army from resting. Finally, racked by fatigue and then by disease, the decimated French troops withdrew, and in 1804 Haiti was a sovereign state.

Although sleep loss is an occupational hazard of the military, its consequences never fully impressed us until World War II. Brigadier General J. G. Hill vividly recalls an incident during the Battle of the Bulge that was not uncommon. He was riding in a jeep with General Clarence H. Huebner, Commander of the Fifth Army Corps, when a wild-eyed sergeant came toward them on the road. They asked where he was going and he replied, "I'm going to the rear and I won't let you bastards stop me." Such a remark had only one meaning. General Huebner gently asked the sergeant to climb into the jeep and drove him to the hospital where the doctors put him to sleep for 35 hours—after which the man returned to duty and served through the rest of the war. In the harrowing jungle contests of the Pacific, troop psychiatrists saw many apparently stable men suddenly come into the hospital tent hallucinating, weeping with anxiety, or suffering from bizarre delusions. Many had been unable to sleep for 48 hours or longer, and their transient psychoses usually vanished after a good night's sleep. Nobody knows what role sleep loss may have played among those veterans who are still reported to bear the marks of battle fatigue.

Reminiscences of World War II are filled with stories of the puzzling behavior of the sleepless. Indeed, the high incidence of battle fatigue provided an impetus that led to intensive laboratory study of sleep starvation. Scientific study had actually begun in the 1890's, but our present knowledge starts with the early 1940's. David B. Tyler of the National Science Foundation studied a group of American marines, and described in detail some of the corrosive effects of sleep loss—intestinal complaints, headaches, irritability, thinking disorders, and even psychotic reactions. Since then our understanding of these effects has deepened, in large part owing to researches directed by Harold L. Williams at the Walter Reed Army Institute of Research. There, in the wooded outskirts of Washington, D. C., in an eccentric old building that was formerly a girls' boarding school, the first scientific wakathons were initiated.

Army volunteers lived in a hospital ward attended by nurses and corpsmen, ready at all hours with coffee, showers, and recreational amusements. Before, during, and after the wakathon, on a regular schedule, scientists recorded the EEGs, tested mental functioning, drew blood samples, and made other physiological measurements. None of these people were awake longer than 98 hours, but that was quite long enough for the research team to map a progressive mental deterioration and psychological change.

The mental symptoms of sleep loss, as followed in these and other studies, occur in a slow and predictable fashion, mounting as time goes on. The Walter Reed volunteers became more and more uneven on tests of performance, showing lapses of attention, weariness, and a tendency to withdraw from the outside world. They stopped making unnecessary movements and began to complain of unpleasant physical sensations—burning or itching eyes, blurred vision, a tight band around the head. Somewhere between 30 and 60 hours they began to notice changes in depth perception. Small objects seemed to dart out of place. Chairs seemed to change size. Many saw a halo of fog around lights. Others saw the floor begin to undulate.

By 90 hours some people were having vivid hallucinations. One man saw illusory dogs in the hall. Another called for help in washing away the cobwebs that seemed to cling to his face and hands. It was hard to tell the time of day or night. Time seemed to stretch or compress like an accordion. To enhance the sense of confusion, thoughts became intermingled with external reality. Brief dreams would intrude, sometimes in the midst of speaking, and it was hard to distinguish these fleeting and imaginary events from those that actually occurred. The men shifted moods, finding themselves laughing for no reason or, more often, growing depressed and irascible. Each day the tests seemed harder than they had before, and the men gave a poorer performance. These symptoms appeared in the quiet of a hospital ward among scientists who were careful to minimize anxiety—a far cry from the strains, frights, and miseries of battle. There was disturbing evidence that sleep loss, alone, must cause some major changes in the function of the brain.

From outside one might have concluded that the mental processes of the subjects were slowing down. They would lose their train of thought, make errors in speech, sometimes meandering off into fantasy in midsentence. Most people associate sleep loss with "slowing down" and realize that it is inadvisable to drive a car or perform any act requiring split-second reactions while tired. Safety manuals often say that reaction time slows down under fatigue. The Walter Reed studies indicated that this is not quite true. After about 30 hours of wakefulness a subject would sometimes react to a signal as rapidly as he did when normally rested, but occasionally he took three times longer. As sleep loss wore on, he was not steadily slowing down like an unwound clock but growing progressively more uneven. He would be told to press a button as quickly as he could whenever a light turned on, or sometimes when a buzzer sounded, an act he did reliably and with ease when rested. But while his overall pattern may have resembled a slowing down, in fact he was missing more and more of the signals during lapses in attention.

When the pacing of the signal was beyond his control the sleepless person did poorly. Still, he could perform well on certain mental tests. He could make computations, add pairs of numbers. He did well so long as he went at his own pace. If pressed to compute rapidly he was no longer accurate. As the studies continued they began to delineate what a sleep-starved person can and cannot do. When playing a communications game, for example, in which one man issued the orders and another executed them, the person who issued the orders made fewer mistakes than the executor. By 70 hours of wakefulness, however, both of them had doubled the numbers of errors they made when rested.

These impairments were seen during World War II. In *Night Drop* S. L. A. Marshall described the airborne troops who saw continuous action after they first dropped into Normandy in 1944—"dull-eyed, bodily worn and too tired to think connectedly." He quotes an officer who related the worst of the story:

> "They were so beat they could not understand words even if an order was clearly expressed. I was too tired to talk straight. Nothing I heard made a firm impression on me. I spoke jerkily in phrases because I could not remember the thoughts which had preceded what I said."

This peculiar lack of memory has been pronounced among the sleep-starved men studied by scientists. In many instances, however, they discovered that the failure was not one of memory. At Walter Reed the volunteers were asked to do a task that required only sustained attention. A man was asked to press a button each time he saw a pair of letters—AX—in a series that continuously paraded before his eyes on a screen. Sometimes he was lying on a cot, wearing EEG electrodes. He might be asked to press the button when he felt a particular vibration among others on his hand, or when he heard a particular sequence of sounds in a continuous series. The volunteer merely had to keep alert for the signal. As sleep loss continued all the men made more and more errors of omission. Their lapses of attention might have been interpreted as simply that, but the EEGs revealed what they were. At the time of the lapse the waking alpha rhythm would slow down, and for two to three seconds there would be a burst of slow waves like those of sleep. The person was having brief sleep seizures, or microsleeps, as they have been termed.

Now the researchers could see why a person erred so badly on certain tasks. He was momentarily asleep and missed parts of the instruction or the signals he was expecting. This was not the man one wanted on sentry duty. He was not a good choice for monitoring radar or sonar, and he would not even be reliable at receiving communications. In fact, as the evidence mounted, it became clear that a sleep-starved soldier might easily misinterpret orders that he merely heard, and could probably do better if he read them.

The laboratory tests were carried out at the same hours each day, and it soon became apparent that there was a rhythm in the performance of the sleepless groups. They were decidedly at their worst during the early morning hours when their body temperature fell to the daily low point, and they would improve in the afternoon and evening of the next day. Under sleep deprivation the daily temperature became slightly exaggerated, and it was during the low point that the men felt most palpably weary. It was then they were most bedeviled by visual distortions, illusions, skin sensations, and their lapses were most frequent. Fragments of thought or reverie often intermixed with reality. It was then a subject was most apt to start a sentence and trail off into the gibberish of a fleeting dream.

The point of the many studies conducted here and abroad was never to press men to the limits in order to examine psychological abnormalities, but to explore their abilities to perform certain tasks during three to four days of unremitting wakefulness. This goes little beyond a common vigil under combat, among seamen or the pressures of meeting deadlines among certain professionals. Those who believe the stories of people who claim they can manage without sleep, the reported feats of excellent performance, may be discouraged by the scientific literature. Sleepless people are curiously inconsistent in their abilities, and the studies of microsleeps have indicated how they could manage to read, compute, write, issue commands, and yet fail to grasp spoken sentences. The studies have contributed findings of immense practical value. Some of these are so plausible as to seem self-evident, yet their important social implications seem to have left little impression on planners. Nobody expects the sleep-starved person to be energetic and efficient, but does he show tendencies that might lead to bad judgment, to lowered standards?

During the long hours between tests at Walter Reed the men quickly gave up any reading or complicated games that required intellectual effort. They abandoned muscular exertions and began spending their time in desultory and listless social conversation. A man who when normally rested would play a skillful game of strategy against a standard slot machine, varying his moves to beat the machine, now changed. He adopted a rigid and predictable strategy, and no longer seemed to try to remember his past moves in order to guess the machine's program. Instead he alternated his plays as if he didn't care, and merely took the course that cost the least mental effort. Fatigue seemed to bring a certain laziness. If given a lot of incentive, however, a person could improve on some tasks.

At first glance monotony seemed to have a particularly strong effect, although it became apparent later that sleep-starved men had a harder time tracking an erratic signal under monotony than doing an even more tedious but utterly redundant task. Other studies, some performed in Cambridge, England, under the direction of R. T. Wilkinson, indicated that the sleepless man reacted somewhat differently to his environment than did a rested man. A hot room, a small amount of alcohol or a continuous hissing sound that would impair a rested person actually improved his performance at a tracking task. Yet a lot of alcohol or a moderately warm room merely worsened an already poor showing.

Within limits, the experimenters found there were factors that could improve performance. Weary men could manage to scan a screen if things happened slowly. They could improve at tasks if told the result of their moves. In spite of fatigue they managed to play a moderately complex game simulating a naval battle. Interest helped, but they could not rapidly cope with added amounts of information. The tired man needed to set his own pace, and benefited from incentive, feedback, interest, or challenge. Many news correspondents say that the challenge of a crisis is what pulls them through a three-day work stint. Eric Sevareid has voiced another recurrent observation. "In this business," he has remarked, "when you are broadcasting steadily you keep going on adrenalin for quite a while." In 1960 a research team led by B. Metz, at Strasbourg, France, published evidence showing that a person excreted higher concentrations of adrenalin and noradrenalin when working under sleep loss than when doing the same work after a normal night's rest. The chemical changes of the body, moreover, appeared to be influenced by what a person happened to be doing during sleep loss as well as his environment at the time. This information simply added to a current picture that has begun to impress some decision makers and military commanders with the genuine dangers of sleep loss, especially when coupled with stress.

Back in 1959 enough had been learned about the effects of sleep deprivation to inspire caution. When Peter Tripp decided to forgo sleep for over eight days, scientists tried to dissuade him from a courageous but risky undertaking. Tripp was determined. He set up broadcasting headquarters in a glass-walled Army recruiting booth in Times Square. Across the street in the Hotel Astor a suite was converted into a psychological laboratory. An impressive crew of psychologists, psychiatrists and medical specialists offered to participate under the direction of Louis Jolyon West, of Oklahoma, and Harold L. Williams, then of Walter Reed. A preliminary checkup and some baseline tests were made to establish Tripp's normal functions. Then a regular daily routine involved medical and psychological tests, including tests of mental ability. EEG recordings were to be made at Columbia University each day, and blood samples and urine collected and analyzed. For more than eight days Tripp was never away from the watchful care of doctors and nurses. He broadcast his regular program and a dozen spot comments on his progress from the booth, and every few hours he was escorted to the Hotel Astor Laboratory where he could also clean up and change clothes. If there was any known safeguard to be obtained under the circumstances, Peter Tripp had it.

Almost from the first the overpowering force of sleepiness hit him. Constant company, walks, tests, broadcasts helped, but after about five days he needed a stimulant to keep going. Although his health was good and he stayed on a high-protein athletic diet, he soon remarked that he felt like "the last pill in the bottle." After little more than two days as he changed shoes in the hotel he pointed out to West a very interesting sight. There were cobwebs in his shoes—to his eyes, at least. West had warned him that he would have visual illusions. Specks on the table began to look like bugs. He thought he saw a rabbit in the booth. He was beginning to have trouble remembering things.

By 100 hours, only halfway, he had reached an inexorable turning point. Now he could perform only one or two of the daily battery of tests. Tests requiring attention or minimal mental agility had become unbearable to him and the psychologists testing him. As one later recalled, "Here was a competent New York disc jockey trying vainly to find his way through the alphabet." By 170 hours the tests were torture. A simple algebraic problem that Tripp had earlier solved with ease took such superhuman effort that he was frightened, and his agonized attempts to perform were painful to watch.

Loss of concentration and mental agility were not the worst, however. By 110 hours there were signs of delirium. As one of the doctors recalled, "We didn't know much about it at the time because he couldn't tell us." From his later statements, his curious utterances and behavior at the time, it became clear. Tripp's visual world had grown grotesque. A doctor walked into the recruiting booth in a tweed suit that Tripp saw as a suit of furry worms. A nurse appeared to drip saliva. A scientist's tie kept jumping. This was frightening, hard to explain, and sometimes Tripp grew angry wondering if this were a bona fide experiment or a masquerade. Around 120 hours, he opened a bureau drawer in the hotel and rushed out calling for help. It seemed to be spurting flames. Tripp thought the blaze had been set deliberately to test him. In order to explain to himself these hallucinations—which appeared quite real—he concocted rationalizations resembling the delusions of psychotic patients.

By about 150 hours he became disoriented, not realizing where he was, and wondering who he was. He developed a habit of glancing oddly at the large clock on the wall of the booth. As the doctors later found, the clock bore the features of an actor he knew, made up like Dracula for a television show. He began to wonder whether he were Peter Tripp or the actor whose face he saw on the clock. Still his teen-age admirers, radio audience, and onlookers would not have guessed his torment. Sometimes he would back up against a wall and let nobody walk behind him. Yet from 5 to 8 P.M. all his forces were mysteriously summoned, and he efficiently organized his commercials and records and managed a vigorous patter for three hours. Although he had passed the breaking point, he never made careless indiscretions, profanities, or the kind of impulsive utterances he made when off the air. His broadcast time occurred at the peak of his diurnal temperature cycle. It was later, when his temperature was low, that he showed the worst symptoms. Although he managed to act awake continuously, his brain waves were like those of deep sleep.

On the final morning of the final day a famous neurologist arrived to examine him. The doctor carried an umbrella, although it was a bright day, and had a somewhat archaic manner of dress. To Tripp he must have appeared funereal. He always insisted that patients undress and lie down on the examining table. Tripp complied, but as he gazed up at the doctor he came to the morbid conclusion that the man was actually an undertaker, there for the purpose of burying him alive. With this gruesome insight, Tripp leapt for the door with several doctors in pursuit. Nightmare hallucination had merged with reality, and the only explanation seemed to be that the doctors had formed a sadistic conspiracy in which he was the victim.

With some persuasion, Tripp managed to get through the day, give his final broadcast, and then, following an hour of tests, he sank into sleep for 13 hours. When he awakened, the terrors, ghoulish illusions, and mental agony had vanished. He no longer saw a visual world where objects changed size, specks turned into bugs, and clocks bore human faces. Now it was no effort to remember a joke and solve simple problems. In 13 hours that unspeakable purgatory had vanished, although a slight depression lingered for three months. The strain and publicity had probably contributed to the ordeal, but it had been a valuable one for research.

It has been striking to see that the symptoms of sleep loss, whether mild or intense, developed in roughly the same way in subsequent wakathons. Rick Micheals, a Michigan disc jockey, stayed awake 230 hours for the Muscular Dystrophy Fund. He, too, was driven from a room in terror when blue flames seemed to spurt at him from a wall. He also suffered an inability to concentrate or perform simple tasks. He felt the tight band of pressure around his head and eventually grew hostile and irascible with his doctors. Micheals was under the surveillance of five scientists from the Lafayette Clinic, under the direction of physiologist Albert Ax. The group had long been interested in the fact that prolonged sleep loss brings on symptoms like those of psychosis. They suspected that biochemical changes must be taking place within the body.

Between 40 and 100 hours there is a turning point; changes become severe and the sleepless person feels an alteration in the weight of his arms and legs, sometimes saying they are not attached to his body. Now the illusions and hallucinations intermittently appear. It is around this time that the body's energy metabolism shows pronounced change. The transformation of food into energy for our nerves, muscles, and all cell activities depends upon the chemical ATP—adenosine triphosphate—

which is the catalyst for energy release in all living matter. As food substances break down into cellular energy, ATP loses one of its phosphates and becomes ADP—adenosine diphosphate. Ordinarily ADP is reconverted and stored so that the supply of ATP does not run down, but after about four days of sleep loss, the emergency metabolism creating ATP seems to decline notably. This is the time when people show most striking changes in behavior.

After only 48 hours of sleep loss, moreover, the body seems to begin generating a stress chemical that belongs to the LSD family (known to produce hallucinations). The new chemical was detected by Arnold Mandell and his associates at UCLA, in people who had received a mild stress, in people who had gone two days without food, and in people who had gone 48 hours without sleep. If this stress-responsive indole has psychological effects like that of LSD, and if it increases in the system during prolonged sleep loss, we may begin to explain why sleep loss produces psychotic symptoms.

The indications are that sleep loss causes some very sizable changes in physiology and brain function. We do not yet know whether they can lead to irreversible brain damage. In a number of experiments, when animals have been kept awake for long periods there have been quite noticeable changes in brain tissue. It would seem reasonable to err on the side of caution in behavior, at least, for one might guess that protracted sleeplessness or long and cumulative sleep loss would leave some permanent traces. What we do perceive now is that a stressed and weary person, totally or partially deprived of sleep, has undergone pronounced biochemical changes in his body, altering the way he musters energy and the function of his mind. These transformations are reflected in the characteristically anguished facial expression of the sleep-starved. A leeched and hollow-eyed stare of suspicion were typical of Cardinal Mindszenty in his trial photographs, of POWs, of accused men after police interrogation. The use of sleep deprivation in so-called brainwashing exploits the progressive symptoms of confusion, delusion, and transient psychosis.

In Korea there were many POWs who did not make false confessions although they, too, suffered the stupor of fatigue and the mounting symptoms. Some studies of these prisoners suggests that a small percentage of men have an unusual sense of purpose and commitment, whatever they may have to endure. Peter Tripp showed this commitment during his daily broadcasts. Loyalty and purpose might be enhanced by training. Nevertheless, a person's tolerance for sleep loss and his behavior may have an individual component—of health, constitution, and personality.

At Walter Reed there were hints that the adjustment of the volunteers was congruent with the personality configurations they revealed beforehand on projective tests and interviews. Researchers found they could predict which members of the group would find the experience toughest and when they would report hallucinations. Some were complainers and others habitually denied symptoms. Still, the people who reported hallucinations were not always the ones who showed the greatest mental impairment on tests or the greatest decline in motor skills. They were somewhat characterized by defensiveness, and by what might be called schizophrenic traits.

Several years ago at McGill University in Montreal, six chronic schizophrenic patients were kept awake for 100 hours. As the time wore on they began to exhibit acute symptoms that had been gone for years; among them, the typical schizophrenic hallucinations, which are auditory. When people refer to schizophrenic hallucinations they usually mean auditory hallucinations. Sleep loss soon exacerbates the symptoms of the mentally ill, and an undefined factor that might be called mental stability seems to be important in tolerating protracted wakefulness. After seven days awake, a disc jockey with some prior mental instability ended in a mental hospital. Quite a few people, other than the mentally unstable, seem particularly vulnerable to sleep loss. Epileptics and narcoleptics begin to suffer from more seizures. Quite a few people do not realize they are vulnerable. One command pilot studied in the Air Force, a man with 6,000 flying hours, suddenly had a convulsion after an inspection duty that permitted him only a few cat naps for 48 hours. There was no family history of pathology, and his neurological examination seemed quite normal. The initial exam was conducted when he was rested; 30 hours of sleep deprivation were sufficient to bring out distinct abnormalities in his EEGs.

One factor that seems to be very important in withstanding sleep loss is age. Peter Tripp was thirty-two years old when he set his record. Five years later Randy Gardner set a new record of 268 hours of wakefulness—11 days. Randy was seventeen when he undertook this self-experiment for a high school science project. It was done in the quiet of home, attended by doctors and friends, and without stimulants or the stress of publicity. Still, mild as they were, Randy's symptoms followed the same progression. After four days he became unsmiling and irritable, unable to concentrate or remember things well. He saw fog around street lights, felt the hatband pressure on his head. By nine days there were transient illusions and reveries, and at one point the sandy-haired boy imagined himself a great Negro football player. He was leaving sentences unfinished, suffering blurred vision, and showing EEGs like those of early sleep. At the end of 11 days he slept over 14 hours and rebounded in a cheerful, refreshed mood. It should be said that subtle aftereffects, perhaps not noticeable to Randy or a casual onlooker, persisted for at least 10 days, and perhaps months.

While scientists at the San Diego Naval Hospital were analyzing the physiological records and measurements obtained from Randy, a group of psychologists at the University of Florida were solving a curious riddle about the role of age in tolerating sleep loss. Wilse B. Webb and his associates at Gainesville had placed a group of young rats on a mesh water wheel, hoping to weary them so that they would fall asleep quickly. The wheel rotated slowly and continuously, and if the animal fell asleep he toppled into cold water. The researchers kept expecting the rats to topple, but some of them managed to stay on the water wheel for 27 days, an unbelievable stretch. However, when older rats were placed on the wheel they fell off in three to four days. By testing rats of intermediate ages, the experimenters could see that the staying power of the animal was directly correlated with its age. Just how a young animal managed to keep moving on the wheel for 27 days was not answered until delicate EEG techniques revealed that they were snatching brief naps of about 10 to 15 seconds as they rode the wheel. For almost a third of their time on the wheel they showed EEGs of sleep. They would nap for a few seconds and then quickly run back to the end of the wheel and sleep as they rode forward. These animals were exhausted when they were taken from the wheel, but they could stay in a wakeful position far longer than their older relatives.

Certain questions about the effects of sleep loss can be answered only by animal studies. Since monkeys know none of our cultural myths and will not try to live up to expectations, some sleep deprivation experiments have been repeated with them. When tasks almost identical to the attention tests given at Walter Reed but adapted for monkeys are given a sleep-deprived animals, they too make errors of omission and seem to suffer increasing microsleeps as their enforced wakefulness continues. With these creatures it will be possible to track effects of sleep loss on responses from deep within the brain. It may be possible to find out whether brain damage occurs after moderate sleep loss, and whether aftereffects linger in proportion to the severity of the symptoms. Man is not likely to drive himself to the limit knowingly, and instances of severe symptoms have come about inadvertently, sometimes in unlikely places.

Many doctors and patients complain that a hospital is no place to find rest, and there seems to be some truth to the allegation. After the development of open-heart surgery, doctors were bewildered by peculiar postoperative reactions. They were psychotic symptoms—delirium, hallucinations, paranoia, disorientation—that set in after several lucid days of recovery. The puzzle was finally disentangled by two psychiatrists and a heart surgeon. In a study of 99 patients, Donald S. Kornfield, Sheldon Zimberg, and James R. Malm at Columbia Presbyterian Medical Center found these symptoms in over a third of their cases and pondered the role of anxiety, anesthesia, and many aspects of the treatment.

Each patient had been taken from surgery to a tile recovery room equipped with special monitoring instruments. He was placed in an oxygen cooling tent, surrounded by a monotonous hissing noise, and could not move much because of cables and wires attached for continuous monitoring of the heart. The ward was a busy place, and to many, frightening. Some adult patients confessed that they were preoccupied with dying and were afraid to sleep, but hourly medical checks and nursing care would have prevented any prolonged sleep in any case. After three to five days in this monotonous and sleepless atmosphere a patient might be overheard making an outlandish remark. One woman began to hear constant rock 'n roll music; she decided it was a plot to torture her. Another saw a landscape in the light reflected from a neighbor's oxygen tent. Another heard her name incessantly called over the loudspeaker system. Rocking or floating sensations were often followed by hallucination and paranoid suspicions, resembling schizophrenia or acute brain syndromes. The symptoms blossomed after three to five days in the recovery room, but usually vanished when a patient was moved to a private room and allowed to sleep uninterruptedly.

The doctors, who concluded that sleep loss and monotony contributed to the mental stress of a severe operation, were now able to suggest that patients be placed immediately in private rooms, in a less monotonous environment, and allowed to sleep through the night with as few interruptions as possible. This study, perhaps not the only one of its genre, took an important step in medicine. Many doctors will welcome a reconsideration of the problems of rest in hospitals. One doctor in Washington, D. C., has said, "I have had only two patients who died of coronaries in the last five years. And these patients complained bitterly of the lack of sleep available to them in the hospital because of extended medical and nursing care imposed upon them. . . ." Hospital organization is likely to be complicated by considerations of sleep, for not all people sleep easily, nor do all people require the same amount of sleep.

If a person wishes to know how much sleep he usually requires, one rough-and-ready method is simply to abandon the alarm clock and count the hours it takes between the time of falling asleep and awakening refreshed. Chronic sleep loss from a habitual shortchanging of nightly sleep does not produce sudden and dramatic consequences in the manner of total deprivation. Long and intensive studies will be needed to track its consequences in behavior and physiology. After days of cutting sleep, however, many a tired person will recall some familiar transformations—irritability, pressure around the head, fog around street lights, momentary illusions.

When a person cuts his sleep short he is changing the kind of sleep he gets. A night that is two or three hours shorter than usual will probably not be a miniature of his normal nightly pattern. In several laboratories where volunteers have sustained a schedule of 2½, 3, or 4 hours' sleep for a number of nights in succession, there has been a marked change in the proportion of time allotted to each stage of sleep. Usually, abbreviation of sleep means a reduction in REM dreaming. Chronic sleep loss thus seems to be a change in the quality of sleep as well as quantity.

It is not necessary to wait for further evidence to form some opinions on the importance of sleep. Sleep starvation can cause unnecessary social waste, expense, error, and tragedy. We have seen how judgment can fade, how strong ethical purposes can diminish, how mental functions decline and finally transient symptoms of psychosis begin to dominate the rational man. Military people have been among the first to recognize that sleep requires the kind of attention usually given to the logistics of food, sanitation, and other essentials to survival. Writers in military journals, and in some industries, are beginning to use the laboratory data for guidelines in planning. Throughout modern society, people are required to make split-second reactions or come to swift decisions on the assumption that their speed and reliability are not impaired. But these are talents of the rested man, and on the whole we make little provision for rest. A tired person might look in office buildings, factories, stores, gas stations and at any hour find a vending machine that sells food, coffee, cigarettes, aspirin, even combs and perfume, but no cot where he could nap. Not even the so-called rest stops on major turnpikes have rest-room dormitories where a tired driver might sleep. Inadequate facilities for rest may bother a host of busy people, but the problem of obtaining rest is more complicated and individual than that, for we do not all sleep alike.

V

POOR SLEEP AND GOOD SLEEP

MORNING amenities are apt to mention sleep, and while these adult conversations are usually banal, they plainly reveal that one man's night of sleep is not just like another's, nor is every night the same kind of experience for any individual. One day a person arises refreshed and vigorous after a night that seemed no longer than an eyeblink. Yet on the next day he may vaguely recall an interminable and fitful night, awakening as if from combat, feeling sodden or perhaps as irritable as a rhinoceros for no sensible reason.

Worry may corrode sleep, depression create a leaden sluggishness, and fever, alcohol, fatigue, the season of the year, temperature of the room, and pressure of the atmosphere all may combine with a multitude of unknowns to create the texture of a night's sleep. For most people life contains a mixture. Many people fall asleep with great ease, slumber soundly all night, and awaken refreshed as a general rule. Others, a more vociferous segment of humanity, complain that they generally do not sleep well. These differences are so common, so ever-present, that they are accepted like personal idiosyncrasies, and the handiest irritant is used to explain poor sleep, while good sleep is often attributed to some virtue, such as a clear conscience, or sound habits.

Sleep differences are hardly grounds for divorce, but incompatible couples often express them to marriage counselors to illustrate their emotional troubles. A well-known counselor in Washington, D. C., has indicated, in a few terse excerpts from case histories, how sleep differences become a weapon in the battle of the sexes:

> "She has to go to bed at 10. I do at midnight. Then when I get to bed she's already asleep."
>
> "He needs more sleep than I do; we can't have any fun."
>
> "She wakes up fast in the morning and wants sex before breakfast. I'm a slow riser and have to get ready for work."
>
> "She likes a lot of blankets. I don't. So we had to take twin beds and that ruined our sex life."

Clearly, such complaints speak beyond sleep itself to the selfishness or compassion of the married partners, to their maturity or childishness. Marriage presupposes an ability to live with differences, and the counselor is interested in the manner in which they are handled. Nonetheless, for all the ludicrous anecdotes and jokes about sleep differences, we have begun to see that they are quite real, and represent pervasive differences in physiology and temperament. They are not the figments of a complaining imagination nor mere excuses for perverse behavior. Current researches may soon tell us why women often want more blankets than their husbands, and why one person requires more sleep than another. We have, as a start, begun to investigate what people mean when they describe their sleep as good or poor.

During the last decade, as sleep scientists have collected nightlong records from thousands of subjects, they have been acutely aware of individual differences, and often troubled by them. A researcher, embarked on an arduous study that necessitates a month of sleep recordings from each subject, will limit his exploration to the study of a few volunteers. He hopes that he has selected them from the great middle group of humanity, so that their reactions may be representative. But variation is the rule, and individual differences among subjects may help to account for some conflicting results among very similar experiments about dream recall, the ability to respond to instructions during sleep and, indeed, the response to dream loss or sleep starvation.

Although some researchers expect to find that there are patterns distinguishing the sleep of men from that of women, and while they are finding many indications that each person writes his own physiological signature at night, these explorations are still young. In some laboratories, seemingly irrelevant problems delay the exploration of sex differences in sleep. Chaperonage has been an issue in laboratories where there are not funds enough to hire nurses or woman monitors, for the sleep laboratory and all that it connotes burdens the doctor-scientist with greater legal risks than examination rooms in the clinic. Only recently has the number of woman sleep subjects begun to increase. In a relatively new endeavor scientists have begun to tabulate some of the physical signals distinguishing between the sleep of normal, healthy people.

One of the first dramatic divisions of a group of people into sound and restless sleepers came about almost inadvertently. It was a side product from a study of eight people who were presumed to be pretty much alike. The team of scientists, then at Walter Reed, was not looking for a division between good and poor sleep. They were trying out a mathematical method of analyzing the EEGs of sleep, a technique known as Markov Chain analysis, by which a person can take one or two steps in a series, and begin to predict what the next step will be. They wanted to know whether the EEG stages of sleep were so orderly that, with proper mathematical analysis, one might see a person in Stage II and predict whether he would drift up into REM, or down into Stage III. In the course of this analysis, John Hammack and his colleagues found that their eight volunteers (each of whom gave four nightlong EEG records) segregated into two groups. Mathematical analysis alone distinguished the two patterns—the restless people who tended to drift upward into light sleep and awaken versus the sound sleepers. Like many incidental findings hidden away in progress reports, this one did not create any stir, although it raised some interesting questions. The researchers wondered whether light sleep and a tendency to arousability might not cause some cumulative sleep loss, affecting the person in his daytime efficiency. Would the restless sleepers be able to sustain alertness as well as the sound sleepers? Would they have other problems?

Simultaneously, in other laboratories, some of these questions were being attacked, and a pioneer study at the University of Chicago provided some startling insights. Lawrence J. Monroe had begun working on his doctoral research program in the early 1960's at the sleep laboratory in Chicago. He had wanted to find out whether there were discernible physiological differences between good sleep and poor sleep, but to seek an answer he had to rephrase his question. He decided to compare the night records of people who ordinarily assert that they sleep well, with those who complain about generally bad sleep.

His procedure was straightforward. He used a local advertisement for good and poor sleepers and offered to pay for two nights of laboratory sleep. All the volunteers were selected by a carefully worded questionnaire. They answered such questions as, "How long does it take you to fall asleep at night?" The response was considerable, and the men were selected so that he had two well-matched groups, all of whom met some health standards, and none of whom represented real extremes of insomnia or exaggerated somnolence.

They were men between twenty and forty. The two groups were matched so that each contained people of comparable ages, education, and athletic proclivities. The spectrum included laborers, students, doctors, and professionals—men who had never gone to school beyond eighth grade and those with advanced degrees. Some were physically inactive, others very active. There were sixteen men in each group. Each person came to sleep in the lab for one night of acclimation before his night of recording, and was asked to fill out two questionnaires. One, the Cornell Medical Index, inquired about physical illnesses and symptoms. The other, a widely known psychological test, the Minnesota Multiphasic Personality Index, was designed to evoke some of the dominant traits and attitudes of the person.

On the recording night, the subject reported to the laboratory some time after 10 P.M., dressed for bed, and sat on a small stool in the anteroom to be decorated with electrodes. This procedure is usually soporific, but the experimenters were surprised to notice that a few of their subjects complained of discomfort. Thermistors, no bigger than the head of a pin, were used to take rectal temperatures all night. Most of the subjects did not notice them, but again, a few complained loudly that they hurt. A few subjects also complained of discomfort in the laboratory bedrooms, although each man slept through the night. At the time, the experimenters were receiving a first impressionistic hint of the difference between their two groups.

At 11 P.M. the subjects went to bed. Because some of the experimental bedrooms also doubled for offices by day, the subjects had to be gone relatively early and were awakened at 7 A.M Excluding the time for preparation and settling down, this gave each subject about seven hours in bed, and a maximum of seven hours' sleep. Months later when the data were analyzed and averaged for each group so that the major trends could be compared, it was clear that the good sleepers obtained considerably more sleep than did the poor. The group of good sleepers averaged a total of 6½ hours of sleep, while the poor sleepers obtained an average of 5¾. The poor sleepers took longer to fall asleep and awakened twice as often during the night.

Although the two groups differed in the amount of sleep they got, the experimenters had actually expected a far greater divergence, judging from their initial screening test. There was an interesting discrepancy here. On questioning, the good sleepers had accurately estimated how long they took to fall asleep at night. In the laboratory the average for the group was about 7 minutes. On the other hand, the poor sleepers had apparently exaggerated on the questionnaire—suggesting that the group would average about an hour before sleep onset. As it turned out, the group fell asleep in 15 minutes on the average, taking only twice as long as the good sleepers. Between the rapidity of sleep onset and number of awakenings, the good sleepers still averaged 45 minutes more sleep, overall. This was not surprising. In fact these differences are the subject of many breakfast conversations and medical texts and are assumed by clinicians. However, when the two groups were compared on other physiological measures, striking differences suggested real distinctions in body and brain function.

Pronounced physiological differences are associated with restlessness and the poor sleeper's difficulty in falling asleep. Higher body temperature and somewhat faster pulse suggested that the poor sleeper was more aroused before sleep, and closer to a waking state during sleep than was the good sleeper. Ordinarily the pulse slows down somewhat during sleep. The average heart rate of the poor sleepers was 66.9 beats a minute before sleep and dropped to 60.5 during sleep. Compare this with the good sleeper. His pulse is not nearly so fast before he drifts off, starting at about 60.7. During sleep his average pulse rate has dropped to about 56.6. That is quite a discrepancy.

The differences in body temperature were exceedingly striking, although at a first glance they might seem negligible. One has to remember that the normal variation of body temperature is rarely more than two degrees in a day. Ordinarily it begins to fall as a person approaches his habitual sleep time. During sleep in a healthy adult, the temperature will vary only by about a degree and four-tenths. Within this small range it was clear that the poor sleepers started out higher and never dropped so low in temperature as the good sleepers. Before sleep they had an average temperature of 98 degrees, dropping to 97.6 at their low point. The good sleepers had a rectal temperature of 97.7 before they drifted off, and fell to an average of 97.2. Even the timing of the fall and rise of temperature differed with the two groups. Toward the end of the night, before awakening, the body temperatures of the good sleepers were beginning to rise. The temperatures of the poor sleepers were still on the decline. It almost looked as if the poor sleepers were following a different clock, and one might speculate that their daily temperature rhythm might be somewhat slower than the rhythm of the good sleepers.

The group of poor sleepers was notably more restless during the night, moving more frequently than the good sleepers, and more often awakening from dream periods. On several other measures—finger pulse volume, the electric potential of the skin, and skin resistance—the two groups diverged.

Brain-wave recordings also accentuated the distinction between the two groups of sleeping men. The poor sleepers spent considerably more of their total sleep time in the transitional light phase of sleep known as Stage II. They distributed their time in the deep delta phase, Stage IV, quite differently, for they used almost all of it up, so to speak, in the first half of the night. It goes without saying that none of the men were deliberately awakened from REM periods for dream narratives, and so nothing could be said about possible differences in dream content; however, there was a very significant difference between the two groups in the amount of time spent in REM dreaming. The poor sleepers, as a group, spent considerably less of their sleeping time in the REM phase of consciousness.

These were important differences, and not merely the result of computing group averages. In a first study of its genre, the evaluation of groups by computing their averages was a valuable way of catching major divergences. Such a process always does conceal some internal variation, however, in the same way that the average U. S. income does not indicate the number of millionaires or families on relief. In this instance the range of individual variation within the groups was not the striking phenomenon. There were only a few men among the poor sleepers who spent about the same percentage of their sleep time in the REM state as the good sleepers. On the other hand,

12 out of 16 poor sleepers had so little REM dreaming that they were significantly beneath the average for the good sleepers. The averages were revealing how exceedingly different these two groups of sleeping men were, in fact. Throughout the night the poor sleepers, for reasons as yet unexplained, appeared to be physiologically closer to waking than the good sleepers.

Their differences did not end there. On a casual introduction, these groups of men might have seemed to be indistinguishable, yet their questionnaires underlined that they were as different in waking as they were in sleep. The Cornell Medical Index is often used for two purposes. While eliciting a quick medical history and assay of physical health, it also reveals tendencies toward psychosomatic ailments and hypochondria. It asks 195 questions, many of them purely objective. "Have you ever had TB?" "Do you need glasses to see things at a distance?" Others are inquiries into less specific symptoms—dizziness, headaches, noises in the ears, clumsiness. Interspersed among questions about medical background, habits such as smoking and drinking, and exercise, are questions addressed to subjective feelings of adjustment. "Do you often become suddenly scared for no good reason?" "Is it always hard for you to make up your mind?" "Do you feel alone and sad at a party?" A person who is healthy and more or less average will give affirmative answers to only about 5 or 6 of these questions about psychosomatic and emotional symptoms. The good sleepers averaged 6.75 affirmatives. By contrast the poor sleepers averaged 23.9. This suggested that they probably suffered more psychosomatic ailments and adjustment problems than the good sleepers. Similarly, an analysis of their responses to the long personality and attitude questionnaire revealed undeniable and large differences between the two groups. The poor sleepers were more anxious, introverted, hypochondriacal, and emotionally disturbed than were the good sleepers. The physiological differences seen in sleep were accompanied by commensurate psychological differences.

These results established very concretely and with unexpected clarity a fact that many sensitive physicians have long suspected. People who generally sleep poorly are psychologically, behaviorally, and physiologically different from those who ordinarily sleep well. The question of cause and effect is not yet answered. Perhaps the poor sleeper needs to adopt a different schedule of sleep, and sleep longer than the good sleeper. Perhaps cumulative sleep loss contributes to neuroticism and psychosomatic illness or neuroticism impedes sleep. Equally well, these may be constitutional differences, genetically inherited and displayed in infancy. Whatever the origins, this first descriptive study of good and poor sleep suggests that a predisposition to sleep well or poorly must be influential in behavior and adjustment to life. If one were to look for the early warning signals of a vulnerable personality—a person whose central nervous system was perhaps overreactive, and who was internally keyed up despite his habitual demeanor—one place to look for these signs might be in his patterns of sleep.

The correspondence between sleep patterns and personality traits has been found, unlikely as it may sound, in cats, during studies which offer some interesting speculation into the neural differences between good and poor sleepers. Pet owners know that cats vary much as people do in their personality traits. Although laboratory animals are generally treated as if they are identical, their individual differences are beginning to become an issue in testing drugs that have behavioral effects. Researchers realize that not all cats are alike, and it is hard to measure the subtle enlivening effect of an antidepressant, for instance, on an animal whose basic temperament and behavioral characteristics are unknown.

Motivated by this unsolved problem, Barbara B. Brown and her associates at the VA hospital in Sepulveda, California, rated the behavioral traits of a hundred cats by a 50-point method known as a Q sort, a method used by clinical psychologists. The cats fell into three rough categories: "anxious," "excessively outgoing," and "average." Given a drink of alcohol, the three groups reacted totally differently and showed distinctive brain-wave patterns. After a long period of research the team could take a new cat and place him in the recording cage, detecting from his brain waves alone the personality grouping into which he must fall.

All of these animals wore electrodes implanted deep within their temporal lobes in a brain region known as the hippocampus. This curious structure curls under on each side of the head like warped antlers. In the cat it lies about a half inch behind the eyes and a quarter of an inch from the ears. During the phase of sleep that corresponds to REM dreaming in man, and under special waking circumstances, the hippocampal region pulsates with a beat known as the theta rhythm. Theta rhythms can be detected from the surface of the head in man, more easily in children than adults. The significance of the theta rhythm is by no means clear, but scientists have inferred that the rhythm may be pronounced when the hippocampal region is strongly active, perhaps in modifying emotion and in processing memory.

The role of the hippocampus and adjacent brain structures in handling memory has been inferred in part from the behavior of a vast number of human patients suffering damages in these regions. These people show an utter lack of recent memory and an inability to memorize even the simplest things. Typically, in their case histories, these patients will complain: "My brain feels like a sieve. I forget everything. Even in my tiny room I keep losing things." Advanced alcoholics frequently suffer damage in the hippocampus or associated regions. Their notorious lying may stem from the fact that they cannot remember what they were doing two hours ago and, when asked, they comb their memories to fill the gaps—but the only available memories may date back six months and are egregiously inappropriate, and are therefore called falsehoods. Indirectly, the study of such clinical cases and experiments with animals suggest that the hippocampal theta rhythm may be pronounced at times when the individual becomes inward and is busily processing his stores of undigested recent memories.

This would be a plausible description of what the brain may be doing during dreaming—reordering recent memories so that they are properly filed away with the old. During the cat's equivalent of the REM state, when he is presumably dreaming, he exhibits a pronounced theta wave from the hippocampus. He will also show a theta rhythm during certain waking situations, perhaps best characterized by anxiety. Theta appears when a cat first orients himself in a new cage, and it seems to persist if he is uneasy.

One of the standard difficulties of the very anxious person is that he cannot absorb new information rapidly. He has trouble perceiving the outside world clearly, and learning. In a very crude sense, he is similar to the REM dreamer—keyed-up yet enrapt in himself and his feelings. During both states—anxiety and REM dreaming—it is hard to incorporate outside information unless it is particularly meaningful, since the individual is highly involved in what is already part of him. Barbara Brown and others have tentatively speculated that the theta rhythm occurs at times of inward concentration, in which crucial portions of the brain are processing information rather than receiving much new material.

When an anxious or an excessively outgoing cat is first placed in an unfamiliar recording cage he will show a great deal of theta rhythm. The average cat will show only a little, before quickly settling down and falling asleep. During sleep, once more, the difference between the animals is striking. The anxious and excessively outgoing creatures will not show any theta rhythm during their first few sleep sessions in a new cage. But the average cat shows a great deal of theta in his sleep.

Although a study of cats cannot tell us what is happening in the human brain, there are some interesting similarities between the poor sleepers and the anxious cats. Like the cats, the poor sleepers took a long time to fall asleep in a strange situation. Physically they seemed more aroused than the good sleepers, more sensitive to the electrodes and attachments, and the laboratory bedroom. Like the anxious cats, moreover, they spent little of their sleeping time in the REM state of dreaming. One cannot ask an overly outgoing cat whether his friendliness covers an internal unease, but the replies of the poor sleepers to test questions emphasized that they were more anxious and disturbed than the good sleepers. No doubt if we had the instruments to listen to their internal rhythms, we would find that, as in the cat, there were clues to different functioning deep within the brain.

Once we begin to consider that the mind is part of the body in which it is housed, that it is inseparable from the central nervous system, we should not be surprised to discover that brain-wave patterns, physiological changes, and personality traits are interlinked. The sleeping person is not separate, either, from his waking self, but there are several reasons why his sleep record may be particularly valuable for diagnosing his mental and physical condition. This is a time when people lie relatively still for many hours, when they are undistracted by the outside world. The night of sleep, with its orderly sequence of changes in the body and brain, represents a complete unit in the person's circadian cycle, a repeated sample of the clockwork of his body. Many researchers have begun to explore the characteristic sleep patterns of individuals, and as the data accumulate we may expect to use a night of sleep to find out about a person's physical well-being, his mental state, his sensitivity to pain or stress, his daytime behavior, his capacity to perform certain kinds of jobs. One of the great potentials of sleep diagnosis, for normal people, is its possible value in preventive medicine. Can we, for instance, judge from a child's sleep record whether he is especially over-reactive and vulnerable to the environment? Will such a vulnerability indicate why some children become neurotic or delinquent, when others in the family do not? Could sleep records help us to catch vulnerable people before they develop neurotic or psychosomatic symptoms?

Russian and European clinicians have long felt that sleep is a useful diagnostic and have applied it to use in preventive medicine and particularly to the prevention of mental illness and psychosomatic disease. Soviet scientists, following a long tradition, have always looked upon the central system as a whole and have expected that disorders of the nervous system would inevitably give indications in sleep as well as in waking. Long before the use of refined instruments for capturing brain-wave patterns, muscle tonus, and a multitude of physiological changes, they sought clues in the rhythms of restlessness that a person might display in sleep. By attaching recording instruments to the bedsprings they obtained "actograms" that would display the nature of a person's movements and quiescence during a night's sleep. This was crude, and often misleading. Recent sleep studies have begun to indicate when body movements should be expected in clusters, and with what EEG patterns they are associated. We have also learned a good deal about what else is happening in the body at this time. Still, the Soviet use of the actogram signified a point of view in which disorders of the nervous system were not expected to restrict themselves to the waking cycle. It was based on the assumption that behavioral disorders, mental abnormalities, and psychosomatic illnesses were all caused by disturbance within the central nervous system. Our research seems to be moving in much the same direction.

Sleep studies have underscored the unity of the person, the interrelationships between mental outlook and physiological functions. We are now accumulating the information and developing the instruments that may give us a very refined early warning detection system for nervous disorders.

VI

ABNORMAL SLEEP

IN the stillness of a darkened street a lonely light symbolizes the person who paces or reads while the rest of his world slumbers. This, in the popular image, is the tormented brotherhood of insomnia. In point of fact, about one out of every two American adults suffers from a mild and transient form at some time in his life, and many older people find that they awaken during the night or early morning. The annual sales of sedatives and tranquilizers testify that sleep difficulty is ubiquitous. People react differently to it, some taking sleep loss in their stride, others complaining vociferously. Particularly during times of pressure or emotional strain a difficulty in sleeping is almost what might be called a normal reaction, and no cause for worry. There are, however, extreme sleep disorders whose persistence and severity exceed the transient and mild sufferings of the average person. Although they have no bearing upon the ordinary insomnia of most of us, these extremes have been of great interest to clinicians and scientists. Beyond a certain limit, the inability to sleep, to stay awake, or a deviation in the daily cycle of sleep can become a torture that alters a person's mood and behavior to a degree we have long ignored, and can disrupt a life with appalling velocity. It is beyond this limit that many doctors are now looking.

Sleep loss is only one facet of insomnia. If doctors occasionally seem heartless, denying sedatives to a weary patient, it is because troubled sleep may arise from many sources. Sedatives would be useless for some insomniacs, and for others truly harmful. An insomniac who receives inappropriate sedation may be accelerated along what is actually the path to mental illness.

"So rarely do we see a recent case of insanity that is not preceded by want of sleep that we regard it as almost a sure precursor of mental derangement." Those words were spoken over a hundred years ago by a well-known superintendent of an Ohio insane asylum, and with some modification the statement holds today. The link between sleep disorder and mental illness was most vivid in the era before tranquilizers. At night, when quiet reigned in other human institutions, the asylum was a darkened nightmare. The writer Albert Deutsch has described a surprise midnight visit to a mental hospital, in which he heard for himself "the occasional shriek, the hysterical crying and senseless laughter, the moaning and muttered soliloquies of the crowded and nervously sleeping inmates," many of whom were bound to bed by leather straps or straitjackets lest they wander and enact their terrible visions.

A mounting storm of emotional disturbance is commonly foretold by sleep troubles, but there seem to be as many varieties of sleep disorder as there are types of nervous illness. Psychosomatic symptoms attack their victims during sleep. Viruses and brain-damaging fevers can twist the rhythm of sleep. Sleep attacks during the daytime and nighttime epileptic seizures are among the many abnormalities now studied in hope of finding the origins of the particular symptoms, and also to discover more about the nature of normal sleep and its relationship to behavior and mood. The study of these abnormalities has again emphasized that sleep is not isolated from daily life and must be considered part of a person's entire rhythm, body chemistry, mental outlook, his experiences, habits, and surroundings. Sleep disorders are beginning to acquire a diagnostic value. They exist in baffling variety, like a night gallery of the nervous ills besetting man. Among them, insomnia is best known, but as we use this word in common parlance it may have as many meanings as the word "love."

Doctors are often importuned by professed insomniacs who say they never sleep, and others who habitually take sedatives. With all due sympathy, they know a few of these people are seizing the excuse to fulminate about an affliction that may be imaginary. Some years ago, internist Arthur Shapiro invited a few of his insomniac patients to spend the night in the sleep laboratory at the Downstate Medical Center in Brooklyn, New York. There, people who couldn't sleep at home managed to sleep quite well dressed in electrodes. Time and again supposed sleeplessness has been claimed within the sleep laboratory. On one occasion a sophisticated psychologist had offered himself as a subject for his associates in an EEG study of sleep and dreaming. Although he was eager to give his colleagues a quantity of useful sleep data, he found the equipment uncomfortable and the situation strange enough so that it was difficult to go to sleep. When he arose in the morning he was particularly exhausted, and disappointed that he had hardly slept at all. Out in the monitoring room, that day, he apologized for having given them so little sleep to study. His associates greeted this statement with loud laughter. Few volunteers in the study had done so much sleeping as he.

A perusal of his nightlong EEG patterns showed that in six hours of deep sleep there had been many interruptions when his brain waves momentarily exhibited a waking alpha rhythm, suggesting that he was at the threshold of arousal. These moments of near-awakening might have fused in his mind, leaving him the feeling that he had been continuously on the borderline of waking. This may explain what happens to many insomniacs who claim they have gone for days, weeks, even months, without sleep.

Over twenty years ago, W. T. Liberson and his associates performed a study that could have been used as arbitration in disputes between patients who claimed they didn't sleep and nurses who insisted they had been snoring. The patients had, indeed, been snoring during brief intervals of deep sleep, but then their EEGs showed that they would alternate, rising for some moments to alertness before sinking back again. At the time, nurses would have insisted that the patients were sleeping soundly, and the patients sincerely believed that they never slept.

The wakefulness of some insomniacs may also be a dream. This has occasioned some entertaining dialogues between researchers and subjects. Donald Goodenough and his associates in studying dream recall, would awaken a volunteer in the midst of sound slumber, after a period of rapid eye movements, and hear something like this:

> "I was up, and I thought I was carrying on a mock conversation . . . negotiating for the United States at a conference . . . for a foreign power, rather, I'm sorry. I overheard a conversation where somebody had gotten a tip on the stock market—watching a board. . . . I asked the person I was negotiating for about it. They said they were too tired or paralyzed. Anyway they were going to sleep. So I lay down in bed and said, well, I'll try it for a whole month, sleeping here. . . ."
>
> "You think you were up when you were having this experience?"
>
> "Yes, just thinking about it. I am aware of where I am, and the hum of the air conditioner, just waiting for the bell."

An experimenter's incredulity might well be excused at some narratives far more bizarre than this, which have been offered very positively as the products of waking thought. At the same time it is possible to explain the confusion of the subject about what is sleep and what is waking. Many show a tendency to sleep lightly, and have said that they control their imaginings in the manner of daydreams. Many were aware of their environment and said they could hear the air conditioner in their bedroom.

Light or fitful sleep and morning fatigue are worrisome, although they are not proofs of sleeplessness. Imaginary insomnia is not a joke, but people who grow agitated over their supposed inability to sleep merely exacerbate their problem of obtaining rest. As the volumes of nightlong sleep records indicate, people vary greatly in their "depth" of sleep. Those who seem to retain greater contact with the outside world and subjectively feel awake while dreaming may indeed believe they are insomniac. A thin line, just now being defined, seems to run between the tolerable light sleep that may be characteristic of an individual, and the poor sleep that may signify illness and mental distress.

An investigation of depressed patients during the 1940's did indicate that they took a long time to fall asleep, and then spent an unusual portion of their total sleep in the "light" phases. A spate of recent studies has emphasized the fact that depressed patients exhibit unusual EEGs during sleep, often shifting from one phase to another in a pattern that might be called unstable.

Depression is another one of our "umbrella" terms. It comes in many guises. It may sweep over a person in the aftermath of emotional difficulties, financial failure, a long futile siege of work, or in the numbing wake of tragedy. It can disappear swiftly or linger and paralyze a person for months or years. It may fume up slowly and mysteriously from within, or arise suddenly and rapidly. In its diverse forms depression is widespread, especially among people of middle age. A great many depressed people do not realize they are depressed, and consult physicians only to obtain sedatives, for insomnia is accepted as a legitimate complaint, as if it were an inevitable penalty for growing older and shouldering responsibility. The doctor with an insomniac patient may have difficulty deciphering the case, since his patient may not help, and indeed may not be frank. "Many of the patients I see regard their difficulties with sleep as *the* problem. They cannot recognize their depression but will talk at length about their sleep." So remarks John N. Davis, a psychiatrist with the National Institutes of Health.

The doctor's job is not easy, for symptoms of depression can be adeptly hidden, in the manner of the spinster who was affable and smiling to friends, and made a virtue of rising very early—and one day bought a gun and tried to shoot herself. An individual may genuinely seem to be suffering from a temporary agitation in his household, the noise of construction work, or a transitory crisis in professional life that would reasonably explain an inability to sleep.

During 1963 and 1964 an illuminating survey of mental patients was performed under the direction of Thomas Detre of Yale Medical School, Peter Spalding of the Norwich Hospital, with the participation of John N. Davis. The psychiatric team issued questionnaires to several hundred patients with psychoses, depressions, and other mental ailments. About 81 percent had been suffering sleep disturbances, and indeed many had only sought medical help for their insomnia and insisted sleep loss was their sole problem. There were three classic kinds of insomnia, sometimes suffered in combination and varying according to the type of illness and severity. There was the inability to fall asleep. There was the complaint that sleep was not sound, but light and fitful. There was also a pattern of falling asleep readily, but being unable to stay asleep and awakening in the predawn hours.

The link between sleep disorder and mental illness is not confined to the United States, nor to urban civilization. Davis has seen the same history of sleep disturbance among natives in the Fiji Islands and in Tahiti. Ordinarily, these people sleep from sundown to sunrise. When they succumb to mental illness, they too complain of difficulty falling asleep or of awakening before dawn.

At the Center for the Prevention of Suicide in Los Angeles, daily questionnaires including detailed inquiries about sleep have been filled out by people in a long-term study. There, too, it is becoming clear that in describing their sleep people may reveal the warning signs of suicidal behavior. At the inception of the program, one elderly woman faithfully filled out her morning reports, but one day she did not submit them. She had killed herself. Edwin S. Shneidman, Director of the Center, feels that today this suicide might have been prevented, for the clues to her declining mood were present in her morning sleep reports. A number of doctors have heeded chronic nightmares as a warning signal of impending suicide. The Yale study suggests that there may be an inherent warning signal when people who normally dream say they have stopped dreaming, or that they no longer remember dreams. This was a striking pattern among the people who had attempted to kill themselves.

A new art of using sleep disorders as guides in diagnosing mental illness is rapidly evolving from psychiatric researches. Heretofore, troubled sleep or insomnia was nonspecific, and hardly pointed to a particular syndrome. Studies by Yale psychiatrists Thomas Detre and Henry Jarecki have begun to outline how particular progressions of sleep disorder correspond to the development of specific mental illnesses. A doctor can always draw out his patient on the topic of sleep, and if he asks the right questions he may begin to pair sleep disturbance with behavior and mood. One example is the manic depressive who may sleep altogether too much during a depressed phase lasting several months, and then may begin to suffer insomnia. Illnesses are progressive and an individual often misses the subtle transformations that occur in him over weeks or months. Using questionnaire and case history data, compiled from studies of hundreds of patients, Detre and Jarecki find that the course of sleep disorder is predictive. A doctor may foresee that an elated and hyperactive patient who has difficulty falling asleep may enter a new stage of depression and nightmares, and in a matter of a few weeks may enter a stage of inactivity and fantasy. A correct interpretation and treatment for "insomnia" is particularly critical to the person with depression, for the wrong drug may worsen the symptoms. The Yale researchers emerged from their study with sobering conclusions: many depressives had originally received tranquilizers or barbiturates for their sleep problems, and among them were significantly more suicide attempts than among the patients who had been correctly diagnosed and treated with antidepressants. Methods of evaluating sleep problems may thus save the life of the person slipping into mental illness, unbeknownst to himself.

It is hard to estimate how many of these people, on the precipice, actually find some pretext to seek out doctors. Interns on duty at night in the accident wards of large hospitals notice some curious patterns. At one hospital in Philadelphia, around five or six in the morning there is an influx of patients who awaken very early, complaining of vague backaches and other pains that cannot be located, and for which no test shows up any organic cause. There are a rare few who are impelled to the emergency room in the dead of night because they have tried and tried to fall asleep without success. The harried intern who is coping with bleeding knife wounds, a fracture or two, a convulsing epileptic, might accept these people as straightforward insomniacs or hypochondriacs.

Not long ago a sleepless panic drove a young woman to the emergency ward of a large hospital in Washington, D. C., at 3 A.M. She was nervous and crying and said her inability to sleep was unbearable. Interns on duty gave her a sedative and sent her home. A week later she returned. This time she showed the suspicious, farfetched delusions that are unmistakable signs of paranoid schizophrenia. Although, to outward appearances, she had not been psychotic on her visit the week before, her sleep disorder had been the precursor of breakdown. It is a common story.

Looking back through digests of schizophrenic histories, one can often see that the mysterious and possibly chemical changes of psychosis first exhibited themselves in corrosions of sleep. Although the metabolic origins of psychoses may defy unraveling in this century, sleep studies may help us to distinguish between psychoses that might have seemed similar if judged only by behavior.

St. Elizabeths is a giant federal mental hospital in southeast Washington, D. C., a vast estate of dark brick buildings, lawn, and dignified shade trees, all a little dilapidated, a little desolate. Eight thousand patients live here. In one of the hospital's modern pavilions, several years ago, a separate ward was established for continued study of sleep among patients. Participation in the sleep ward is voluntary, and quite a few patients refuse, thinking they will be electrocuted or that their inner secrets will be read. Those who are persuaded to join the experiment move into a special ward, where they spend the better part of two weeks getting to know the staff and becoming familiar with the procedure. They are invited into the laboratory to watch the affixing of electrodes, instructed in the function of the EEG machine to whatever extent they can understand, and allowed to watch the gathering of data. As their apprehensions of the nighttime surveillance begin to abate, their own behavior is watched in some detail.

Ridiculously simple regime has enabled the psychiatric team to predict a great deal about each patient's behavior. An attendant, doing rounds of each bedroom every half hour, simply peeks in and jots on his pad whether the patient is sleeping, awake, or in an indeterminate state. This nightly chart reveals mounting sleep disorder, and if a patient were found to be awake increasingly often over a series of nights, his daytime symptoms almost inevitably grew more severe.

The schizophrenic patients, when given no tranquilizers or sedatives for the purpose of the study, quickly began to lose sleep. The insomnia that had been the harbinger of illness was still with them, whether they had been hospitalized for just a few months or for several years.

They took a long time falling asleep, and then the EEG record did not show an orderly progression through the cycles of night. The patient might enter a REM state in just a few minutes after falling asleep or not for several hours. It was almost impossible to forecast the EEG pattern from the behavior of the patient.

One young boy, who had been studied at the very beginning of his illness in another hospital, lapsed into REM dreaming within ten minutes of falling asleep. He was a Negro boy who had just won an athletic scholarship to a university when he suffered his breakdown. His rapid plunge into REM dreaming did not indicate outward agitation. Most of his day he sat like a statue, hearing voices, ignoring the people around him. When electrodes were taped to his head he sat rigid as a stone, and had to be lifted into bed and molded to the pillows.

Among the acutely ill patients, hallucinating and acting out agitated delusions to explain their bizarre inner vision, the St. Elizabeths team and investigators elsewhere have noticed signs of an intensity during REM sleep that corresponds to the intensity of the symptoms. The eye movements seem to occur more often and more wildly than in the normal sleeper, suggesting a discharge of extraordinary excitement within the brain. An acutely ill person in a stage of hallucination might have bizarre mannerisms, like the man who paced the hall talking to a fantasy menagerie of reptiles, monsters, and dinosaurs. The animals were concealed behind the tile wall, he believed, and as he passed, talking to them, he would suddenly pound the walls, infuriated by their misbehavior. Some patients, after recovering from a lapse into such severe sickness, might show an increase in REM dreaming; others do not.

In general, the poor sleep of the schizophrenic did not resemble the poor sleep reported for normal people. Brain-wave patterns shifted rapidly from one stage to another, and intervals of REM dreaming were frequently interrupted by another stage of light sleep. Studies elsewhere suggested that the schizophrenic, before sleep and during REM intervals, has a fast brain-wave rhythm that differs from the normal waking or REM background tempo. The nightlong EEG record of a sleeper may someday be enough to tell a psychiatrist that the person is schizophrenic.

There are a few schizophrenics whose sleep would not suggest psychosis. Their behavior would not distinguish them from the majority of schizophrenics but they sleep as soundly as babies, at times when their symptoms are acute. One youngster of eighteen, for example, a foreign ambassador's son, spent almost every waking moment in communication with the inhabitants of other planets. He kept his elaborate code a secret, suspicious of people around him. Despite the obvious signs that he was very psychotic, this boy showed no sleep troubles. Another paranoid, an attractive physicist in his thirties, also slept magnificently. He, too, acted upon a secret and protected system of his own that the psychiatrists were unable to decipher. For many hours at a time he sat, immobile and distant, believing that all people around him were dead and he was the last man alive. During these periods his face wore a look of wracking anxiety, heartbreaking to observe, yet by physiological measures his body showed none of the characteristic signs of stress and apprehension. One might expect that this man and others like him who do not reflect their sickness in troubled sleep, might be people unable to express emotion. But this is not quite true. The physicist, for all his stony detachment, would break into a storm of anger when intruded upon, and let loose with volcanic language. All the psychiatrists who saw him expected to find serious sleep disturbances and were surprised at the normal appearance of his nightly records. The concurrence of excellent sleep and acute psychotic symptoms may be a marker that singles out a group quite different from the majority of schizophrenics, although they are classed as schizophrenic. These may be people in whom anxiety and agitation is not expressed through the usual channels.

The relationship between strong emotion and sleep is, indeed, strange. Healthy people commonly show the effects of heightened feelings, of intense anxiety, in their sleep. People with psychosomatic ailments may act self-possessed and calm during the day, yet suffer from angina or asthma or ulcer pains during sleep. One theory of psychosomatic disease postulates that a particular organ which happens to be constitutionally vulnerable to the chemical expressions of stress in the body acts as a shock absorber. There are other disorders in which strong emotion, even anger, may actually induce sleep.

One of these, a curiosity among illnesses, does not even have a familiar name. Textbooks describe narcolepsy as a rare illness of inappropriate sleep. It may not be so rare as we once thought, since many people endure the symptoms without having a name by which to call them, and without seeking help from a doctor. In mild form, they seem unduly sleepy, and fall asleep at the wrong times in peculiar places. They are not to be confused with the exhausted businessman who inevitably drifts off to sleep at the bridge table, or the bored housewife who is put to sleep by the vacuous chatter of friends. Narcoleptic sleepiness happens rapidly. It is often the observer who will find the naps strange, as a physician points out.

"The secretary of an important business executive complained to me of her boss's strange symptoms. In the middle of dictating a letter he would suddenly and mysteriously fall asleep, arousing himself some seconds later."

In the safety of an office this may be disconcerting but relatively harmless. Many people, however, rationalize their sleepiness, and do not obtain medical help until they are carried to a doctor after falling asleep at the wheel of a car. There is no saying how many automobile or industrial accidents have been caused by narcoleptic attacks. If the symptoms are severe, however, the victim is generally aware that something is wrong. He is likely to fall into a swoonlike sleep whenever he feels strong emotion. This is even more disconcerting to the bystander.

"My mother pulled into the driveway, and this friend of mine went over to the car to say hello. She must have cracked a pretty good joke. They were both laughing, and then, all of a sudden, he faints dead away in the driveway."

It was not a faint, but a seizure sometimes called a cataplectic fit. About 60 percent of narcoleptics suffer from this peculiar reaction to emotion. They cannot laugh at a joke, spank their children in anger, mourn, or exhibit certain strong feelings without becoming literally weak with emotion and collapsing like jelly. Others cannot dance or perform rhythmic activities without the same consequence. Additional symptoms of narcolepsy include transient hallucinations and a state of apparent paralysis, an inability to move upon awakening from sleep. Naturally enough, many narcoleptics have assumed they must be insane or epileptic. Quite a number have deprecated themselves for being "no-count good-for-nothings" with an intractible lazy streak. Some resorted to the ophthalmologist, claiming eye troubles, or to the optometrist, from whom they requested glasses that would cure a nasty case of double vision. Their eyes, sometimes unable to focus, were merely diverging as they do in sleep. Doctors have, indeed, taken skin conductance recordings of narcoleptics who were wide awake and answering questions, yet if these records were scanned by a doctor who had not seen the patient, he would have judged that the person had been deeply asleep.

The cause of narcolepsy and the brain mechanism that instigates seizures are not yet known but the onus of mystery has been removed, and the symptoms no longer seem so weird. EEG studies show that each symptom is a facet of sleep. The unveiling of the syndrome was largely accomplished by the collaborative work of three young scientists, Allan Rechtschaffen of the University of Chicago and William C. Dement and George Gulevich of Stanford University. A surprising number of the people who responded to their newspaper advertisements and came into the laboratory to be studied had never before seen a doctor although their symptoms were pronounced.

EEG records promptly dispelled any association between their cataplexy and fainting fits. They were unmistakable seizures of REM sleep. A normal person falls asleep gradually, and there is an hour or 90-minute wait before he drifts into REM sleep. The narcoleptic would plummet from waking into REM sleep. The plunge was so instantaneous that it was often difficult to study.

Dement repeatedly tried to observe the transition in one woman. She was seated in the recording room with a magazine as he hurried toward the control room. By the time he reached the door, she would be sound asleep. He awakened her and urged her to stay awake for a count of ten, but by the time he had dashed to the EEG machine, the record already spelled out the familiar low-voltage script and rapid eye movements of dreaming.

Any normal person who, in the midst of daily activities, plunged so abruptly into REM sleep would collapse in a limp heap and might believe he had fainted although he remained fully conscious. The collapse is caused by a sudden loss of muscle tone throughout the body, which is pronounced during REM sleep but which people do not notice because the relaxation happens slowly and in bed. A normal person may feel himself relaxing when he is sleepy, but a narcoleptic is more likely to say he experiences weakness. Cataplexy places a strain on his life, for he must control his natural feelings lest he be struck into a seizure by a hearty laugh on a street corner, in the midst of making love, or during an angry attempt to curb dangerous antics in his children.

Not only at the beginning of sleep but at the other end, awakening, the narcoleptic may experience a bizarre few moments. He may be fully awake, yet be unable to move. Many normal people have endured this transient immobility on awakening and describe it as a paralysis. It is not. The return of muscle tone has been delayed. By some error of timing, the body remains limp as in REM sleep although the mind is alert.

The ill-timed sleep mechanisms of the narcoleptic sometimes intrude upon his waking life with what seem to be fragmentary hallucinations. Perhaps they are dreams. One does not have to be narcoleptic to be invaded by vague mental excursions, images, fragments during times when one feels subjectively alert. Even when brain waves begin exhibiting a pattern of drowsiness many people feel wide awake. An EEG study of drowsiness by W. T. and Cathryn W. Liberson at Stritch Medical School in Hines, Illinois, suggests that it may be quite normal for the mind to briefly withdraw from the demanding reality of the present. Perhaps it is even biologically necessary to blur the outside world periodically. Vague thoughts and dreaming are so common in daily life that nobody pays them any heed, and most people hardly remember that it happens. As we look more closely we may discover that these momentary withdrawals of attention follow some regular timing, some clock of their own.

The conspicuous signs of narcoleptic attacks have shown some regularity, often appearing at intervals of four to six hours. This periodicity hints that the attack may be caused by a metabolic cycle—as yet unknown. There is some evidence that susceptibility is inherited, and the symptoms generally begin at puberty or after, frequently in the wake of emotional trauma such as that caused by a death in the family.

Narcoleptic seizures appear to be misplaced interludes in which the brain seems to act as if it were in a REM phase of sleep, and some narcoleptics have less than the normal amount of nightly sleep in this phase. Ironically, the amphetamines they take to stay awake merely suppress nightly REM sleep. It has been thought that narcoleptics need the very opposite, a drug that could amplify their nightly REM time. Even normal people or animals, when deprived of the REM interval, will compensate later, spending much more time in REM sleep as soon as they are uninterrupted. In part, the narcoleptic may also be compensating for loss—and having daytime REM periods.

This does not explain the syndrome, or the mysterious link between emotion and a seizure of REM sleep. In a primitive brain center, a nub of tissue known as the pontine reticular formation at the base of the brain, stimulation can generate the paradoxical state of consciousness we know as REM sleep. Abnormal metabolism might periodically act upon this brain-stem region and trigger REM seizures. There are scientists who conjecture that the locus of sleep seizures lies elsewhere, far forward in a brain area called the amygdala, within the temporal lobes. This region appears to be important in memory and emotion, and EEG studies of chimpanzees and man suggest that it plays some part in pacing out the stages of nightly sleep.

Even though we have not pinpointed the biochemical chain of events and the exact brain cells that generate narcoleptic attacks, sleep studies have made diagnosis simple, and suggested a regimen that reduces the symptoms. EEGs taken at the beginning of sleep will distinguish between the instant dreamer and the average person. One revealing test is absurdly simple: Can the patient tell a funny joke or genuinely laugh at the doctor's jokes? Until such time when "REM-enhancing" drugs may be safely given at night, a careful use of available drugs and the avoidance of sleep loss will aid the narcoleptic, for whom it must be relieving to hear that eccentric as his symptoms may seem, they are merely ill-timed periods of dreaming sleep.

If narcolepsy has displayed facets of sleep during wakefulness, epilepsy has told us about the nature of brain-cell activity during sleep. Epilepsy has many degrees of severity and takes many forms. It is thought to be congenital in part or to result from brain damages left by a childhood virus disease. Until recently it was considered an ailment of geniuses or saints, and was imbued with strange and visionary overtones. The popular image of an attack was as Dostoevsky described it, beginning with an inexplicable aura of emotion and fear, mounting to convulsions, foaming at the mouth and finally coma. Grand mal seizures of this sort are rare. More commonly, epileptics will experience what are known as psychomotor seizures, moments of irrational behavior that the person will not remember. One pretty college girl, for instance, felt a pain in her stomach while rehearsing in a play. For no reason she was overcome with terror. She smacked her lips for several moments, flung her arms out, and fiddled with buttons on her dress. A frightened classmate led her to a couch where she promptly fell asleep and awakened refreshed, remembering only the stomach pain and senseless fear, which had come from nowhere and defied description. An EEG diagnosis made it apparent that she was not insane, as she thought, but epileptic, and drugs ameliorated the symptoms.

Sometimes momentary seizures are so mild that they escape medical attention, passing as lapses in attention or daydreaming. Very often, seizures seem to follow a timetable, occurring at intervals of a week or fortnight, and at particular hours of day or night. Some kinds of seizures can be instigated by emotion, by a hearty laugh for instance. The attack is usually followed by sleep and, indeed, often occurs during sleep.

During the nineteenth century, when the brain was believed to fall into slothful inactivity during sleep, the sleep attacks of epileptics suggested that this theory was wrong. Quite a few epileptics suffer all their seizures during sleep. The only traces may be a few drops of blood on the pillow, a bitten tongue, sore muscles. Some rise from bed and perform elaborate acts before a member of the household returns them to bed, but these are things they do not remember. The biting of the tongue, the slight convulsion, begins when a sudden volley of electric discharges emanates from certain brain cells to stimulate nerves that cause particular muscles to contract. This might be called the essence of the epileptic fit, whatever its form. The problem is that these excessive discharges do not remain restricted to a few abnormal brain cells but can spread to others, causing a wave of excitation in a portion of the brain. Since this happens frequently in sleep, the cells of the sleeping brain could not be inactive as we once thought. Indeed, each epileptic, perhaps because of the particular location of the defect, will show seizures in a characteristic phase of sleep. During nightlong EEG studies, the seizure will show up as a series of jagged spikes on the brain-wave script. These have been observed at every stage of sleep, but most rarely during the REM phase that resembles waking in so many ways.

A number of scientists have implanted microelectrodes, so small as to seem almost invisible, within single brain cells in animals. Edward V. Evarts and Peter Huttenlocher, of the National Institutes of Health, have begun to suggest that the activity of brain cells in deep sleep may be, if anything, less controlled than in waking. Their recordings have shown that cells exhibit different kinds of discharge tempos during each phase of consciousness. Evarts' work on the motor system suggests that some cells seem to be inhibited during waking, and only during sleep do they fire off in rapid and irregular volleys, as if some brake were released—sometimes causing muscle spasms or convulsions. Recordings from discrete neural cells in different locations in the brain are beginning to suggest why the epileptic is particularly vulnerable to sleep seizures.

In parts of the world where sleeping sickness is common, irresistible drowsiness is a frightening omen. Attacks of somnolence that last days, weeks, even months, can come from many causes, among them brain tumors, brain lesions, damages from malaria, chicken pox, German measles, syphilis, and other high-fever diseases. The most feared and one of the most peculiar is the virus disease encephalitis. It takes a multitude of forms, generally starting with fever and delirium, often followed by periods of insomnia and agitation that lead to stupor and coma. Encephalitis raged through Europe in the aftermath of World War I, often taking its grip after a weakening bout of influenza. This epidemic was an important impetus to modern brain research on sleep, for the range of odd symptoms and brain damages revealed by autopsy immediately started scientists wondering about the role of the brain in causing sleep or waking.

Autopsies showed that the ravaging virus did not restrict its marks to one small spot in the brain, although lesions—neural scar tissue from dead cells—were often located in the hypothalamus. This is a knob of tissue about the size of an acorn and located above the roof of the mouth in a human being. Within this primitive center are controls for the body's routine survival functions, temperature, hunger, respiration, heart rate, sexual functions, and rudimentary emotions. As one might imagine, viral damage within the hypothalamus alone provoked an array of preposterous symptoms, depending upon which brain cells were destroyed.

Encephalitis victims have been known to sleep as long as five years, a fact that may imply a destruction of arousal capacities. One of the most revealing and important of the symptoms, however, is a shift in the diurnal cycle, frequently observed in children after fever. Sometimes the cycle inverted, and the patient slept by day and was awake by night. This abrupt inversion strongly suggested that the circadian rhythm of sleep and waking must have residence within the brain, perhaps in a region that acts as a brain clock. The ugly abnormalities and sufferings of the epidemic victims caused scientists to conjecture that the brain contains a center of sleep and waking. As they looked they found not one but many. Cell systems that could produce sleep or arousal were situated in regions concerned with hunger, emotions, sex, and they responded differentially to the many chemicals known to exist in the body.

The unraveling of specific connections may take a hundred or more years, still the neurophysiological researches have begun to clarify how the strange disorders of sleep might arise, and how disturbances within the body, malfunctioning in the brain, could be mirrored in strange behavior. They explained, in principle, how a person's behavior might generate sleep difficulties and how they might originate from within and influence his behavior. Many relatively minor sleep disorders, such as teeth grinding or bed-wetting, or even the more dangerous sleepwalking, are often described as psychological in origin. A great many insomniacs have heard that tension and worry prevent them from sleeping. An example may indicate generally how a psychological habit, a behavior, affects the body.

Stress and fear impel the hypothalamus to send impulses to the pituitary glands in the base of the brain. In response, the pituitary releases a chemical, a hormone known as ACTH, which travels through the blood and starts action in the adrenal glands just behind the kidney. The adrenals release adrenalin and stimulant stress hormones, among them cortisone. As these hormones travel through the bloodstream affecting nerves and muscles, they mobilize the body for stress, perhaps augmenting arousal and thereby interfering with the progress of relaxation and sleep. A thought or feeling can trigger this action. Brain damage or malfunction in metabolism may also have the same effect.

Occasionally the consequence is circumscribed. The tense bruxist, who grinds his teeth by night and pays the dental bills by day, exhibits his intensity mainly during the REM period of dreaming. Such people might benefit from a drug that relaxed the masseter muscles controlling the jaw, and sometimes show less tendency to grind their teeth after psychological therapy.

Although many transient sleep problems might be reduced by conquering emotional disturbances, the tailoring of remedies to fit the ailment should not add to the elaborate gadgetry that has been promoted against nuisances that are quite normal. Snoring is extremely common, if annoying, in the relaxation of the musculature in sleep. Alarm systems and uncomfortable chin straps, usually futile, also hinder rest. Sleep talking is another common event, a behavior once thought to be rare and to signify a disturbed mind. On the contrary, as experimenters have manned their sleep laboratories over thousands of nights, they have intermittently heard the mumblings of subjects in all stages of sleep. Usually indecipherable and toneless, these utterances sometimes become more distinct and emphatic during REM dreams. Children and disturbed people may cry out with nightmares' shrieks and pleas and commands, but it would seem that everyone talks gibberish in sleep now and then.

Bed-wetting is also more common than most of us would like to imagine, and less innocent. The Army has found that about one man in a hundred wets his bed, and a cautious estimate indicates that about 2 percent of the adult population is enuretic. Until very recently texts asserted, and almost everyone assumed, that wetting was caused by dreaming and dreams.

As research teams have studied EEGs of sleeping enuretic children, they found that wetting did not occur during the active REM period, but rather in the sleep preceding or following this interval, very often a deep stage of sleep from which dreams are only rarely remembered. Enuretic children have been, in general, heavy sleepers who are hard to awaken. While their emotional problems are often cited as the source of wetting, many have shown other physiological disorders as well. Some seem to evince abnormalities in the EEG. A good many are also somnambulists, and quite a few suffer from urinary irritations, complaining of pressure, pain, and frequent need to urinate.

Healthy on most counts, a number of these children have shown an unusual amount of nitrogen in the urine, and thus many of them seem to be more than recalcitrant youngsters defying toilet training or reacting to family strains. One medication that has been tried on enuretic children is imipramine, a drug which effectively lightens sleep so that the child can awaken when he needs to get up. Unfortunately, while keeping the bed dry, the drug also produces an irritable child, for it affects not only depth of sleep, but mood. When administered to depressed patients it has an enlivening effect, but it seems to raise the normal person to an irritable level of excitability.

A most eerie and fascinating sleep performance, often associated with enuresis, is sleepwalking. Somnambulists have been known to perform remarkable feats, to stride across narrow walls, pick their way through furniture, and even march into a city store and do their shopping. In the centuries before Lady Macbeth's sleeping perambulation through the castle of her evils, the sleepwalker was considered bewitched.

The evils of sleepwalking have been very real indeed, for in a state that resembles the dissociation of a narcotics addict, unaware people have driven cars and even committed murders. A sixteen-year-old girl, dreaming of burglars as she later said, took the family revolver in her sleep and killed her father and brother, injuring her mother. In 1946, an Arkansas father awakened from a nightmare into greater horror, when he found that he had warded off an imaginary attacker with a heavy flashlight—and killed his only daughter, a four-year-old. A Berkeley housewife rose one night at 2 A.M., threw a coat over her pajamas, and gathered the family dachshunds into the car for a long drive to Oakland, awakening at the wheel 23 miles away. Lore about somnambulism is abundant. Perhaps one of the most amusing tales is that of an English lady who awakened one night. There was a thud on the bed, and she was so frightened she fainted. When she awakened in daylight she found that her sleepwalking butler had set the table for fourteen on her bed. Each night thousands of Americans wander out of their beds without awakening, and return to bed. Perhaps four million Americans walk in their sleep.

It is not a safe habit. People have injured themselves badly. One young Frenchman, who often arose in the morning with bruises and bad wounds, yet claimed he had slept soundly and restfully. His wife knew otherwise. He spent a part of his nights in a pitched battle with the furniture—breaking things, bumping things, and even throwing chairs as he shouted. He seemed to be re-enacting a shipboard trauma suffered as a very young man, during which he found himself forced to take command and quell a fire and mutiny on his tanker.

A good deal has been conjectured about traumatic experience, worked out during sleep. Psychiatrists have considered sleepwalking the result of unresolved Oedipal conflicts, the enactment of sibling rivalry, or hysterical reactions to deep conflicts within the personality. There have been almost as many conjectures as sleepwalkers, many of them postulating emotional disorder and the re-enactment of significant events.

Until recently, most of our conjectures were based upon reports made in retrospect, for nobody had systematically watched a sleepwalker perform and correlated behavior with brain waves and other physiological measures. Because people reported dreams, sleepwalking was presumed to occur during dream intervals. A typical and not so funny case was reported in newspapers throughout the country in 1965, when a twenty-three-year-old Australian woman was found at night in a Sidney street by the police—with broken legs. As she explained, she had had a vivid dream about eloping with her fiancé. He had placed a ladder against the window of her third-story bedroom and she stepped out onto a ladder that, sadly enough, existed only in her imagination.

In 1963, with the help of new EEG equipment that would permit movement without disrupting brain-wave recordings, a team of young scientists at UCLA took a hard look at eleven somnambulists over some 80 nights. They found at once that sleepwalking did not begin in the REM stage of dreaming but in the deep and usually dreamless Stages III and IV. The children and adults in the study wore a garland of electrodes connected to a long cable, allowing them to rise, leave their bedrooms, and wander throughout the laboratory while their brain waves were continuously recorded. Each of them spent many nights in the laboratory and when they left, the team had collected over 100 somnambulistic incidents. In each instance the subject began his movements in Stage III or IV, and most of the time did not remember having budged.

As the sleeper moved, the large rolling delta waves diminished, and the EEG showed a combination of new wave forms. During the longer incidents that sometimes lasted up to seven minutes, the tracings occasionally showed a rhythm like the alpha wave of relaxed waking. Ordinarily this rhythm vanishes when a person opens his eyes, but the sleepwalker's eyes opened wide, and the rhythm did not evaporate. Often the sleepwalker wandered into the control room, feet shuffling, eyes wide open yet giving no sign of recognition, apparently oblivious to the experimenters' presence. One child wandered to the end of the laboratory, into the kitchen, into another bedroom, and as if he found nothing he sought he retreated without bumping anything, retraced his footsteps back to his own room and clambered into bed. Ten minutes later when an electrode connection came loose and he was awakened to repair it, he remembered nothing.

Allan Jacobson and Anthony Kales, who led this study, compared the sleepwalking children with normal children of the same age. On many tests they were similar, but on one they diverged in a startling manner. A normal child, lifted to his feet during slow-wave sleep, would do nothing. A somnambulist could be induced into sleepwalking by this manipulation. If it were done in REM sleep he would awaken, but during delta-wave sleep he could be induced to start sleepwalking.

This EEG study at UCLA, and one other performed in France by H. Gastaut and R. Broughton, give a new picture of the way somnambulism happens. The initial brain waves are those of deep sleep, changing to a background rhythm suggestive of arousal or perhaps hypnotic trance. How do these people wander around, avoiding furniture, apparently seeing—yet giving no signs of recognition, no signs of perceiving? Why do they not remember what they have done?

Scientists have shed some light upon this paradox. By analyzing the averaged EEG responses of a person to clicks or touches in the many stages of sleep, they have found signs that sensory information enters the brain during deep stages of sleep, but there is an alteration in the response from the central regions that finally transmit this to the cortex, making information into sensation, or perception. The brain of the sleepwalker may receive a bombardment of visual information, yet the brain does not consciously experience this as it does in waking.

A state resembling that of the somnambulist but arising from REM dream periods has been seen in older people with chronic brain damage. It may explain the odd night wanderings of some elderly people, which often lead to hospitalization. A retired businessman in his late seventies, for instance, who was sometimes a little confused and disoriented, was found walking on a main street in Washington, D. C., at 3 A.M., in a hurry and wearing pajamas under his coat. He told the police officers he was racing to get to synagogue on time. He often meandered around the house at odd hours of night, inevitably giving his family the same explanation—that he was hurrying to synagogue or a business appointment. This is not uncommon among aged persons, who often suffer psychotic hallucinations and delusions in addition.

One signature of declining mental abilities in old age has been a slowing down of the EEG alpha rhythm. Another common characteristic is disturbed sleep. Irwin Feinberg and a team of psychiatrists at St. Elizabeths Hospital have made a four-year study of senile patients whose symptoms are commonly grouped under the rubric of "chronic brain syndrome." While disoriented and often confused, some of these patients did not have psychotic hallucinations. They simply showed the perverse behavior we resignedly call senility. The patient included an eighty-two-year-old fireman, a retired businessman of seventy-five, an army officer, a sixty-five-year-old service station operator, a physician of seventy-nine, a housewife of sixty-eight, and a barber of eighty-one. All but two had arteriosclerosis. It seems ironic that the mental impairment, disorientation, and perilous night journeys of these elderly people should be the fault of cardiovascular disease. Its ultimate effects upon the brain were painfully evident in the actions of these formerly active and competent people. Two of them, when tested, showed what could only be described as a marked drop in intelligence, in addition to confusion of time and place, past and present.

Most of them had disturbed sleep and awakened frequently during the night, a few showing a very small proportion of REM dreaming. Characteristically they awakened swiftly, much faster than a young adult. Four of them did something in the laboratory bedroom that might have explained their unmanageable nighttime wanderings to their perplexed families. During every REM interval each would awaken like a shot and start tearing off the electrodes. As a doctor or attendant rushed to their sides, they would be leaping out of bed in breathless haste, with a hurried explanation. Each time it was the same sort of explanation. "I've got to meet that train, my daughter is on it." "I've got to get to work." "I'm late for synagogue." Although this almost never happened in any other stage of sleep, inevitably the REM period would arouse them to this agitated and hurried race to meet one of the everyday situations of their past lives.

There were other peculiarities in their sleep, less dramatic but equally suggestive about the nature of their brain damage. They showed bursts of muscle activity, independent of body movements or twitches, bursts that had not been seen in other patients. These might be related to cramps, prickling fingers and some sleep pains that have been reported by patients after middle age, sometimes thought to be associated with circulatory problems or changes in body hormones. Characteristically, these older people awakened often and their total nighttime sleep was indeed abbreviated. The doctors found this fact was at least circumstantially related to their diminished mental acuity.

A systematic comparison of these senile patients with healthy young adults revealed that the elderly patients were sleeping about 20-odd percent less than the younger persons. Some years earlier, a study had been conducted to ascertain the rate of brain metabolism in old patients. It measured about 23 percent lower than that of the younger person, a decrement that matches almost exactly the drop in total sleep time. This slower brain metabolism and reduced sleep time also corresponded to lower intelligence. A group of very bright and active older people had been studied, ranging from sixty-five to ninety-five years. "The ninety-five-year-old," remarked the doctor, "was the whiz of the lot. His memory was better than mine." These bright elderly people spent about as much time sleeping each night as the normal young adult. Moreover, the older person who is still in peak health shows the same rate of cerebral metabolism as the young person. It may be circumstantial evidence, but the findings do offer a strong suggestion that total sleep time, cerebral metabolic rate, and IQ may go together.

Excepting for an occasional alcoholic or drug addict, elderly patients with senile dementia who have been studied in mental hospitals have almost all suffered from atherosclerosis, poor blood circulation in the brain, from cerebral hemorrhages and other concomitant neural damage. Here is a disorder characterized by disorientation, neurosis, a drop in intelligence, and even psychotic symptoms, which is not just the inevitable fatigue of age and might be reduced if circulatory disease were caught in earlier life. Thus, in the study of sleep, we are beginning to find that even the senility we have long accepted with resignation develops along a traceable physiological path before it corrodes the central nervous system. There are numerous ways to wreak havoc with the central nervous system, and some of these we enter upon through neglect, others by deliberate and voluntary action. If the nighttime wanderings of the senile dramatize the extent of his brain damage, there are other patients whose odd night behavior comes from a self-inflicted nervous damage, by alcohol or drugs.

VII

DRUGS

MILLIONS of Americans who would never dream of injecting themselves with heroin have recently begun to ply themselves with sedatives, tranquilizers, alcohol, and stimulants—casually and without apprehension. Many of these are new drugs and invaluable in medicine. They have revolutionized the treatment of the mentally ill. Yet their precise physiological action is almost as mysterious today as in the 1950's when so many of them were spawned. Except for their chemical structures and a few effects in animals, we know little about the manner in which they play upon the human brain. In balance with their medical merit we now witness the gravity of careless handling and abuse, often arising in poor sleep habits or relatively mild sleep difficulties associated with psychological problems.

Doctors administer barbiturates to some twenty million patients each year, and stimulants such as dexedrine to about ten million. The upward surge of demand for and dependence upon such drugs has been noticed in England and in other European countries as well. Americans pay about $100 million for prescription sedatives each year—about $350 million if over-the-counter drugs and hospital purchases are included. About $250 million are spent on tranquilizers, and the yearly purchase of

Americans' foremost psychotoxic drug—alcohol—amounts to nearly $13 billion.

These figures barely suggest the extent to which these drugs have been used to substitute for a well-balanced nervous system. The U. S. Food and Drug Administration has estimated that about half of our barbiturates and amphetamines are diverted from the legal market. We produce about 6 to 10 billion barbiturate capsules and 8 billion amphetamine capsules a year. Illegal traffic in "pep pills" alone amounts to something between $200 million and $400 million a year. Alcohol is unrestricted, of course, and may be considered our primary addiction, maiming about five million lives. Nevertheless, for every five deaths caused by acute alcoholism there are now four deaths from barbiturate poisoning and an ever-increasing highway toll caused by drivers intoxicated with amphetamines and other drugs.

The cliché portrait of a drug addict describes a febrile and skinny misfit in a slum, piercing already scarred thighs with a syringe of Mafia poison, who either collapses dreamy-eyed on a shabby stoop or sets out on a ravening course of rape and murder. In point of fact, the addict is quite as likely to be a wealthy suburban housewife or a respected professional. For every person hooked on narcotics there are about twelve who are hooked on barbiturates. In 1962, Senator Thomas Dodd of Connecticut remarked, "A virtual epidemic of "nice-drug" addiction is sweeping the country." He proposed a bill for the control of psychotoxic drugs, and Senate hearings have opened to the public one of the saddest stories of our era.

The new trend in addiction may be blamed in part on the misguided Harrison Law of the early 1900's, when narcotics were taken out of the hands of doctors, thereby inhibiting therapy and sending drug distribution underground. Law enforcement made serious narcotics hard to obtain. As heroin became scarce and increasingly diluted, addicts began to take combinations of sleeping pills to enhance the effect of heroin, or tide them over when none was available. Psychiatrist Marie Nyswander told a *New Yorker* reporter: ". . . these substituted drugs are more dangerous than heroin. They can alter judgment, cause mental deterioration, and bring about convulsions." Sleeping pills are abused and illegally purchased in every level of society, not just by a million or so known addicts who are neatly roped off by law. Widely dispensed by doctors, accepted in society, these medical drugs are considered to be safe and comfortable—assurances of needed sleep, calmed nerves, a backstop of alertness and courage for long stretches of duty.

Many people depend upon these handy pills to a degree never anticipated by their doctors, but one seldom reads of housewives or ordinary men, quietly going about their lives, in the headline stories about drug addiction. Juvenile delinquents, college students on sprees, and truck drivers seem to monopolize the newspaper stories, complete with details about the motels or restaurants where the drugs have been illegally disseminated. Unfortunately, this publicity merely cloaks the massiveness of a problem that cannot be categorized with crime and delinquency. In testimony for the Senate subcommittee investigating psychotoxic drugs, Commissioner George P. Larrick of the Federal Drug Administration cited the instances of famous people, some of them entertainers, who took amphetamines to stay awake and barbiturates in order to sleep, in a vicious circle that eventually destroyed them. On investigation several of the famous cases of barbiturate suicide revealed a history of excessive drug use.

Inordinate reliance on drugs is kindled by a slow and beguiling process. Amphetamines and barbiturates develop tolerances in the individual, which is to say that the body adjusts to repeated doses so that they no longer instigate their original effects. Tolerance is an essential physiological survival mechanism. It permits the body to adjust to natural toxins in the environment. A person may get sick after drinking water in a new town where the concentration of minerals is unusual, yet after repetition his body can adjust so that he no longer falls ill from drinking water. When a person takes a sleeping pill he desires the effects of the "toxin," yet the same tolerance mechanism slowly diminishes the effect so that he is forced to take ever more. Millions of people drift down this path so gently they do not realize what may be happening to them.

Most of the adults taking sleeping pills, amphetamines, or tranquilizers are not thrill-seeking nor suicidal. Anxiety and tension are probably their common bond. They may start with insomnia or a pressured schedule that leaves them too wound up to sleep. The long-distance hauler who moonlights to earn extra money, the television producer in a deadline crisis, the student taking exams, the intern on 24-hour duty in a hospital—all must stay alert during an exorbitant schedule. An individual who makes a steady diet of amphetamines may simply need to stay awake, or he may be combating depression, or attempting to control appetite to lose weight.

Amphetamines are central nervous system stimulants best known in the form of Benzedrine or Dexedrine. They come in various strengths, occasionally in spansules that last between 6 and 18 hours, and are referred to as pep pills, bennies, footballs, co-pilots, and Miami turnarounds. Teen-agers and college students have combined them with alcohol or other drugs for jags, but it is the truck drivers who account for 90 percent of the black-market trade. They buy pills for 10 to 35 cents each at truck stops, motels, and restaurants. By using these drugs they can drive for long periods without rest or make more trips each week, but they fail to realize that the drugs are mendacious. They do not eliminate physical fatigue. They merely mask it. Ultimately the driver suffers impaired reflexes, hallucinations, periods of semiconsciousness while at the wheel and believing himself to be alert.

In 1963 a young Air Force sergeant and his family were crushed and charred beyond recognition when a truck behind them failed to stop and ground them under another truck ahead. The heedless driver was uninjured, and by blood test was found to be high on amphetamines. He carried three bottles in his suitcase. This kind of tragedy on the road has become more common than people would like to admit, and worries bo truckers' associations and the Interstate Commerce Commission.

Intemperate use of amphetamines can lead to behavior almost indistinguishable from that of the paranoid schizophrenic. Appetite is diminished and the user generally does not eat normally. Like any addict, he functions under illusion. Amphetamines have no odor and leave no smell on the breath, yet the police are learning to identify this new species of drunken driver. As one police spokesman testified before a Senate subcommittee:

"A person driving under the influence of amphetamines indicates his condition by erratic driving. He thinks he's better than he really is, consequently exhibits a startled response and exaggerated quickness. He'll cut someone off too short, changes lanes a great deal . . . telltale signs for the arresting officer will be extreme pupillary dilation, nervousness, agitation, giddiness, talkativeness."

Even though the tired driver exudes a false sense of well-being, he suffers an inability to concentrate. As the drug wears off he increases the dose, and then has no impulse to sleep, and he may suffer headaches, dizziness, and irritability. When he stops the drug he will feel depressed and hung over. If he combines the drug with alcohol or other drugs, the wallop is augmented. A combination of amphetamine and antihistamine can even knock a man out. Drivers on heavy doses of amphetamines think they are very acute, yet before they collapse they may report mirages on the road, visions that can cause them to swerve into another vehicle, hallucinations that are similar in some respects to those of the alcoholic with delirium tremens or to the visions of the sleep-starved. Often they are, indeed, sleep-starved.

Wherever amphetamines are consumed to excess, they are likely to be accompanied by sedatives, a combination often employed by ambitious people busily impelling themselves toward greater success, or among quiet, circumspect individuals who can hide a drug habit more easily than solitary drinking.

Nobody is shocked to hear that a person has swallowed a "dex" or requires a sleeping pill at night. Well-intentioned faculty members have suggested an amphetamine to students preparing for doctoral exams, and kindly friends or neighbors will readily dispense their sedatives to individuals in crisis. So the drugs spread from person to person, often, if not always, outside medical channels. Even when amphetamines are prescribed for weight control, the reducer often finds he cannot sleep without a barbiturate. Because the sedative leaves him feeling soggy and sluggish in the morning, he may double his dose of Dexedrine. By nighttime he may need a larger dose of barbiturates in order to sleep, and so he enters the ascending spiral. Soon he may suffer a temporary psychosis due to a combination of amphetamines, alcohol, and barbiturates. Mental hospitals treat a number of physicians with such psychoses, many of whom began their drug dependence in an effort to lose weight, and others who used drugs in their intern days. A few years ago, there was a well-concealed, embarrassing incident at a well-known psychiatric institute. A group of interns arrived to do their residency acting so peculiarly and erratically that Institute officials began to investigate. They soon discovered that the young doctors had sustained themselves through their difficult schedules of internship on a diet of Benzedrine. By the time they arrived for their residency, they showed full-blown amphetamine psychosis and had to submit to a withdrawal procedure before they could go on to complete their psychiatric training.

Barbiturate reliance frequently evolves from the genuine miseries of insomnia and a visit to the doctor's office. A sleepless person whose desperation impels him to the accident ward of a major hospital at night may discover that the only soporific in stock is a barbiturate. Of the twenty-one or so barbiturates listed for use in the United States, phenobarbital is outstanding for its potency and duration. Nembutal, Amytal, and Seconal are most commonly prescribed for insomnia, nervous tension, hysteria, psychiatric treatment, and anesthesia. There are many other sedatives with different properties, among them chloral hydrate. By any past standards the array of sedatives on the market looks misleadingly sophisticated, for there are about 60 kinds of sedatives and 200 kinds of tranquilizers. A few are sold, without prescription, at drugstore counters. They go by trade names such as Dormin, Nytol, Sleep Eze, and Sominex. The soporific ingredient is usually an antihistamine or scopolamine, which is made from belladonna. These are mild and harmless enough if ingested according to directions. But the mildness is a problem, for the drowsiness caused by an antihistamine would hardly benefit anybody with severe sleep difficulties. In large doses they induce side effects—dizziness, blurred vision, nervousness, blood changes. In turn, these side effects often produce sleep disorders, tempting the individual to multiply his dosage or combine the soporific with alcohol, inviting yet more side effects. Quite a few insomniacs have been taking tranquilizers, yet some of these also produce dependence, as we have begun to learn. Equanil, Librium, and Miltown have been notably overused, although there are others that have given no signs of addiction in years of use. With all these drugs on the market, and the growing certainty that insomnia's chameleon symptoms can spring from multitudinous origins, this treatment of sleep disorders must be considered relatively primitive and sometimes sloppy.

Harry C. Solomon, a renowned professor of psychiatry at Harvard Medical School, became something of a legend for his success with older patients suffering mental disturbance. He found that patients over fifty were coming to him for neurological examination, prompted by mental confusions that were often caused by bromides or barbiturates prescribed for insomnia. He would remove the drugs and the patients regained their lucidity. Barbiturates have a cumulative effect in older people, perhaps because they are not metabolized sufficiently rapidly.

In an era when it was thought to be impossible to run a state mental hospital without barbiturates and nurses made nightly rounds carrying a bucket of sedatives, Solomon banned the use of barbiturates at Boston Psychopathic Hospital. If a patient could not sleep, staff members would talk with him, smoke cigarettes, and keep him company until he was tired. Patients were forced to get up in the morning, and began to find themselves tired at night. One factor in the insomnia was poor habits and this was resolved by the new regimen and attitude. Many elderly people who assumed they had brain damage discovered that their confused thinking was merely the cumulative result of nightly sedation.

A Yale study of mental patients has emphasized that tranquilizers and barbiturates should not be administered to certain insomniacs, whatever their age. As one of the doctors has said, "Depression is a potentially fatal disease, and about 15 percent of psychotic depressives die as suicides." Surveys have indicated that they are more likely to have attempted suicide if they received tranquilizers or barbiturates than if given an antidepressant. People may not know they are depressed and insist on sedatives, yet sleeping pills may not help their insomnia. A prominent woman gynecologist who was testifying in an important criminal trial, and was too haunted to sleep, obtained a mild sedative from her psychoanalyst. It helped her fall asleep, yet she could not stay asleep—and in desperation one night she took the entire bottle. Subsequently, she received a remarkable drug that banished her glum mood and gave her rest. It was not a sedative, of course, but an antidepressant that might have kept a normal person awake. With the help of this drug, normal rest, and psychiatric counseling she soon regained her usual composure and healthy outlook on life.

Although a cursory review of sleep disorders sketches out the multifarious nature of insomnia, it is not easy to persuade a patient that sleeping pills will do him no good. One lobbyist who entered a Virginia hospital in a manic attack insisted on sedation, and by accident received a dose that would put a normal person to sleep for 24 hours—but he raved on, unable to sleep a wink until he received a very different compound to calm the mania. A man in this condition might easily kill himself with an overdose of barbiturates, while merely seeking rest. There is no inherent safety device in this path to oblivion. The alcoholic must stay awake to continue drinking, but barbiturates are swallowed in advance, absorbed slowly from the intestinal tract into the blood, and may often have a delayed effect. In 1963 about half of the U. S. suicides were from barbiturates—10,000 deaths. Authorities, psychiatrists, and coroners estimate that as many as 5,000 were not intentional deaths in the sense that the victims did not plan to die. The combination of alcohol and barbiturates is particularly treacherous, a fact emphasized in 1965 by the apparently accidental death of the newspaper columnist Dorothy Kilgallen. Taken together, the drugs have enhanced power, and a quantity that seems harmless enough on some occasions may suddenly prove fatal.

Barbiturates can have psychological effects that may indirectly cause a fatal overdose. They can emulsify a person's sense of time and perception of his surroundings. Addicts and some middle-aged people who begin experimenting with their doctors' dose may never notice the subtle metamorphosis, but outsiders and family may detect a slight expansiveness, errors in judgment, discoordination. The person may begin to lose his train of thought while speaking, may slur words as if drunk. When daily intake begins to approach a gram or two the deterioration is likely to be obtrusive—a staggering gait, slurred speech, confusion, intermittent aggressiveness, and finally paranoid delusions in a form of temporary psychosis. A lamentable death may occur long before this stage when an insomniac awakens, unable to recall how many pills he took and how long he slept. In a state of confusion he may swallow more, without counting.

Deliberate or involuntary, the person in barbiturate coma presents a dilemma to the hospital. Occasionally a person will be carried into the emergency room, as was one young woman whose neighbor found her on the stairs, inarticulate and semiconscious. To the doctors who saw her lying unconscious and breathing with difficulty, she appeared to be in the throes of acute pneumonia. Treated accordingly, and placed in an oxygen tent, she died four hours later.

The person who survives without mishap a growing addiction to barbiturates is more difficult to wean away from his habit than the heroin user. Harris Isbell, Director of the Addiction Research Center in Lexington, Kentucky, has said, "Treatment is far more serious than for morphine addiction. It can be done only under hospital conditions lasting anywhere from three weeks to six months." If barbiturates are withdrawn too suddenly, the addict commonly suffers from convulsions and dies. Withdrawal can be an agonizing process, incurring terrible apprehension, insomnia, weakness, nausea and cramps, circulatory difficulties, vomiting, rapid respiration, and accelerated heart rate. People sometimes become dehydrated, so rapidly that they have been known to lose 10 pounds in three days. Hallucinations, convulsions, and disorientation are commonly attended by fever, and the individual is on the threshold of death throughout such a crisis. Only a slow and careful procedure can avoid these dangers. People who abuse sleeping pills, amphetamines, and tranquilizers resemble the alcoholic, but unlike the heavy drinker they may not realize what penalties they court.

Why is it that these valuable medical drugs are handled so destructively? Many factors have contributed to their abuse. A fraction of the blame must rest upon those few unscrupulous doctors who have sold outright quantities of drugs or prescriptions. That is rare. Less rare are the doctors who have listened to a patient's complaints of fatigue or insomnia and prescribed drugs casually and liberally. Some reach into their top drawers and hand out samples received for clinical testing from drug companies, saying, "This is new and I'm not sure how it works—but you might try it." This is utter carelessness and the patient who accepts such free handouts often cherishes the illusion that the modest doctor actually knows a great deal about the new drug. A more pervasive medical contribution to drug abuse, if less reprehensible, might be summarized as unrefined usage among practicioners.

Most doctors have been inadequately trained in handling pharmaceuticals. They are bedeviled by a crop of new samples from drug houses every few months. Moreover, they often fail to spend time tailoring doses to the individual patient, despite the fact that people exhibit constitutional individuality in responding to drugs—even to alcohol. Many doctors, through no fault of their own, fail to diagnose the patient's symptoms. General practitioners and psychiatrists are beginning to receive information about the multiple sources of sleep disorders that look the same on the surface, but much of this is very new. The medical profession can be charged with some misuse of drugs, and the AMA did not diminish the problem by opposing for years the law proposed for controlling psychotoxic drugs. Still, drug abuse in its epidemic proportions is largely the fault of individuals who tamper casually and ignorantly with their own nervous systems, abetted by a competitive society that impels them with breakneck speed along the route to success without regard for the tempo of the human body and mind. Somewhere on the forehead of each person there should be an invisible legend that appears each time he sees his face in the mirror: CENTRAL NERVOUS SYSTEM WITHIN—HANDLE WITH CARE. Once drugs have begun to substitute for the usual functions of the brain, the individual may no longer possess the ability to care.

The study of sleep has not revealed why people become addicted, but the study of drugged sleep has brought into sharp focus certain changes in the nightly pattern that are correlated with altered behavior. Alcohol, barbiturates, tranquilizers, and amphetamines all reduce the normal amount of REM sleep when taken in the usual dose range. The reduction is especially noticeable in the early part of the night when the drug is at the height of its potency. Taken regularly in sufficient quantities, these drugs inevitably cause a substantial reduction in rapid-eye-movement sleep. A person might never miss a few truant dreams from his night's vivid cycle, but their absence would seem to have a physiological, perhaps a biochemical import. Interference with the REM cycle implies interference with an entire chain of physiological and neural events that would normally recur with almost clocklike regularity throughout sleep. Some scientists feel this may account for the psychotic symptoms of the addict. Does the bottled-up REM activity finally burst through into wakefulness like compressed steam, disrupting behavior, invading the day with fragments of dreams? A number of psychiatrists have conjectured that the delirium tremens of the alcoholic might represent extended REM deprivation finally reaching a discharge point. This is a figurative explanation, and doubtless too simple a theory to accommodate all the chemical and neural transformations that are implied, yet it may be the first glimmering of an insight.

Case histories in a study of 500 alcoholic patients have indicated that insomnia often precedes a bout of heavy drinking, yet as drinking increases so do the sleep disturbances. Milton Gross and a team of other psychiatrists, psychologists, and physicians at New York Downstate Medical Center have begun to track the progression of the alcoholic's sleep disorders. At first the alcoholic seems to drink heavily in order to sleep. Gradually he develops nightmares. In time, he begins the night with a huge drink and drops into a heavy, stuporous sleep, but nightmares begin to awaken him and he returns to sleep only by drinking more. As addiction continues, he may spring out of a horrifying dream uncertain whether he wakes or sleeps, feeling suffocated, and continuing to hallucinate. If he can no longer keep alcohol down at this point, or has decided to quit, he may enter a state of sleeplessness and hallucination and seek help in a hospital.

In 1963 the Downstate team began a series of long and grueling observations and EEG recordings of alcoholics in the early stages of withdrawal. These monitored sessions, running from 48 to 72 hours, were the first concerted study of alcoholic sleep and did suggest that the suppressed REM activity might be bursting forth and expressing itself as the drug was removed. The four men who entered the hospital had a psychiatrist in constant attendance, and a family member present when possible. While they were encouraged to eat and drink fluids, all medications were withheld as long as possible. They were young men, in their thirties and early forties, and only one had been alcoholic over a sustained period. Two of them never showed signs of sleep on their first day. When they closed their eyes, however, the waking alpha rhythm was occasionally punctuated by eye movements and unpleasant hallucinations. One man sat up in a sweat, scarcely able to breathe. As he later said, he was watching gremlins, midget dogs, cats, and mice. The other sleepless patient hallucinated with his eyes open, hearing threats on his life, observing doctors amputate legs while blood squirted in all directions and lizards devoured snakes. These two men, with full-blown DTs, could fall asleep only after receiving a dose of paraldehyde, a valuable sedative that is often avoided because of its foul smell. The sleeplessness and convulsions may have reflected the fact that these two had not been drinking in the 24 hours before they entered the hospital and were in advanced withdrawal.

Another patient who had managed to drink earlier in the day and had not yet descended into the full maelstrom of withdrawal, exhibited a first-night sleep record unlike anything in the annals of the sleep laboratory. He spent the entire time in the REM state. When he awakened, his dream continued and he attempted to enact it in the manner of an elderly patient with chronic brain syndrome. For half an hour he insisted that he was back in the old barroom where he used to work. When reminded that he was in the hospital his only concession to reality was to convert the laboratory into the bar, leaving the psychiatrist's status intact by making him bartender. In his eyes, the medical staff were customers, and since the taproom of his dream was crowded, he peopled the room with an imaginary horde in his delirium. By the next night, however, he was sleepless and his hallucinations were worse.

The fourth patient followed a similar pattern. He had drunk

a fifth of vodka on the day before he entered the hospital. He spent fully half of his sleep time in the REM state that night, and on the following night was sleepless and hallucinating.

Muscle recordings taken during the sleep of these men disclosed another facet of the impact of alcohol, for the usual flaccidity of neck and head muscles did not occur during REM sleep. Unlike the normal dreamer, these men moved about, talked, and gestured a great deal, with unusual signs of excitation. They often seemed to dream of eating. Throughout an intense REM dream one alcoholic furiously moved his eyes, mouthed, chewed, sweated, and dripped saliva, while his hands made occasional gesticulations as if preparing food. When these men continued enacting their dream after awakening, they were not racing to some mundane appointment but to relieve a basic drive. It was sleep behavior that did, in toto, lend corroboration to a theory that has been casually proposed for many years. If extended drinking had set a lid upon the expression of the REM cycle, it might break through with a vengeance once the alcohol was removed.

Once entered upon the agonies of withdrawal, the alcoholics barely got any of the deep, slow-wave sleep known as delta sleep or Stage IV. Clinicians in numerous sleep laboratories have noticed that mentally ill patients seem to need delta sleep. After it, they begin to show improvement. This was true among the alcoholics. As withdrawal advanced, and there was little alcohol left in their systems, they showed less delta sleep and finally could not sleep unless given paraldehyde. This sedative restored delta sleep and improvement followed.

It must seem curious that drugs as diverse as alcohol, amphetamines, tranquilizers, and barbiturates all suppress the normal rhythm of the REM cycle. Exactly how they intercede in the chemistry of the body and brain, and where they make their impact on the brain is still a matter of speculation. Still, their common effect of suppressing the REM interval seems to lend a clue to the psychotic symptoms these diverse drugs can produce. The answers probably lie in the unfolding areas of neurochemistry and neurophysiology, where researches have indicated that REM deprivation can produce negligible, serious, and sometimes psychotic symptoms.

For about a decade, animal experiments have hinted that interference with the rapid-eye-movement cycle will eventually result in most peculiar behavior. Michel Jouvet and his laboratory team at Lyon have used surgery to destroy a small group of cells in the base of the brain. They lie in the primitive region known as the pontine reticular formation, so designated because of its netlike reticulum of white nerve fibers. When a small nucleus of cells is ablated in this region a cat no longer shows its usual repertoire of REM sleep. Unless the damage heals and the phase of sleep returns, the animal will begin to paw around its cage, scrabbling as if to grasp invisible objects in what appear to be hallucinations, and eventually will die. Ingenious nonsurgical methods have been adopted to delete REM sleep, and after a period of this deprivation, the animals again behave oddly. This pontine reticular region appears to be important in the excitation of REM sleep.

Although there is no coherent biochemical theory of the REM cycle, many scientists suppose that it must be triggered by body chemicals. Its almost clocklike recurrence in sleep suggests that it may be part of a regular body metabolism that discharges periodically. Drugs that inhibit or prevent this cycle may be interrupting a fundamental process of body and brain.

This tentative hypothesis may offer a first approximate key to drug psychosis. Nonetheless, the drugs that suppress REM sleep are heterogeneous in chemical structure and effect. For many years barbiturates and tranquilizers were both used in mental hospitals to produce a calming and sedative effect. On close inspection it was clear that barbiturates could help a schizophrenic patient sleep but they often seemed to exacerbate the psychotic symptoms. Tranquilizers, by contrast, ameliorated symptoms among the schizophrenics who had trouble sleeping.

A relatively simple test has indicated that the barbiturate must act upon portions of the brain involved in intellectual function, while tranquilizers seem to depress mechanisms in the brain for arousal or attention. A segment of a widely known IQ test asks a person simply to match numbers and symbols. A normal person would show a drop in intellectual function, as judged by this task, after taking barbiturates, but no change in ability after taking tranquilizers. If he were asked to perform a task requiring only sustained attention—detecting certain pairs of letters as they appeared in a steady stream of letters on a screen—he would be quite as attentive as usual after the barbiturate, but a tranquilizer would cause him to make errors of omission. In the manner of sleep-starved people who have taken this test, he would show lapses in attention. Schizophrenics who performed these two tasks under barbiturates and tranquilizers differed in one important dimension. The tranquilizer did not appear to diminish their sustained attention, hinting that one of their problems may be an excessively high state of brain vigilance, over-arousal.

Another important difference between barbiturates and tranquilizers has been observed in sleep studies of psychotic patients at St. Elizabeths Hospital. Both drugs suppress REM sleep. However, phenobarbital, a long-acting barbiturate, also diminished the number of eye movements that occurred during the dreaming periods, perhaps signifying that it suppressed the intensity of neural discharge. Even more revealing than this was the difference in sleep after the drugs were withdrawn. Psychotics who had been taking tranquilizers immediately showed an increase in REM sleep, in compensation, when they were not on the drug. Psychotics who had been on barbiturates exhibited no such rebound during undrugged sleep, a clue perhaps to the exaggerated symptoms caused by barbiturates.

From another quarter comes a possible explanation for the intellectual decrements, the confusion caused by barbiturates and also the sluggish hangover that annoys many people after taking them. A group of scientists collaborated at Yale University several years ago in a study of the relation between our subjective sensations and the physical stimulation of the outside world. When we say that one touch is stronger than another, does our nervous system reflect the actual and measurable difference between the two physical events? Can a person accurately report the measurably hotter sensation of a warming iron? Would his brain waves reflect the mounting intensity of the heat sensation? Burton S. Rosner, Truett Allison, and William Goff used electric shock to explore this question. Electric shock can be delivered in precise intensities and timed to the split second. Volunteers received mild shocks to the wrist during waking, in every stage of sleep, and under drugs.

By analyzing the brain waves that followed each intensity of shock, the research team established that people do feel changes that correspond to the actual intensity of larger shocks, and this is reflected in their EEG responses. At a certain point, however, there is a notable change—and this is the point of pain. This discovery may enable a surgeon to track a person's brain-wave reactions during periods when he might look unconscious or impervious to pain.

The transformations in brain-wave patterns are very complicated and not merely a matter of size. To analyze the brain-wave responses the scientists divided them into parts, although the entire morsel of EEG response lasted only a fraction of a second. Each time they delivered a shock the EEG showed its brief, instant reaction. They repeated the same shock many times, superimposing the EEG responses and averaging them to get a clear picture of that brain's reaction to the particular stimulus. The first waves of the response, analogous to the first letters of a long word, told that the shock impulses had traveled up the nerve from the wrist, through the spinal cord and into the brain. Thus, the first letters only said that the specific sensory nerve paths had registered the shock at the gateway of the perceiving brain. The letters at the end of the response told about activity in the center of the brain that integrated this message and transformed it into feeling. These end letters are thought to signify integrative processes among regions known as the diffuse projection system to the cortex—the thinking, conscious brain.

Without this final activity a shock message may enter the brain yet the person never feel it.

One of the tactics the scientists employed to decipher the meaning of the different letters in the EEG response was a process of elimination. They would try to exclude certain letters, by excluding those phases of brain activity. They found that they could completely obliterate the end letters of the EEG response to shock if they administered a light barbiturate anesthesia. The barbiturate apparently halted activity in the integrative areas of the brain. This tailless EEG response was not that of normal sleep, not even the deepest Stage IV sleep. Throughout sleep they had delivered shocks so mild that the subjects ignored them, and in each stage of sleep the brain had a characteristic reaction to the shock. Even in the oblivion of Stage IV, the shock evoked an EEG picture that showed integrative activity continuing in the central regions of the brain. It was larger and slower and later than during light sleep. Nevertheless, central regions of the "thinking and experiencing" brain still responded, suggesting some kind of mentation. Since barbiturates abolish or diminish this activity, their sedation is not natural sleep.

When a barbiturate abolishes the end letters of a brain-wave response it eliminates or reduces certain brain activities, and this may mean that the entire body is missing some of its usual regulation, for it is the action of the brain that seems to control myriad body processes during sleep, metabolism, heart rate, and the innumerable physical transformations that ceaselessly occur during life. An effect upon these processes may help to explain the barbiturate hangover. It must seem obvious why people under barbiturate sedation show a loss of mental sharpness, even confusion, disorientation and poor judgment, if this drug attacks the integrative brain centers so crucial to their mental faculties.

Barbiturates are, of course, only one class of sedatives, but all sedatives must exert their influence by acting upon the central nervous system. Eventually a wise use of soporific drugs must rest upon discovering how and where in the brain they perform their hypnotic work. It will be quite a while before there is any such assay of even our most commonly used drugs, although a great many researchers have begun using EEG methods to analyze them. Most of these studies have to be conducted on animals, especially when we need to track changes at locations deep within the brain. For example, at MIT, hair-fine electrodes have been implanted into regions of the brains of cats, and scientists have watched how differently Nembutal (a barbiturate) and chloralose (an anesthetic) affect the motor brain. A touch on the paw instigates a larger than normal response under chloralose, and smaller than normal under Nembutal. Such facts are meaningless in themselves but they are beginning to define the specific sites and characteristics of the many drugs we use. Ultimately, doctors will make use of this information as they select an anesthetic or sedative for the needs and constitution of a particular patient.

Drug companies, needless to say, have grown sophisticated about this burgeoning research. Their advertisements in trade magazines describe a new tranquilizer as having no effect upon the thinking brain and maximal effect on the primitive limbic system. Since the unwanted effects of Dexedrine are widely known, a new drug for appetite reduction is advertised as having no stimulant effect on the central nervous system. It may sound as if we could design drugs to have only a single effect—to depress appetite cells within the brain—but neurochemistry is still in its infancy, and any drug that achieves its impact by influencing brain cells is likely to touch more than just the function of appetite cells. When drugs become truly specific we should hear less about side effects. Drug companies issue folders for doctors, describing the side effects and contraindications of each drug. Anybody taking a central nervous system drug should glance at the manufacturer's folder to the pharmacist and doctor. A single look will indicate that the compound cannot be truly specific, and a quick review of side effects may reduce the temptation to begin self-medication. There are, in addition, effects that the drug company could not be expected to know until the compound has been in use for quite a long time. Tranquilizer advertisements, for instance, may end with a postscript saying that euphoria and addiction have not been observed—yet. Most of us do not read these items. We will accept and ingest a new drug with less interest than we would give the purchase of a new candy—and we rarely ask whether there are alternatives.

Fortunately, scientific ferment, growing awareness of drug defects, and mounting evidence from sleep laboratories has caused a search for alternatives among academic experimenters. One substance that has attracted considerable research attention is a family of compounds with some unusual properties. Gamma hydroxybutyrate, or GHB, belongs to a chemical family related to a naturally occurring amino acid in the brain, GABA. This structural relationship suggested to chemists that the body might convert GABA naturally into a hypnotic under certain conditions. They hoped they might be on the trail of one of the body's own soporifics. GHB is used in France as a hypnotic for anesthesia. Its action seems almost the opposite of the barbiturate. Indeed, this is one of its disadvantages for the person in pain. After heavy barbiturate sedation a person slowly drifts back to consciousness through a long murky cloud of sluggishness and confusion. He will not feel the full sting of pain, nor will he try to get up and move around. His "thinking" brain has been affected. When GHB wears off, however, the patient is completely alert, likely to move, and be attacked by the utter sharpness of his pain. GHB does not perform its action upon the integrative central regions of the brain. It appears to stop sensory signals at what one might call the gateway to the brain, somewhere before they ever reach the "feeling and conscious" regions—on the specific nerve pathways.

Sleep induced by this chemical is very different from barbiturate sleep. It does not appear to reduce REM sleep; indeed, it can be used to enhance the amount of REM phase. When injected into cats it has actually elicited REM sleep, a most unusual property among sedatives, but one that has not been demonstrated with people.

There is one particular form in which this compound appears to act with particular speed as a hypnotic. Samuel Bessman and William Fishbein at the University of Maryland Medical School have found that GHB is converted into this variant, GBL, by an enzyme in the liver, and might account for the drowsiness and apathy attending some liver diseases. We do not know whether this hypnotic variant is normally produced by body tissue, however. If so, our present instruments are too slow to detect it. When injected into an animal the substance metabolizes like lightning and does not wait for biochemists to track it. One can see why it might induce sleep swiftly and wear off rapidly: it metabolizes so fast that it can be detected in an animal's breath seconds after it is injected.

If this chemical and its related compounds can produce anything like natural sleep they might become invaluable for people who have a hard time falling asleep, but who stay asleep once they have let go. It is too early to know whether this hope will materialize. The biochemical causes of insomnia are not known. They may arise from the overproduction of arousing brain chemicals, from deficiency among the hypnotic brain chemicals, or from disturbance in a metabolic cycle—or the body's inability to neutralize some natural but potentially toxic substance. Into this unknown chemical condition we send drugs to do their work in a variety of ways. Some duplicate brain chemicals, others interfere with the synthesis of particular brain chemicals or prevent them from accumulating or from being released from storage. Drugs often work by blocking the action of an undesirable brain chemical at receptor cells in the nervous system or by enhancing their breakdown in metabolism.

Our knowledge of the disorder we treat and drug action is almost entirely indirect. It is drawn from EEG studies, from behavior, from using brain lesions and histological analysis of brain tissue—almost entirely in animal brains. We have frequently found generalization from animals to humans inappropriate, and human studies are essential, usually following a legion of animal studies, although occasionally data are obtained from accidents of nature or clinical reactions of patients.

From studies of human volunteers, we have learned a good deal about the effects of the stimulants, sedatives, and tranquilizers we so promiscuously use. These volunteers gave no more thought to ingesting small quantities of drugs than they did to taking a drink of Scotch. Ironically, drug abuse and its destructive aftermath is a natural consequence of our casualness. People accept prescriptions and take drugs without question. Rarely do they wonder whether the dosage is exactly right for them. A recent series of experiments in pursuit of a REM-enhancing drug has dramatized what a difference the dosage makes and how extensively people vary in their response.

For some years scientists have conjectured that a REM-enhancing drug might help addicts and narcoleptics and certain psychotics who show less than the usual REM phase in their nightly sleep. LSD seemed to be a likely candidate since it causes hallucination in waking subjects. One of the first experiments to use LSD with hopes of REM enhancement was performed on cats. Instead of augmenting REM time, the scientist found that it made the animals wakeful. Since then it has appeared that the wakefulness was caused by too large a dose.

At Columbia University School of Medicine, Joseph Muzio, Howard Roffwarg, and Edward Kaufman decided to take a long shot with a dozen volunteers and initiated an arduous year-long study. Each of the volunteers would come into the sleep laboratory at night, receive a dose of LSD that was recorded, and then his nightlong EEG patterns would be studied. At first it seemed doubtful that the drug would increase REM sleep. After every drug session the volunteer had to wait at least a week before returning for a different dose. This precaution meant there would be no trace of the drug left in his system, and that he would not have a chance to develop tolerance, but it made the study a very long one. In one instance it took repeated attempts, spaced out over almost a year, before a particular, infinitesimal dose showed an effect upon the volunteer's dreaming. The doses were adjusted within an almost microscopic range—between 0.08 and 0.73 micrograms per kilogram of body weight. This amounted to the equivalent of roughly 1/500th of an aspirin. When the individual received the dose that was right for him, the results were indisputable, even spectacular. There were several instances of phenomenal increase in the total REM sleep. Early in the night when the drug's action was at its peak some volunteers were doubling or tripling the length of their REM periods.

The Columbia volunteers required only minuscule amounts of LSD in order to augment their REM dreaming, yet another scientist in a distant laboratory also elicited more REM sleep by giving his volunteer 300 micrograms, an amount that was between 8 and 30 times the dosages used at Columbia. One may assume that the differences between these volunteers arose from more than just body weight. Body weight is only a crude guide for drug response as it is a rough and fallible guide in trying to purchase clothing. Anybody who has ever tried to purchase a bikini for a girl weighing about 120 pounds is suddenly confronted with the many dimensions of fitting the suit to the wearer. The fitting of drugs to an individual constitution is analogous but more difficult, for the dimensions are less visible.

Scientists, in their study of sleep disorders and drugs, have emphasized the need to tailor doses. As they search for special drugs to answer the needs of particular ailments, they have been focusing upon the biochemistry of the body itself in the hope that we can discover the body's own hypnotics and mimic them without creating toxic aftereffects.

VIII

THE NATURAL CHEMISTRY OF SLEEP

We all know that drugs can act upon our chemistries to influence our sleep and our behavior yet few of us imagine what normally goes on underneath our skins. We are constantly affected by migrations of substances in the blood and brain, such as the familiar hormones, or enzymes, or acids and salts. Somewhere within us an elixir of mortal juices helps to prompt a wholesome nightly sleep, or sometimes makes us unable to sleep. As we begin to face, in some detail, the task of countering nature's mischiefs, we must know how body chemistry influences our spirits and sleep.

Three lines of current research offer a heartening prospect, although they are so new they presently offer hypotheses rather than definite conclusions. Roughly speaking, they can be grouped together as explorations in the biochemistry of sleep. Some experimenters have been touching chemicals directly to the brain and inducing sleep or wakefulness in animals. They are hoping to discover the master chemicals of brain activity, and their anatomical sites of action, in order to decipher the brain's chemical codes. Other researchers have begun to search for chemicals generated within the brain or body during sleep or other states, substances that may influence our ability to sleep and which we may one day learn to synthesize. A third approach is the intensive psychiatric or biochemical study in which drugs are administered, and their effects carefully tracked. Unfortunately, some of the most dramatic and memorable clues to the body's many chemistries of sleep issue from the abnormalities of sickness. They emphasize how vulnerable we are to slight shifts in the chemical balance of the body and brain.

Perhaps the most thoroughly understood kind of sleep—from the biochemical standpoint—is the unpleasant and ominous sleepiness of people with severe liver disease. Depression, lethargy, disorientation, odd behavior, and sleepiness are symptoms of cirrhosis, and eventually lead to coma. In the late 1800's they were known as symptoms of meat poisoning. Ivan Petrovich Pavlov, the great Russian neurophysiologist, performed an experiment on dogs that seemed to clinch this diagnosis. By a clever device he prevented the blood from the intestines from passing through the liver as it would normally. The dogs survived so well they seemed not to need their livers—until they were given a meat dinner. Then they began acting peculiarly, growing sleepy and finally falling unconscious. It was later found that all protein foods—such as meat, milk, nuts—contain nitrogen, and these would cause a cirrhosis victim to fall unconscious. Before he lapsed into coma, however, he might act as if he were insane. In one famous case an English minister astounded his adoring congregation one Sunday. He stopped in the middle of his sermon, descended from the pulpit and proceeded to urinate on it. He was taken to doctors, who found that he had liver disease. Each time he ate a big dinner of cheese and meats, his behavior became very peculiar. In many respects the strange behavior and disorientation of the person with diseased liver resembles the first stages of sleep onset, and the symptoms are prevented by a very restrictive diet.

The unpleasant sleepiness and behavior problems of the liver patient must be blamed upon the familiar chemical ammonia. The ammonia forms out of the nitrogen of ordinary protein foods in the intestine. The disabled liver cannot detoxify the ammonia, which begins to accumulate and surge through the bloodstream to the brain. Samuel and Alice Bessman and their associates at the University of Maryland Medical School have now shown how the ammonia influences the brain. It exhausts the brain's supply of one of its most essential metabolites, thus by a form of natural theft interfering with normal behavior and consciousness.

We can and do, by our own actions, profoundly influence our chemistry and consciousness, pleasantly or unpleasantly depending upon the course we take. At all times of the day and night people catapult themselves into contented slumber, although this is not the goal of their enterprise. During the mounting passion of making love no couple considers the compelling chemical transformations that drive them to a climax, nor do they ask why they fall into a contented sleep after the surge of hormones and neural firings. What combination of chemicals prevails in the sleep of lovers? Is there a relationship between hormones that help to inspire the convulsion of the sex act and the sleep that follows?

Researchers suspect that a number of the body hormones may influence both sleep and mood, but the term "hormone," by itself, resembles the name "Smith." Without more identification it might refer to a secretion of the thyroid gland, a pituitary substance that elevates blood pressure, the pancreatic hormone insulin, the growth hormone or a number of related substances that are produced throughout the body and are conveyed through the blood to stimulate activity elsewhere. Hormones are the abundant chemical messengers of the body. The steroid hormones have a particular structure related to that of fats. All hormones contain amino acids, the building blocks of protein. A well-known group is produced by the yellowish glands near the kidneys, the adrenals, and are released in quantity under conditions of stress or fright. Commands from a portion of the brain cause the pituitary gland to release a hormone that acts somewhat like a Western Union messenger, traveling to the adrenals and causing them to pour their stimulants into the bloodstream. The insomniac who tries to capture sleep by force may in his rage be adding stimulants to his own bloodstream. The many sex hormones of the human body also appear to exert a powerful influence over states of consciousness as well as sexual behavior and reproduction.

One of the most common of all "sleep disorders" has been described repeatedly in books on prenatal care. A. F. Guttmacher, in *Pregnancy and Birth* recites a classic version.

> In some women, one of the earliest signs of pregnancy is an overpowering sleepiness. Sleeping late in the morning and napping in the afternoon do not prevent the pregnant young wife from yawning in her husband's face and from dozing, even at her own dinner parties. This excessive need for sleep disappears after the first few months.

The placidness and somnolence of a pregnant woman does not resemble the blankness of an epileptic seizure, the narcoleptic attack, or anesthesia—and yet there may be a chemical link between them.

Sex hormones have been used experimentally as sedatives within the laboratory. At one dosage they may be soporific, but in higher doses they can produce anesthesia and convulsions. This range of reactions has been produced with progesterone, the hormone that helps to develop the mammary glands and to form the placenta. It is secreted in unusual quantities during pregnancy. Working together at the Brain Research Institute at UCLA, Gunnar Heuser and George Ling have observed that progesterone injections do more than induce a deep and lengthy sleep. The quality of sleep in cats given this hormone was notable for unusually plentiful episodes of rapid-eye-movement intervals, the activated sleep of dreaming. During pregnancy the cat produces more of this hormone than usual, and a study of pregnant cats has shown that there is an increasing incidence of REM sleep as they near delivery and during the immediate postpartum period after giving birth. Scientists have wondered, of course, whether the sex hormone causes sleep indirectly by setting off a chain of chemical reactions, and whether it could cause sleep if injected directly into the brain. Heuser has indeed demonstrated that progesterone, applied directly to the preoptic region of the brain, puts a cat to sleep.

Hormones could be partly responsible for the exhausted sleep that follows giving birth. There are about 12 sex hormones in the normal human adult, and a number of them have been shown to produce sedation. Viadril, a synthetic progesterone, is being tried out as a hypnotic to be administered before anesthesia. But female hormones are not the only sex hormones with a soporific effect. Ling and Heuser have used the precursors of two male hormones to produce sedation in laboratory animals. In high doses, like progesterone they induced anesthesia and convulsions. Sleep appears to lie on a continuum, with anesthetic states and convulsions at the other end. Experiments with finely graded doses of sex hormones may clarify the way these natural body substances sometimes change in concentration, producing strikingly different effects upon our state of consciousness. Such studies may explain certain abnormalities. Narcolepsy, for instance, often begins during adolescence, and it is not unreasonable to think that hormonal imbalance may have something to do with the onset of seizures.

Over the long span of a lifetime, the balance of sex hormones is slowly changing. Nightly sleep patterns also show distinct metamorphoses in infancy, maturity, and old age. The life-span is too long a period to search for a correlation between hormone levels and sleep patterns, since the shifts are slow and progressive, but short-term shifts might be observed in women. Some women must undergo a monthly hormonal change of unusual strength, for their fluctuations of mood around menstruation are so extreme, so close to the precipice of mental illness, that they require medical aid. All normal women experience some transit between exhilaration and depression at the onset of menstruation, and initial studies of nightly sleep in women suggest that there may be a monthly rise and fall in their amount of REM dreaming. It is too early to say that it parallels the rise and fall of any particular hormone.

If there is a strong connection between sex hormones, sleep, and mood, it is not an academic matter for the women who take contraceptive or fertility pills every day. These are concentrates of female sex hormones whose action takes place within the brain. The contraceptive action occurs when the synthetic hormone influences a neural region that affects the pituitary gland in the base of the brain, and prevents it from releasing its usual train of hormones that liberate and nourish an egg in the ovary. Instead, the brain acts as if pregnancy had already begun. Just as a few women react extremely to menstruation or pregnancy, a few women react to some of these hormone compounds with irritation or depression, and in high doses even with transitory psychosis. The compounds are making their impact upon a region of the brain that functions to promote the fertility process —but also influences emotions, and sleep.

No direct link between fertility and sleep quality has been observed in human beings, but it has been seen under a special circumstance in the rabbit. Altered sleep patterns were, in fact, important in the research that has tested the effect of such double-purpose drugs as Enovid—a combination of a progesterone and estrogen that can be used to prevent fertility or to enhance it. The experiments were performed largely on rabbits, in whom ovulation can be controlled. Unlike the human, in whom ovulation begins spontaneously according to some metabolic clock, the rabbit only releases eggs into the ovary after sexual stimulation. Ordinarily, ovulation occurs after coitus. In the laboratory, artificial stimulation and direct brain stimulation substitute for coitus quite adequately, at least from the scientist's point of view, for he can control the time of ovulation.

Charles Sawyer and his associates at the Brain Research Institute of UCLA found that the hypothalamus, in the rabbit's brain, contained discrete, or separate, centers controlling sexual behavior and reproduction. When the fertility center was electrically stimulated she would ovulate, but if it were damaged her ovaries would waste away and she could no longer ovulate. This fertility center was susceptible to sex steroids. Moreover, it was possible to see almost immediately whether the steroids made her infertile. Sawyer and his associates would administer the drug, stimulate the rabbit, and then watch her sleep patterns.

After coitus—or its substitute—a fertile rabbit would lapse into sleep and soon show the unmistakable EEGs of the REM phase. However, when she was given an antifertility agent, this REM interval would not appear as usual after coitus. When this distinctive change in sleep pattern was first discovered, the EEGs of the REM state were thought to mean waking. The scientists would dash from the EEG machine to inspect their animal, fully expecting her to be wide awake and ready to leap from the table. Instead she would resemble a rag doll. No EEGs are necessary to see REM sleep in the rabbit. During other sleep the ears are held erect and back, but during the paradoxical REM phase they lose muscle tone and flop over with a ludicrous limpness. Presuming rabbits dream, the dreaming rabbit provides an ultimate symbol of relaxation.

Using the sleep pattern of the female rabbit as a marker, Sawyer and his team tested a number of drugs, among them a commonly used tranquilizer, barbiturates, and morphine. They all suppressed REM sleep after coitus, suggesting that they might also suppress ovulation—creating, in effect, infertility. Although it is unwise to generalize from rabbits to humans, these findings raise questions about the impact of many drugs on fertility. It is interesting to note that women morphine addicts tend to be infertile, and to have irregular menstrual periods. In a world where drugs are widely used, and in which fertility is likely to be controlled by drugs, their many effects on the central nervous system may become an issue to millions of people.

Do sex steroids and other drugs affect the hypothalamus so as to alter mood, sleep patterns and personality? Sleep patterns seem to be so sensitive to changes within the brain that nightlong studies of people may suggest answers. For the present the question can be asked but not satisfactorily answered. There are no EEG records of lovers' sleep, no concerted sleep studies of pregnant women, no nightlong studies of women who take contraceptive pills. We know only what the animal studies have disclosed, that sex steroids can alter sleep patterns and that they can act as potent hypnotics.

There are other steroid hormones in the body that can have antithetical effects upon sleep. These are the products of the adrenal glands and some of them are well known because of their usefulness in medicine. Prednisone is one that has been widely prescribed for patients with severe kidney disease, and occasionally it has a dramatic impact upon both mood and sleep. People with a malfunctioning kidney tend to feel lethargic, tired, and even depressed. One of the pleasant secondary effects of certain adrenal steroids is that they counter a dreary mood, on occasion to an extraordinary degree. In one instance a high concentration of prednisone was given to a University of Pennyslvania professor suffering from nephritis. From the doctors' standpoint the purpose of the drug was to prevent the kidney membrane from acting like an open sieve and passing through large molecules as waste. From the viewpoint of the patient, the drug was an outright gift of time and energy.

He recalled the day the drug took effect. He had gone to sleep around 9:00 P.M. in the hospital and arose, refreshed as if from twelve hours of sleep. It was a marked contrast with the fatigue and apathy he had felt during his illness. "I felt about twenty-five years old, and remember going to the window thinking that it must be about eight in the morning. I wondered why it was so dark—it was two A.M." That night he read an entire book. On the subsequent night he read another book and the following day he sent to his university office for the piles of manuscript material that he had been planning to write later during the summer. For one month, on high doses of adrenal steroids, he enjoyed a schedule that was the wonder of the hospital staff and the envy of his doctors. He would retire at

9 P.M. and get up at 1 A.M., working through the night and most of the morning, until lunch. Then he would relax and entertain visitors. During this time he wrote about 600 pages of letters, about 275 pages of scientific manuscript, ate voraciously, and told his doctors that he felt his life was like "fishing on a tide that always comes in." He was sleeping two hours less than customary and sailing on the euphoria and boundless energy that have, in modified form, been characteristic of the drug. Why did he have such energy, and why did he sleep so little?

One prequisite for liveliness appears to be a good circulation of adrenal hormones. Until recently, there was no scientific demonstration of a link between the brain chemistry causing high spirits and the adrenal cortex, whose hormones might help give them physical energy. A part of the answer has begun to materialize at Rockland State Hospital in Orangeburg, New York, where a team of scientists have discovered a new connection between brain chemistry and the activity of the adrenal cortex. The story began with drugs for the treatment of depression. Certain compounds which alter brain chemistry appeared to enliven the mood of the depressed person, probably because they caused the adrenal glands to suffuse the body with stimulating hormones. The study of depression begins to explain the euphoria sometimes seen in patients taking cortisone, the vitality and reduced sleep of patients on other adrenal steroids.

Informed scientists who generally offer a pessimistic forecast about the control of mental illnesses now feel that at least this widespread affliction may become a misery of the past. Research on brain amines may soon allow us to conquer the symptoms of depression by drugs. The amines are compounds that include noradrenalin, serotonin, dopamine, and tryptamine, and are chemically related to ammonia. The amine molecule contains nitrogen and hydrogen attached to its structure, and is related to the amino acids that combine to make protein. Indeed, it is believed that certain protein molecules known as enzymes—whose catalytic action causes substances to break up and recombine—may release the potent amines from the protein food of the brain.

The level of these amines in the brain appears to be an important factor in dictating emotional tone. A drug that depletes the quantity of brain amines can make a man depressed. A drug that enhances their activity can make a depressed man cheerful. As the amine levels change, so does the timbre of a personality and also sleep. Indeed, the chemical treatment of depression may be yielding clues to the chemical nature of "restful sleep."

For many years Nathan S. Kline has persistently explored the chemical treatment of severe depression, as a research director at Rockland State Hospital and in his private practice in New York City. Many of his patients had been morose and wretched for years, their intellectual performance diminished, feeling constantly fatigued, insomniac by night, lacking appetite by day. Many brooded through their waking hours, hunched under the burden of invisible incubi, expecting unnamable disaster, unable to concentrate, bedeviled by past failures, guilts, feelings of worthlessness. Under this plague of miseries quite a few felt suicidal.

Kline confirmed that their insomnia was a decided clue to the nature of the depression. Patients who could not fall asleep at night often suffered their depression as the side effect of some other disorder, or perhaps real tragedy. Those who characteristically awakened too early, on the other hand, seemed to be suffering from a fairly specific metabolic disorder. In 1956, Kline and his associates began exploring a drug for these early awakeners that had been previously used at Rockland State Hospital. It was known as an MAO inhibitor—a monoaminoxidase inhibitor. It blocked the action of aminoxidase compounds, enzymes that break down brain amines. By stopping the demolition, the MAO inhibitor may be effectually increasing the supply of brain amines. The results surely hinted that the MAO inhibitor was promoting a more efficient brain metabolism.

Patients taking the drugs began to feel more chipper in about two weeks. They told Kline about their new sense of well-being —yet reported that they still slept very little. Oddly enough, they didn't seem to mind, and felt they didn't need as much sleep. Kline listened to these remarks with a seasoned psychiatric skepticism. He knew that people needed sleep. Indeed, he had been trying desperately to administer drug combinations that would give his patients eight hours of sleep each night. Week after week, nevertheless, they returned to his office, overtly cheerful and alert, insisting that they still didn't sleep very much. Kline began to wonder whether eight hours of sleep were critical after all. Curiosity finally impelled him to take the drug, himself, and for two productive months he found that he was sleeping only three hours a night. He did this, of course, as a researcher, realizing that he might be risking long term effects, for the long term impact upon normal people was not then known, nor is it yet known. Kline, therefore, stopped taking the drug. Until the long range effects are determined for normal people it would be foolish for anyone to risk using MAO inhibitors merely to change their sleep patterns.

During the early 1960's psychiatric researchers discovered that the already potent MAO inhibitors were even more powerful when accompanied by either of two substances. One was tryptophan, an amino acid used in tissue repair. The other was one of its breakdown products, 5-hydroxytryptophan, known as 5-HTP. 5-HTP is a biochemical building block in the construction of an exceedingly important brain amine, serotonin. By using 5-HTP with an MAO inhibitor, it seemed possible to increase the level of brain amines in two ways at once. The 5-HTP was presumably adding to the store of brain amines by enhancing production, while the MAO inhibitor prevented the depletion of amines by blocking the enzymes that normally destroy them. Thus this seemed to be a combination of chemicals that would effectively augment what the brain could do with its protein. Patients with dire depression, some of them suicidal, might finally be offered instantaneous relief. In this hope the combination of an MAO inhibitor and 5-HTP was tried.

The results of an initial study were so striking as to be almost flashy in some of the patients. Interviews with patients revealed that the drugs had a very quick effect. One patient, himself a scientist, a thin, sandy-haired man in his mid-fifties, had been almost paralyzed by depression for a year. Agitated and anxious, he had been forced to leave his job, but he had so lost interest in life that staying at home with his family merely caused him constant irritation. He was always fatigued, complaining that two or three hours of fitful sleep were all he could dredge from any night. The drug changed all that in four days. Alert again, he was taking an interest in his home. Now, although he slept only four hours, he said that he felt more rested than he had felt in former years after six hours of sleep.

Despite their rising spirits and capacities, a few patients complained about the lack of sleep. A middle-aged housewife who had been depressed for almost eighteen years was no longer unhappy, but moaned, "I was always a good sleeper—eight hours. I never slept so little before. Now I don't know what to do with myself at five o'clock in the morning."

Others considered the time a gift. A commercial artist described his nine years of depression as "living at 10 percent of capacity." He recalled that he had been drinking heavily and sleeping a great deal, feeling drugged most of the time. Now he slept only four hours a night. "Even nine years ago I'd have been busted on that little," he said. "I used to get eight hours' sleep and feel I needed nine." The extra time was allowing him to make up for the lost years in his career.

Quite a few patients have done well for over a year on these drugs, although they have not averaged more than about four hours sleep a night. Others with long histories of insomnia responded to the drugs by increasing their sleep. In both instances the patients felt better. They had psychic energy. Kline began to refer to the drugs as psychic energizers, a name that is widely used today and almost literally describes their effects.

Judging from the behavior of the patients who did improve by taking it, the psychic energizer seemed to have increased the efficiency of brain metabolism, making available more of the brain amines that support cheer and alertness. Simultaneously they seemed to make sleep more efficient, providing rest despite fewer hours of slumber. Although it is hard to generalize about brain metabolism, data from many quarters imply that the rate of brain metabolism must be crucial to the individual's ability to function. During childhood, when the brain's metabolic rate is indeed very high, we see a capacity for rapid learning. Healthy children are typically alert, cheerful, energetic, and rise refreshed from their sleep. The action of the MAO inhibitors may help to explain how certain adults manage energetic and vital lives yet spend less time than the rest of us in sleep.

MAO inhibitors appears to be psychic energizers in the most literal sense, possibly by augmenting the release of energy in the body and the utilization of energy substances. One way in which they may do this is via the adrenal hormones. A research team at Rockland State Hospital has found that when MAO inhibitors are used to increase brain amines, the adrenal cortex will release into the bloodstream the many hormones so essential to activity. The augmented amine concentration may touch off action in the adrenal glands by the usual channels. First the brain activates the pituitary gland in the base of the brain. The pituitary then sends ACTH through the body to the adrenals where it activates the adrenal cortex. One of the products is adrenalin, which helps to release energy from stored carbohydrates and effectually increases blood sugar levels, as well as stepping up heart rate and respiration.

Clearly, the action of body hormones must be an element of psychic energy that allows a person to act vigorously rather than merely entertaining cheerful thoughts and daydreams without the ability to express them. Many puzzling gaps remain in our understanding of the links between brain amines, restful sleep, and good cheer, but the satisfying aspect of evidence for a connection with the adrenal glands is the emerging unity of body and mind. We often speak as if psychic energy and vitality were a mystical endowment when it is, after all, a state of biochemical balances.

A person can have all the energy in the world, and sleep very little—yet once in 24 hours he must sleep. The most elemental explanation for this inevitable rest is given by mothers to tired children: "You must sleep to restore energy." Doctors pronounce the same message for patients in slightly more sophisticated language. For as long as scientists have worried about the purpose of sleep, the same theory has recurred. Sleep must be restorative, and vast expenditures of mental and muscular energy finally, so to speak, poison us into slumber so that the body may rebuild its supplies. There is one flaw in this plausible idea that bothers everyone. Why does an Olympic runner sleep no more than a lazy sales clerk, and why doesn't he fall asleep after his four-mile sprint, instead of waiting for nightfall? Somewhere within our chemistry there must be a clock, the metronome of our circadian rhythm that puts us to sleep once in every 24 hours. The idea has always made sense and yet the physical manifestations of such a mechanism have eluded pursuit until recently. No one clock has been located, but biologists have found clues.

One of the critical brain chemicals—serotonin—rises and falls within the pineal gland in a circadian rhythm. Solomon H. Snyder and Julius Axelrod, at the National Institutes of Health, have demonstrated in the rat that this rhythm could be eliminated by a drug that depletes brain amines, or by cutting certain nerve fibers. Apparently this daily chemical rhythm in the pineal gland takes its cues from a "clock" elsewhere in the brain.

Within the brain are two distinct kinds of cells. The nerve cell or neuron might be called the active computer, and most people mean to refer to this cell when they speak of brain cells. Surrounding the neurons, however, there are glial cells. They are thought to nourish the nerve cells, but until recently they were never given credit for participating in the transmission of neural messages. Experiments by W. R. Adey and his colleagues at UCLA have employed microrecording methods to measure electrical impedance in and around neurons. Their researchers suggest that the glial cells may be very important in the electrical wave transmission of the brain, for the glia seem to modulate the excitability of the neurons. Changes in the glia could make the neuron more responsive or less responsive, thus altering its discharge. The seizures of epileptics during many phases of sleep, and recordings from single neurons in sleeping animals have revealed the curious fact that certain brain cells become erratic, tend to fire in volleys, as if the controls that regulate them in waking are removed during sleep. Now we have learned that at least certain groups of neurons and glia show a fundamental change during sleep—a clue, if not an explanation, of the rhythm of sleep and the behavior of "sleeping" brain cells.

Holger Hyden and P. W. Lange at the Institute of Neurobiology in Göteborg, Sweden, have been looking at an enzyme found in all living tissue, body and brain. The amount of new energy any cell can generate is proportional to the quantity of the enzyme. Within the lower part of the reticular formation in rabbits, this enzyme shows high activity in neurons and low activity in glia during sleep. In waking the situation is reversed. Because this exchange of activity was not found in certain other brain regions, the scientists concluded that the brain-stem reticular formation must be a center in which the energy metabolism oscillates between neurons and glia, in a circadian rhythm.

The lower portion of the reticular formation does not comprise the clock, although it may be a link in the chain. It can have a damping effect upon the brain that generates the slow brain-wave rhythms of sleep. Perhaps it is triggered by a chemical produced on a cycle of 24 hours in the body's abundant metabolisms. What substance could trigger sleep? The search for the body's natural soporific has followed a course like that of the familiar nursery rhyme, for one must not only kill the giant, but catch the dog that killed the cat that ate the rat that lived in the house that Jack built.

Scientists have been looking for a hypnotoxin since early in the century; some expected to find a product of fatigued muscles, others anticipated a drained energy metabolism. Many researchers have involved transferring spinal fluid or blood plasma from an exhausted animal to a rested one or from a sleep-deprived animal or a sleeping animal. Unfortunately the recipients of these injections often gave signs of sleepiness or depression after any kind of injection whatsoever. Furthermore, there was the well-known blood-brain barrier. Many of the large colloidal particles in the blood will not pass through the membranes into the spinal fluid.

Recently, however, brain blood has been taken from a sleeping animal and passed through a fine sieve process known as dialysis, removing all the large particles so that it could be injected into the brain of a wide-awake animal. The alert one was put to sleep. This intricate procedure, conducted by the Swiss team of M. Monnier and L. Hosli, included safeguards that definitely showed the induced sleep was not merely a reaction to injection. Although subtle artifacts are hard to exclude, it would seem that the brain blood during sleep bears some hypnotic agent. Even purified blood contains a huge admixture of compounds, and so this research eliminates large molecules, but does not say which of the remaining multitude cause sleep.

A body chemical could, alternatively, trigger sleep without ever entering the brain. Serotonin does not pass through the blood-brain barrier. However, there are small structures at the base of the brain, just above the spinal cord, that respond to this chemical. A series of delicate surgical maneuvers led to this discovery. Werner Koella and his associates at the Worcester Foundation in Experimental Biology in Shrewsbury, Massachusetts, established that serotonin can put a cat to sleep when it touches this outpost of the brain. The responsive cells discharge impulses in the next station of the brain where serotonin cannot go and presumably set off a bioelectric chain reaction into the reticular formation and thence to the rest of the brain. Thus, this important and widespread chemical could trigger sleep, even though it was forbidden entrance directly to the brain.

Does serotonin or some other compound accumulate out of our body metabolism each 24 hours and start our nightly sleep? Even if we found some staple hypnotic or some trigger chemical was generated in a circadian rhythm, we would know we had not found the sole origin of sleep. There are many kinds of sleep, inspired in part by a host of compounds. It may be the ammonia sleep arising from a sick liver or sleep in the aftermath of childbirth, presumably contingent upon sex steroids. It may begin and be modified by a myriad of special-purpose chemicals. We may uncover body hypnotics, but this does not tell us what chemicals control sleep within the brain.

Whatever happens takes place within that intricate and elegant brain we so proudly wear upon the stalk of our spine. It contains billions of neurons and glial cells, interconnected by millions of nerve fibers. Despite its baffling intricacy, we know that it must be a very economical instrument. It operates by codes, and it probably does not utilize a different chemical for every shade of sleep. From separate corners of sleep research two well-known scientists have advanced an appealing conjecture that obeys the rules of economy: asserting that the brain must operate by master chemicals, like master keys, and that one chemical activates a system inducing sleep and a different chemical activates arousal. Raul Hernandez-Peón, of the Instituto de Investigaciónes Cerebrales in Mexico City, and George Ling, Chairman of the Department of Pharmacology at the University of Ottawa, have speculated that the brain could rely on two master chemicals in a dual balance system of sleep and wakefulness. Using cats as experimental animals, they have seen that the natural brain chemical acetylcholine induces sleep, whereas noradrenalin causes arousal. They do not have this impact just anywhere in the brain: Reaching from the forebrain down to the spinal cord, there seem to be two systems of cells, a sleep system coming into action when touched with acetylcholine, and an arousal system awakening the creature when touched with noradrenaline.

In the 1920's, when W. R. Hess of Zurich launched modern brain mapping by delivering mild electrical impulses directly to the brain, he touched groups of cells that produced special behaviors—rage, eating, signs of bliss, or sleep. Twenty years later, Giovanni Morruzzi and Horace Magoun delivered pulses to the reticular formation that awakened sedated animals. Scientists then spoke of sleep centers and an arousal center in the brain, but as stimulation methods became widely used, the centers for sleep and arousal multiplied like a rash. Electrical stimulation had the disadvantage of arousing more than one kind of brain cell. By developing tiny hollow guide shafts that could be implanted, like electrodes, it was possible to touch a layer of cells with a single crystal of a chemical. Since scientists were trying to evoke the natural response of those cells, they used as stimulation compounds found at nerve ends throughout the body and in the brain, chemicals released in nervous transmission, that might ordinarily activate the neural cells—acetylcholine and noradrenalin.

After tamping acetylcholine into hundreds of brain sites in hundreds of cats, Hernandez-Peón concluded that the many known "sleep centers" were all part of a pervasive sleep-inducing system in the brain. This sleep system sends impulses in two directions, upstream and downstream in the brain. In what we might call voluntary sleep, the cortex or thinking brain may transmit its commands to sleep—downward to the primitive visceral brain or limbic system, thence to the brain stem and spinal cord. Similarly there is an upstream route, bearing impulses from the skin, the senses, the body, up from the spinal cord through the brain stem and limbic system. This two-directional pathway of sleep cells seems to use acetylcholine normally in transmittting neural impulses. Not only did it respond when stimulated by the compound, but it seemed to release the chemical along its pathway. This was simply demonstrated. An electrical stimulation directed at a particular point would cause sleep. Then an agent preventing the action of acetylcholine would be fed in at this point, and the electrical stimulation repeated. This time the cat would not go to sleep.

One might not expect to find that the protean diversity of sleep could be elicited with a single compound, yet acetylcholine in various strengths, touched to different locations on the pathway, created a startling range of effects. Cats are inveterate nappers, to begin with, and an animal placed in a familiar cage will sniff around for a few minutes, then curl up, and in less than 20 minutes be asleep. When acetylcholine was tamped through the permanently implanted tube into the hypothalamus, the animal was asleep in two to five minutes. In another region, however, the chemical touch had an almost instant effect. The cat was eating his dinner with some relish. When the stimulus came he literally fell asleep, his head dropping into his food dish. In one region the stimulus caused a half-hour nap, yet in another, the same stimulus caused a four-hour slumber. With a very strong concentration of the compound the experimenters could produce a sleep so profound that the cat was not awakened by loud noises or even pinching, only by direct stimulation to the arousal region of the brain.

Geography is important in an economical brain code, as numerous experimenters have demonstrated. The small hollow guide shafts used in chemostimulation are usually designed so that they can be left in place for months like electrodes, and at the surface of the skull there is a screw setting that can move the tube from one layer of cells to another a millimeter away. Acetylcholine has been used to put a cat into deep slumber at one setting of the tube, yet when it was screwed down one notch so that the chemicals touched cells a millimeter away, the same chemical caused a cat to hiss, flatten his ears, arch his back and strike out in rage. It is, indeed, by this method of repeatedly adjusting the guide shaft and inserting chemicals, then watching for the effect, that experimenters have been exploring the brain to discover its systems of sleep and arousal. Along the same path on which acetylcholine induces sleep, noradrenalin has caused arousal. It was applied through the same cannula, but now instead of falling asleep the animals would wake up and act alert.

It looks very much as if there are upstream and downstream pathways of arousal in the brain that are activated by noradrenalin. These arousal paths are thought to extend, like the sleep circuit, from the spinal cord up into the forward reaches of the brain, and are being explored by repeated chemical stimulation. The anatomical relationship of the sleep and arousal pathways may begin to illuminate a phenomenon that everybody senses—negative emotions of anxiety, frustration, pain, anger or fear usually cause one to be wakeful, whereas pleasurable sensations of warmth and patting, security, and happiness are more conducive to sleep. It is thought that the pathways of sleep and arousal run parallel at some levels in the brain's convolutions, and even overlap at certain junctions. Both nerve pathways appear to send their fibers through certain junction points, near the fibers of motivational centers.

In nonscientific language these centers have become known as pleasure and pain centers. Their existence came as an unforgettable surprise to many people when they were first demonstrated in the 1950's by James Olds. Since then, scientists have been intensively exploring in the primitive brain region known as the limbic system, probing for reactions to electrical or chemical stimulation. Today we find that there are a number of centers where stimulation evokes pleasure or pain, perhaps interconnected as a motivational system, the system that drives us toward certain actions but causes us to avoid others. The cells of pleasure and pain must be struck into action, coloring our experience by the code that associates them with other brain cells —those active in eating, drinking, sleeping, and the many specific behaviors and memories of our lives.

We know of the existence of brain centers controlling rudimentary behavior and nonetheless it is dramatic to see them activated directly, from outside. A small white rat, wearing a crown of metal electrodes, begins to eat as an electric signal touches his brain, and eats and eats until he has almost eaten his own weight in dry laboratory chow. Wearing this same small crown, with an implanted electrode touching a "pleasure center," the animal could be seen hunched over a bar, delivering a small shock to his brain cells with each press of the bar. Hungry, he would ignore food. Weary, he would press on, until he reached a point at which bliss turned to aversion. Implanted in this manner, he would skitter across an electrified grid that shocked his toes, in order to reach the other side where an electrical or chemical stimulation would give a direct reward to his brain. If the electrode touched a "pain center" the animal would do all in his power to avoid the stimulus.

In some experiments, acetylcholine has been used to activate pleasure, whereas noradrenalin has evoked pain. It is interesting that sleep and pleasure have been elicited by acetylcholine, and that arousal and pain have been induced by noradrenalin, and that these systems appear to have junction points in the brain. Such discoveries do not explain the impact of emotions on sleep, for the brain is more complex than a few paragraphs can indicate. No doubt, when a full explanation arrives it will contain a few unexpected twists, since chemistry and anatomy are very crude aspects of brain function, and brain cells operate by bioelectric codes and electric wave transmission. Moreover some scientists expect to find that the brain uses more than a single code chemical for sleep. Sleep itself comprises two radically different states of consciousness, not one but two egregiously distinct conditions.

No matter how sleep is induced, normally it will be punctuated with intervals of irregular brain waves, roughly similar to those of waking, with rapid eye movements and vivid dreaming. This paradoxical cycle of REM sleep bears many lineaments of arousal, and can be triggered by compounds associated with brain arousal—at least in cats. Freud speculated that dreams were the guardians of sleep, holding a person quiet at times when he was biologically attempting to wake up. Perhaps dreams are not the crucial and relevant factors in maintaining sleep, but rather some unusual organization prevailing in the brain. In a sense, Freud could have been describing what we now see in the sleep laboratory.

REM intervals have so many earmarks of attempts to awaken that some scientists have described them as tests to determine whether or not it is time to awaken, a feedback system within the body. Perhaps the body and brain metabolism accumulate the chemicals of arousal on a regular schedule. When the stimulant manufacture reaches a certain level, they may almost cause the arousal system of the brain to reassert itself and take over. In some sick people, this may be what happens, for they commonly awaken during dream periods. But in the normal body, perhaps the metabolism and the chemistry of sleep continue to inhibit our activity and our awakening until they run out of hynotic fuel, so to speak.

From this point of view, our nightly sleep appears to oscillate between the systems of sleep and arousal, with sleep dominating the balance. As the night wears on, the REM periods grow longer. In normal people, researchers notice that there is a notable difference between the first and second halves of the night. Most of our deep, oblivious delta sleep occurs in the first half of the night, while REMS cluster toward morning. The reported thoughts of awakened volunteers also differ in quality and content as the night wears on, becoming progressively sharper toward morning. Some researchers have remarked that REM narratives have the fuzzy thoughtlike quality reported from other sleep phases in the early night, but that the sleep thoughts of deeper phases begin to resemble REM dreams in clarity and vividness by morning. These disparate observations do not themselves imply that REM dreaming is a form of arousal, yet they serve to buffer surprise that experiments associate REM dreaming with a chemistry of arousal.

The cat's equivalent of our REM sleep has been triggered by an injection of noradrenalin into the thalamus, in a study by

George Ling, performed at UCLA. In Lyon, France, Michel Jouvet and his associates have employed a clever process of elimination and indirection to test the chemicals of paradoxical REM sleep. Their experiments once again suggest a relationship between sleep and the brain chemistry of mood, for they were altering the brain's supply of crucial brain amines.

Jouvet employed reserpine to eradicate all traces of REM sleep in the cat. Reserpine has an effect that is opposite to the psychic energizer. It depletes the brain of amines and can cause depression in man. It is a derivative of *Rauwolfia serpentina,* or snakeroot—one of the world's first tranquilizers. Centuries ago, snakeroot was used in India to calm or sedate people, and today the drug is valuable in preventing wild fluctuations of blood pressure, dangerous in hypertensive patients. There are, of course, numerous compounds that diminish REM sleep, among them barbiturates, amphetamines, and alcohol, but their influence looks trivial next to the sledgehammer impact of reserpine. A single injection was enough to obliterate REM sleep in a cat for four or five days.

If reserpine accomplishes the opposite of the psychic energizer, depleting brain amines, perhaps it also has the opposite effect upon the adrenal glands and damps their output, thus reducing the stimulating hormones circulating in the body. What chemical would counteract the reserpine and restore REM sleep to the cat? Jouvet injected DOPA, a chemical from which noradrenalin is constructed. When this amine was injected the cat started showing his REM phase again. Moreover, when DOPA was administered to a fresh unmedicated cat, he showed a veritable orgy of dreaming.

Human beings can be expected to react somewhat differently from cats, although human beings also seem to show a correspondence between their amount of REM sleep and level of certain brain amines. Arnold Mandell, Mary Mandell, and Alan Jacobson at UCLA have conducted a difficult study of two young men in whom they were able to increase REM sleep very markedly. The two volunteers slept many nights in the laboratory. One of them had been a subject in several sleep studies and his usual pattern of REM dreaming had been tracked for over 100 nights. On some nights the subjects received no medication, on some nights a placebo, but on several nights they received oral and intravenous doses of 5-HTP, the compound that showed such potency as a psychic energizer when given to depressed patients. This compound, a chemical building block in the formation of an important brain amine (serotonin), apparently helps to increase the supply of amines and promote efficient brain metabolism. It induced an extremely notable increase in REM dream time. As the dosage was increased over several nights in the one thoroughly studied subject, his dreaming rose from its usual 22 percent to over 30 percent of his sleep.

Although the specific chemical triggers for sleep and for dreaming may differ among the species, experiments on the chemistry of dreaming do suggest a unifying principle in cat and human, even though they are far apart on the phylogenetic scale. The amount of REM dreaming appears to be related to the brain amines that so profoundly affect our moods, our efficiency, our vitality. The efficiency of sleep, cheer, and vitality are enhanced by the available supply of these amines in the brain, and these amines in turn seem to influence the activity of the adrenal cortex and the supply of its hormones in circulation. The story of mood and sleep seems to come full circle in these studies of the REM dream interval. We can begin to see—in this incipient biochemistry—why dream suppression may accompany mental illness, and why dream-depressing drugs can have an ill effect upon mood and behavior.

IX

THE BODY OF THE DREAMER

IT was a gray winter morning on the top floor of a modern hospital as a young mechanic awakened from sleep to the sound of a buzzer, and gasped into the microphone, "I never thought I'd make it." He had been trying to swim out of a deep-sea cave, his lungs bursting. On the verge of coma, the buzzer saved him. "I knew I wouldn't make it. I was clutching for air."

A voice from the adjoining room asked, "Do you remember what happened before that?"

Although sleepily yawning, the young man searched his memory, trying to earn the $15 he was paid as a volunteer. He remembered walking in a redwood forest on a vivid autumn day. It was more vivid than any movie. He felt the sun hot on his shoulders in open spaces between the trees, and the chill of the shade. He breathed the aroma of the redwood bark, the needles underfoot.

"Can you remember how you got to the sea cave?" asked the voice.

"No, sir, I can't. I just remember I was down too far—I was going to pass out, and I felt like my body took control of the dream." The experimenters searched through the EEGs and the records of pulse, respiration and blood pressure to see if the body ferment matched the dream. Were nighttime medical crises related to dreams?

Dreams can be so vivid that the valves of memory seem to have opened the entire life history of a person, down to the smallest details of smell and touch. This sensory experience is awesome in itself, but the condition in which man dreams is perhaps stranger still—and for that we have no memory. It happens nightly, four or five times. Out of quiescent slumber, the body acquires some of the aspects of terrible fright—the pulse quickens, breathing becomes uneven, the eyes dart and the cadences, responses, and temperature of the brain resemble moments of intensity in waking life. The limpness of the body in seemingly impenetrable slumber hides wild internal activity, as if some of the usual government had disbanded and the person were invaded by unusual storms of nervous activity.

The exploration of the physical state of the dreamer, a relatively recent endeavor, has been the focus of the preponderance of sleep research. The most vivid dreams of life appear to occur during this peculiar, recurrent cycle—a cycle that can be at least partly suppressed by drugs and alcohol, altered by unusual sleep schedules and sleep loss, and affected by emotional disturbance or mental illness. Slowly, over the last dozen years, we have begun to unravel the story of a mysterious biological rhythm in our lives. It is a cycle whose importance to our well-being, to our survival, extends well beyond the psychological value of the dream. In fact, the dreams we remember may only be part of a periodic release of other energies and vital systems in the body. Their purpose and precise organic mechanisms pose too profound a puzzle to have been deciphered once and for all within such a short time in the history of science; yet diverse studies already have drawn together attributes of the dream cycle that suggest theories contributing significantly to the understanding of man's mind and its physical organization. These new discoveries hold out immense potential for all of medicine and for individuals in their exploitation of their own selves. Briefly outlined in this chapter is a composite of the many concurrent changes that normally take place in the body of the dreamer.

For all man's interest in dreams, little attention had been paid to the body of the dreamer until the early 1950's, when Eugene Aserinsky and Nathaniel Kleitman demonstrated that cycles of rapid eye movements and emblematic brain waves punctuated nightly sleep, and that people awakened at this time almost inevitably recalled a clear and vivid dream. William C. Dement, while a graduate student at the University of Chicago, began probing this incredible finding with gusto, luring students, professionals, and housewives to sleep in the laboratory for a small payment. Then, and even today, the laboratory nights held an element of surprise as a buzzer from a control room would ring a sleeping volunteer out of the dark reality of his dream through the mists of sleep. As one man remarked on his fifth awakening, "Doc, you hit it on the button every time—I sure enough was dreaming!"

As the lined graph paper unrolls the unmistakable signature of rapid eye movements and an irregular low-voltage brain-wave pattern, the experimenter can easily mark the onset of the dream with his pencil, giving the volunteer five minutes by the clock before sounding the buzzer. As the night wears on, it may take a louder alarm or the repeated calling of his name before the sleeper will answer. He often sounds trapped in the quicksand of slumber, sighing into the microphone, regretful to wake up. Occasionally his first words will resonate with the dream, with the ebullience, the intoxication perhaps, of a man who is still out on the town with a buddy, leaving a bar and spotting a very sexy girl on the street.

> "I noticed I had a hole in the bottom of my left shoe, and we were deciding which way to turn. My friend said 'Right,' and I said, 'No, left.' Then I saw this girl in *skin tight brilliant yellow leotards* coming across the street. I said I didn't care which way, right or left—'I am going that way.' I was feeling pretty good, like I'd had a few drinks and wanted to play all

night, really enjoying myself, clowning around—not a care in the world."

Into this reality, with its colors, its details, sights, smells, and sounds of everyday, intrudes the experimenter. Each night there are four or five of these capsule experiences and yet, by morning, they have faded into the distance. At home, without the experimenter to awaken them, people rarely know all this has happened.

In the mid-1950's a furor was created by the proof that dreams could be spotted from outside and captured. Hundreds of laboratory nights were recorded and truckloads of dream tapes analyzed. The unbelievable regularity of the dream periods, so startling when Aserinsky first noticed it, gave an even more startling picture en masse. We saw that everyone normally dreams in this state every night, approximately every 90 minutes for a total of about an hour and a half. There was worldwide exhilaration at the discovery of a handle for extracting dreams, yet the spectacle of regularity caused the interest to shift from dreams themselves. It was discovered that cats and other mammals showed very similar signs periodically in their sleep. The cycle of dreaming began to take on the proportions of an almost universal biological phenomenon.

Around the world, scientists began to inspect the sleep of many species, from the reptile on up the phylogenetic scale. The macaque monkey, commonly used in laboratories and popular with zoo visitors for its almost human facial expression and hazel eyes that mimic man's, showed like man the same alternation between sleep and the REM condition. The chimpanzee also showed this cycle, but so also did the dog, the rat, the sheep, the goat, mouse, and even the primitive opossum, although the amount of time spent in this condition varied from species to species.

Recordings from the opossum suggested that it spent about as much time in REM sleep as in waking. The detection of the familiar REM signals in the opossum hint that this cycle of nervous activity must have begun far back in the evolution of animals. The opossum, like the kangaroo, is a marsupial whose young are not nourished in the placenta of the womb but outside, in a pocket. Marsupials and placental animals parted company in evolution some 130 million years ago. Unless the neural mechanisms of the REM cycle began independently in the two branches of the animal tree, we must presume that they were already established in that prehistoric time. Were the minds of these primitive creatures shaken by internal fantasies and emotions?

Do animals dream as we do, about the world they experience, the sights or, perhaps dominantly, the smells and actions of their lives? Over two thousand years ago, the Roman poet Lucretius observed: "You will see stout horses, even when their bodies are lying down yet in their sleep sweat and pant without easing, and strain their powers to the utmost as if for the prize, or as if the barriers were thrown about open. And often during soft repose the dogs of hunters do yet all at once throw about with their legs and suddenly utter cries and repeatedly sniff the air with their nostrils. . . ." Animal lovers have observed their favorite creatures sniffing, whining, yelping, miaowing, wagging or flapping their tails, moving paws, sucking, licking chops, breathing heavily and evincing a gamut of emotions that suggest dreaming. Still scientists have hesitated to infer that this means dreaming. Rapid eye movements do not necessarily mean the eyes are scanning dream images, and the external motions do not necessarily attach to internal hallucinations. Animals cannot be awakened and asked to recall their experience but, by indirection, a clever laboratory procedure has suggested that animals probably dream—monkeys, in any event.

What tentative evidence there is arrived serendipitously while the researchers pursued something else. Charles Vaughan, Harry Braun, and Robert Patten at the University of Pittsburgh had been attempting to find out whether sensory isolation or monotony affected monkeys in the way it reportedly affected human beings—causing waking hallucinations. By an elaborate procedure they trained monkeys so that they would signal if they started "seeing things." They acclimated the monkeys to a restraining chair inside a remodeled telephone booth, where they learned to obtain automatically dispensed food and water, and where they were shocked on the leg if they did not press a bar very rapidly every time they saw an image on the screen before them. A variety of slides were projected, including patterns of dots, pictures of people, food, and outdoor scenes. The monkeys became very reliable bar pressers, and would press at a rate of 3,000 times an hour whenever an image appeared. Then they were shut into the booth for several days, surrounded by a uniform waterfall sound and wearing contact lenses that created a dim sameness wherever they looked. The experimenters waited for the beginning of hallucinations.

Unfortunately, as the scientists saw through the booth window, the monkeys would fall asleep soon after they were closed in. Their eyes would slowly roll for a while and then begin to make rapid darting movements like those of a person reading a newspaper column. Simultaneously, the monkeys would start pressing the bar at their accustomed velocity as if seeing images. They would continue for many minutes, often breathing deeply, flaring their nostrils, grimacing and barking audibly as they pounded away at the bar. The bar pressing meant that they were "seeing things" in their sleep. When the isolation test was over, the experimenters ascertained that this bar pressing was no accident. Each monkey again pressed the bar as he had been taught, whenever images were projected onto the screen of the booth.

Similar techniques may be used to train animals to tell us what they dream about, perhaps by pressing certain bars for smells and other bars for special objects. We need to know more about the sleeping experiences of monkeys and cats, animals whose brains differ greatly from our own, but who act as our substitutes in many studies of the sleeping brain. We need to know how they differ and in what degree they are similar to us. As scientists enter the body of the dreamer, attempting to piece together the anatomy from which dreams are formed, the trained animal who lacks an artificial language and logic may help to show us how the raw experience of life becomes transmuted into the treasured hallucinations of sleep.

When the REM cycles of human beings had been gathered and clocked for the first time, many people expected to find that the bodily changes that accompanied dream periods were indeed caused by visual dreams. Studies of animals and infants have modified this assumption, and it no longer seems so straightforward. Newborn infants spend about half of their sleeping time—and sleep occupies most of their time—in a REM condition. Observant mothers have noticed that babies switch from a visage of peace and serenity, suddenly moving their fists, their feet, grimacing, sucking, their chests heaving, in a sleep that almost resembles struggle. REM sleep occupies about 90 percent of the newborn kitten's sleep, and is predominant in many infant animals. At a stage of infancy when they can barely see, vivid visual dreams do not seem the likely cause for their bodily commotion.

If the shifting blood pressure and respiration of the dreaming adult had seemed to be a consequence of his dream emotions, the same kinds of changes were observed accompanying REM periods throughout the infant and adult animal kingdom. It looked more universal than a physiological reaction to particular kinds of dreams. Some rudimentary mechanism was generating these cycles of change throughout the mammalian world. It was built into the brain and perhaps into fundamental metabolism. Its symptoms, moreover, were so incongruous and stunning that further examination made the REM phase stand out from the rest of sleep like a tree on the desert. It was not merely the dream that distinguished this condition, for people report dreams of various sorts when awakened in other phases of sleep.

The REM period was physiologically so different from quiet sleep that many scientists began to refer to it as a third state of being—a condition of consciousness that was neither sleep nor waking. It resembled a lost continent of the mind.

The nature of the dreamer's bodily ferment began reaching

print in the late 1950's, beginning with the intensive research of Frederick Snyder and his team at the National Institutes of Health. There, volunteers wore a blood-pressure cuff and sensors to measure breathing and heart rate, as well as electrodes on the scalp and face. Each night, at the control console, the paper tape unfolded roughly the same pattern. Uniform blips showing heart rate would slow down. Respiration recordings made gentle swells, one exactly like another, until, suddenly, the REM stage began. Then came erratic changes. Occasionally the sleeper's blood pressure would shoot up above his highest recorded waking levels. The even, fence-post marks of the pulse would lose their uniform spacing. The regular swells of breathing would exhibit sudden dips or heights. To some extent these irregularities appeared in all REM periods, but occasionally they were so extreme that, on paper at least, they seemed to mimic the changes that would occur in great fright or anxiety. Yet the awakened volunteers often gave a disappointingly innocuous statement. "Oh, dear! I'm so tired I keep falling back to sleep—I don't know—I can't remember this one." Reports were interspersed with sighs and yawns. "I was just a child in a candy store." Or, "I just saw lemon juice spilling on Grandmother's tablecloth." Of course the dream may say very little to an outsider yet evoke the echoes of a lifetime in the dreamer. It was difficult to determine whether the reported dream truly lacked emotional significance.

In another laboratory, Donald Goodenough and his associates held long morning interviews with their subjects, whose rich associations to their nighttime dream reports revealed how cryptically a dream story expressed the elaborate emotions and memories of the individual. Still, the extreme physical changes in the dreamer are not yet explained by the intensity of his dreaming emotion. Studies of other parts of the body portray a curious condition during REM sleep, in which storms of activity suggest an element of disorganization, as if a switch had been thrown in a theatre and its lights began to dim and blink erratically.

Any observer can get an inkling of this activity by watching a pet or an infant sleep. After a spell of quiet, it will move. The eyes, whether shut or half-open, will show jerky movements. The body will twitch, the chest heave in visible breathing. Oddly enough, this is not deep panting and at first may be very shallow and rapid. During the REM state, blood oxygen may drop as low as it would if the person held his breath to the fainting point. This may help to account for the strange pattern of inhalations. In patients with the progressive lung disease emphysema, nighttime breathing is a serious problem. When studied throughout sleep, these people have shown recurrent periods of low oxygen saturation in arterial blood, 15 to 30 minute intervals of very shallow irregular breathing that were probably related to REM periods. The irregular breathing may not stem from emotion but from a whole system of which emotion is only a single component.

During REM periods, insofar as scientists can clock such events, the oxygen consumption of the body seems to rise suddenly from its usual low level in sleep. Oxygen consumption can be measured indirectly: a person inhales measured air and his exhaled carbon dioxide is also measured. Studies of gas exchange, by which we gain some notion of body metabolism in sleep, have required volunteers to sleep with an oxygen-measuring device digging into an earlobe, or with gas masks, or with their heads under plastic hoods. Results from several independent researches suggest that during REM intervals oxygen metabolism is high, meaning that consumption of oxygen and burning of energy is rapid—hardly an image consonant with our past notions of passive, inactive sleep.

If one looks at other body functions during the REM interval, the old notions of utter passivity and energy conservation go down the drain altogether. There are cues of internal frenzy that resemble the signs of emotional upset. During most of the relaxed phases of sleep, for instance, tiny blood vessels at the fingertips dilate with each contraction of the heart and fill with blood, but during REM sleep, as during tension or stress, these vessels tend to constrict, to dilate less than usual with the pulse.

Many adults are sadly familiar with the variety of gastrointestinal changes that can afflict them during stress and there has been some controversy about the manner in which emotional upheaval and tension may strike off gastritis, ulcers, and companion miseries. At UCLA a team of young scientists, Armstrong, Burnap, Jacobson, Kales and their associates, have indicated that there may be a rhythm to the occurrence of visceral changes in sleep. Duodenal ulcer patients may come to blame REM dreaming periods for their nighttime pains. A comparison of severely ill ulcer patients and healthy volunteers was performed by inducing both groups of subjects to sleep with tubes in their stomachs. Normal people do not appear to secrete gastric juices in any quantity at night, but it is well known that the ulcer patient does. As the intubated subjects indicated, these abnormal secretions usually occur in spurts that peak during periods of rapid eye movements.

By the time blood or gastric juices have been drawn out of a tube from a sleeping person, it is hard to say exactly when the changes occurred. Nevertheless these approximate trackings of the sleeper's chemistry are beginning to show that REM periods must be accompanied by many tranformations in the vital juices of the body. The adrenal hormones become plentiful in the blood around the times of REM periods. Ordinarily, the adrenal glands release these so-called stress steroids into the blood during emergencies, but their concentration in the blood normally follows the circadian rhythm. The group known as the 17-hydroxyketosteroids, largely cortisone, is in lowest concentration at nightfall and rises during the night to peak concentration in the early morning, as if to start the day's activity with a full supply. Without an adequate supply of these hormones a person will feel lethargic, and eventually begin to behave strangely.

Elliot Weitzman and his colleagues at the Albert Einstein College of Medicine in New York have managed to pursue the blood concentration of these hormones throughout the sleeping night. Each of the volunteers was either a physician or psychologist, nonetheless a bit uncomfortable at the prospect of sleeping with a catheter in a vein of the arm. Once it was inserted, however, the volunteers did sleep, and the experimenters would creep into their room on tiptoe every half hour for a blood sample. At first they may have had some doubts, suspecting that any hormonal changes they found might be the by-products of anxious subjects, wakeful because of the discomfiting experiment. But the EEGs and remarks of the volunteers were reassuring. They had not feigned sleep. As one doctor commented cheerfully the next morning, "I slept amazingly well—but then you fellows didn't disturb me excepting once when you came in to take a blood sample." It was an amusing and a heartening observation. Weitzman informed his volunteer that he had actually been in the room fifteen times for blood that night.

This exploration of the blood of the sleeper gave a very different portrait of rising hormone concentrations than one might expect. Most medical practitioners would have anticipated a slow and steady rise. Instead of the traditional curve, the concentration rose in a series of peaks in the latter half of the night. The increases paralleled the increasing amount of REM time in the night's sleep.

Sleep watchers of an earlier era understandably did not pursue changing oxygen metabolism, gastrointestinal secretion, or hormonal output during dreaming; yet one of the most obvious and curious of all the REM events has merely been hidden by bedclothes and the human habit of sleeping curled up on one side. Men often speak of a bladder erection upon awakening in the morning, presumed to arise from the need to urinate. Actually, this so-called bladder erection is a regular occurrence that may have nothing whatsoever to do with urination. It is probably a remnant of the individual's last REM dream—no matter what that dream was about.

Twenty years ago several German scientists recorded a pattern of nightly erections in men, remarking that some would last for almost half an hour. More recently, this phenomenon has been put to careful study by Charles Fisher and his colleagues at Mt. Sinai Hospital in New York. They have shown that almost all of a man's REM periods are indeed preceded by an erection that may last for the entire interval. Indeed, the unusual instance is the REM dream that lacks an erection—usually a dream of anxiety. It might be amusing to credit the entire male population with a richly erotic night life, but it hardly seems that visual erotic dreams account for all these erections, since they are observed in the newborn, and persist into advanced age. Ismet Karacan, working in another laboratory, found that if REM intervals were prevented, the erections would stubbornly appear in other phases of sleep at the very time when the REM period was due. Here, in sleep, unbeknownst to the individual, his most apparent erotic reflex rises to the beat of some internal clock, strangely unrelated to the subjective associations that he has been taught to expect.

The rhythm of nightly erections has not been explained, but we have clues to the nature of the answer. At present it looks as if a primitive region of the brain, the hypothalamus, known to exert controls over sexual behavior, is inflamed by neural excitation during the REM interval. Animal studies of the hypothalamus certainly suggest that this archaic structure, with its control centers for sexual function, becomes active during the REM state, and one aspect of its excitation may result in erections.

Despite all this, the body of the dreamer is remarkably relaxed. The surface limpness is all the more striking when one is aware of the fury within. He looks asleep. Test him and he will not even show some of his usual spinal reflexes. Indeed, he would have a hard time lifting his head from the pillow. Although his extremities may twitch sporadically, his body has a silken relaxation. This dramatic reduction in muscle tone appears to come from activity within a certain brain-stem nucleus, just above the spinal cord. It may explain why somnambulists do not rise from bed during REM dreaming. People snore in other phases of sleep, but not during REM intervals. Postural muscles and the muscle just under the chin become slack, although some facial muscles retain tone.

Without general muscular inhibition to hold the dreamer in place, he might act like a patient with chronic brain syndrome or an alcoholic in the violent stages of withdrawal, agitatedly moving in an enactment of the dream. If a dreamer were, indeed, to have his eyes partly open—an occurrence not so rare as people once believed—he might appear to be awake, his eyes looking about the room as if tracking the movements of objects.

Cats and dogs commonly sleep with their eyes partly open, and a pet owner might think he could imagine the dreams of his animal by watching the twitches, the flicks or wags of the tail, convulsions of the paws, cries, and especially the furiously moving eyes. At times they fix upon the observer as if seeing him, then abruptly move on. One can wave a hand before the face of the animal, but the eyes do not pursue. Sometimes the pupils dilate suddenly, pools of black enlarging as they would for a sardine or piece of steak; then again they constrict. Although pupil dilation has been associated with intensity of attention and interest, these dilations occur in abrupt bursts, and it seems unlikely that they signify the attention of the dreamer.

The tracking movements of the eyes have intrigued quite a few scientists. The first plausible explanation seemed to be that the sleeper watched dream events and moved his eyes as he would in real life. A number of ingenious EEG studies have tested this idea, by comparing the dream reports of volunteers with the patterns made by their eye muscles on the EEG script. In one instance a young subject described ascending five steps just before she was awakened. Her recorded eye movements showed five upward glances just before she was aroused.

When people outside the experimental situation have been asked to take the transcribed dream stories and draw the eye movements they would expect to see on the script, their drawings have coincided neatly with the actual record made by the eye electrodes. The coincidence has been so close that it might be tempting to conclude that we scan our dreams with our eyes. Still, the visions within cannot be the sole cause of the eye movements, and may be only coincidentally related. We do not actually watch an inner motion picture. Some of our eye movements seem uncontrolled, too gross and furious to occur in waking life. Moreover, a sensitive use of recording instruments reveals that they occur in congenitally blind people during REM intervals. These people do not have visual dreams but dreams of sound and touch. Despite this negative evidence, it is true that a person's eyes may move when he hears or feels something in a particular direction. The eyes of the dreamer, blind or no, could be reacting in reflex fashion to directional cues generated by the image-making apparatus in his brain.

If the eyes are not scanning dream images, why else might they move? Sleeping cats have offered some clues. A large number of brain-wave recordings have been taken from various points along the optic tract and in the visual brain of the cat. Quite suddenly at the beginning of a REM interval, the EEG shows a new and unmistakable series of bursts from these regions. This energy invades the neural station to which the nerve fibers of the retina bring their messages, the visual cortex, where these millions of retinal impulses are transformed into perception. The spikes emanate from the nerve cells controlling the eye muscles and also from the brain stem. Presumably these extraordinary brain-wave patterns do not come from the eyes, from mental images, or indeed the visual brain—for even if all these have been destroyed, these spikes issue from the brain stem about eight times a second. This rhythm can be produced in the last optical receiving station of the retina, not by stimulating the eyes, but by stimulating the brain stem; and at that, the stimulation succeeds during REM sleep only—at no other time will it be effective. The rapid eye movements observed on the face of the dreamer almost always occur during this rhythm of spike discharge, suggesting that they may be initiated by the brain stem. Perhaps the images of our dreams follow from the electric spasms that move our eyes, rather than the other way around.

Everyone has urgent questions about the nature of dreaming, where dreams spring from, how they are formed, how they bear upon real-life experience. Bits and pieces of answers are flowing out of laboratories of brain research. Although they may not seem to satisfy our age-old curiosity, they are beginning to form a portrait of the dreaming brain that is far more fantastic than any of our conjectures.

Studies of the dreaming brain have revealed a function so extremely dissimilar from the rest of sleep that REM existence hardly seemed part of sleep. The brain not only acted awake but in a high pitch of arousal and concentration. Experimenters who had injected sensing devices into the cerebral cortex of animals were finding that the local resistance to electric current, the direct current potentials of the cortex tissue, and blood flow through the cortex resembled that of waking arousal. When temperature-sensing devices were placed within the brain they showed that brain temperature remained relatively constant during most of sleep, but at the beginning of each REM interval the temperature leaped up. It would rise above the brain temperature of quiet waking, sometimes to levels that were extremely high for the narrow range of the brain.

The "hot" brain of the dreamer suggested a high rate of brain metabolism, rapid conversion and use of energy. High brain metabolism is essential to the keen functioning of the mind, to intelligence, and acuity of perception. Perhaps, in the discovery of brain heat during REM intervals, we were receiving an explanation of the vividness of REM dreaming by contrast with the rest of the night's fare. In any event, as the temperature and rate of brain metabolism rose, the EEG waves grew smaller in amplitude. There seemed to be an inverse relationship between brain temperature and the size of brain waves, suggesting that EEG patterns might be an index to brain metabolism. During most of sleep the EEG waves are relatively large and slow. During waking and REM periods, the cortical waves shrink, dwindling into a desynchronous, swiftly changing pattern of very low voltage, smaller as the brain grows hotter.

The salient property of the dreaming brain, which refutes our early presumptions about sleep, is its resemblance to the brain of a waking person during his most intent and active moments. The cells of the brain do not slow down in their activity. Indeed, when microelectrodes have been implanted in individual nerve cells in the visual cortex or vestibular regions important to balanced motor activity, the frequencies of discharge sometimes surpassed those seen during quiet waking, more nearly resembling moments of crisis or rage. But even individual brain cells have traits that distinguish their activity in dreaming from that of waking.

A single brain cell may seem to have a limited vocabulary, yet its code has room for expression. The cell may fire a little or a lot, frequently or infrequently. It may fire off its infinitesimal electric charge with the uniform beat of a metronome, or it may discharge in sudden pulses, separated by long silences. In a sense this can be described as a code like Morse code, but composed solely of dots and pauses. The messages depend upon its rhythm and changes or rhythm. José P. Segundo and his associates at UCLA have been trying to decipher this neural code by listening carefully to the pulses of certain giant cells in primitive organisms. At the National Institutes of Health, Edward Evarts and others have performed the painstaking job of tracking the rhythm changes of single brain cells—as a monkey rested, scratched himself, reached for food, slept, and lapsed into REM consciousness. During REM states, the cells often discharged as frequently as in waking, but analysis revealed a difference in tempo. It was characterized by greater evenness during waking, longer pauses and more sporadic bursts during REM sleep, when the cell seemed to have escaped from its usual control and would explode from extended silences in volleys of discharge. This erratic tempo, this appearance of uncontrolled activity, might imply that the brain would be fragmented, discoordinated, highly vulnerable to any breath of air or distraction that touched it.

Yet the dreaming mind seems to be almost undistractible, exhibiting a force of concentration that most people could not sustain half so long when awake. Flashing lights, bells, electric shocks, blasts of air, recorded voices and barrages of sensory stimulation have been aimed at dreaming cats, rabbits, monkeys, chimpanzees, adult and infant human beings while EEGs recorded the brain's response to the stimulus. In REM sleep the EEG responses resembled those obtained during waking attention.

The alertness and focus that we ordinarily describe as attention appears to have a physiological meaning that can be seen in brain studies. Hernandez-Peón has studied the responses within the brains of human patients with electrodes implanted in their optic systems during diagnosis for neurosurgery. He would watch their brain-wave patterns as they saw a flash of light. If they were sitting idly, the flash evoked a sizable EEG response, but when they were busy adding a column of numbers or trying to recall some childhood memory, the same flash of light evoked only an attenuated response from their brains. This attenuated response is analogous to the brain's reaction to sound or touches during REM sleep, and might be described as an attribute of attention.

During attentive moments the brain appears to be only narrowly receptive, censoring out all irrelevancies. Without this faculty there could be no organized behavior. One modern scientist has eloquently likened the mind to a black sky pierced only by a thin beam of light that shrinks to a knife's edge during serious concentration.

The apparent censorship of the dreaming brain is very strict, and may occur at several levels in the nervous system. Throughout life, sensations from the skin and interior regions of the body travel along nerve pathways that converge into larger transmitting, or relay, stations. There are several such echelons through which specific sensory pathways travel into the brain. By implanting electrodes in animals at different positions along these pathways, and then testing with touches or sounds, neurophysiologists have seen that these gateways respond more during quiet slow-wave sleep than during the REM phase. This lack of response during dreaming has been described as "censoring." In part, it may be accomplished by muscles. During REM sleep, for instance, the fine muscles of the middle ear show the kinds of changes one would notice in an animal who was intently watching his dinner being prepared. General muscular relaxation in the body may also help to mute the impact of sensory signals. Everyone knows, subjectively, that if he is tense in the dentist's chair the drill will hurt, but if he is quite relaxed, he will not experience much pain.

Under most circumstances animals and people are remarkably hard to awaken during REM sleep, leading some scientists to argue that it is the deepest slumber of all—the widest separation from the outside world that we normally experience. An average conversational voice measured on a scale of loudness would be about 60 decibels. When a jet flies overhead with a momentarily deafening roar, the sound is about 100 decibels. Although a 60-decibel tone has awakened volunteers from sleep, during REM dreams they have sometimes needed an 80-decibel blast, a sound that is uncomfortable to most people at close range. Yet these same people would awaken when their names were spoken.

The dreamer may exclude the intrusions of the outside world, yet his brain responds to meaningful events. Like the subjects who slept through laboratory noise yet awakened when their names were mentioned, mothers commonly sleep through the cacophony of automobile traffic noises and the drone of air traffic overhead yet wake up to the slightest cough from their infants. This is the stock example of the brain's ability to make discriminations in sleep and shield itself from all but the most pertinent sounds. Animals have exhibited the same faculty, of course. Within laboratories experimenters have attempted to load one signal with meaning while leaving another neutral—the payoff of the experiment coming when the animal or person discriminated between the two signals during a REM dream.

Curiously enough, sleep discriminations have been encouraged more readily by punishment for failure than by reward, possibly because laboratory rewards have been insufficient to the cause. Alternatively, the response to punishment may reflect the construction of our brains. An alarm system that arouses us from the deepest self-immersion is probably designed to promote survival by detecting threats, and not by interrupting our sleep for frivolous pleasures. A delighted cooing can be quite as audible as an infant's sneeze, yet how many young mothers are catapulted out of bed by the sheer joy of eavesdropping on their babies? The REM dreamer seems to be as internally aroused, yet as intent and single-minded as a pilot who is landing a plane in a heavy crosswind. If the dreaming brain acts awake in some respects, it also shows distinct differences from its waking state.

Thirty years ago, when EEGs were used to diagnose neural damage and were scanned by the naked eye, the brain waves of the REM state were almost always confused with waking. Today, computer analyses emphasize that there are enormous differences between the brain-wave configurations of waking and dreaming, clues from the surface that the brain within must be altered in its functioning. One clue that may be significant when we consider how much the sleeping brain can learn comes from studies of implanted cats. Certain neurons in the cats' cortex grow progressively less active during sleep, and their activity does not revive during REM intervals. These brain cells happen to be associated with the corpus callosum, a dense bridge of nerve fibers that spans the long fissure dividing our two cerebral hemispheres.

All mammals have two brains, joined by fiber bundles. Occasionally an entire hemisphere must be removed, and the human being or animal will function surprisingly well. When nerve fibers joining the twin brains are severed the right brain cannot know what the left brain may be perceiving. Split brain operations have actually improved life for some epileptics, by preventing their seizures from spreading from one side to the other. Most of the time these people have both eyes open, and thereby function normally, since both sides of the brain receive the same picture at once. Still, the twin brains do not appear to be identical in man. Ordinarily, the left hemisphere is dominant and controls the expression of speech while the right hemisphere is mute. Furthermore, it is not clear that memories of events are stored immediately in duplicate. Recent memories may have to be transferred through the fiber bridge from one side to the other.

Throughout waking, the nerve cells associated with this giant neural communication system show intense activity. Their diminished action in all sleep might reduce the integrating function of the fiber bridge. If so, communication may be altered between the two halves of the brain, and we should suspect that sleeping thoughts differ from waking mentation—perhaps suffering from severe restrictions.

Brain studies do not yet explain the quality and content of our dreams, but they have provided some useful hints. The instinctive quality, the occasionally childish or brutal animality of dreams in the gentlest human being, seems less paradoxical after surveying the neural regions that seem most active during REM dreaming. Momentum for the dream cycle seems to issue from the primitive lower reaches of the brain, while dreaming itself involves the elaboration, the refinement, the brilliance and nuance that is provided by higher centers in the cortex.

The folds of the brain comprise almost a layered history of evolution. It begins with a simple wormlike form, the spinal cord, to which is added a brain stem, centers for smell, body control, emotion. As animal life became more complex than a matter of smelling out prey and ripping it apart, new units evolved upward in the archaic brain to heighten other senses, modulate rudimentary instincts, incorporate longer memory storage—and nucleus upon nucleus, layer upon layer, modulating structures grew, until finally in the human form this whole machine could respond to refinements from the outermost layers, the neocortex. The rudimentary rhythm of the REM state appears to require no more brain than that of the opossum. The human being in a REM dream is nonetheless capable of concocting experiences of great poetry.

The supreme refinements of the cerebral cortex must remain somewhat accessible to us at these times. Indeed, it may be responsible for some of the stumbling blocks of dream research. Experimental subjects, jarred by some deliberate stimulus in the laboratory or uneasy about exposing their innards to strangers, have occasionally refused to dream, bypassing dream periods in their sleep, or have spent an entire night in an uncharacteristic procession of innocuous thoughts during REM periods. People have pressed buttons during REM dreams. They have incorporated suggestions in dreams and have demonstrated to varying degrees that cerebral volition is still there.

Physiological researches have shown us that the cortex appears to be excited during this time. Its pitch of activity may be due to activity within one of its major service centers, the thalamus beneath. The thalamus, resembling a Brazil nut on either side of the brain, does much of the sorting of sensory information as it filters in from the outside, feeding it to regions of the cortex by a vast network of nerve fibers. The thalamus might be likened to a research editor, organizing reports from the senses and drive centers below and sending this digested material to further editorial centers above. Finally, in amended form, it goes to the supreme editor, the cortex, from which the final nuance, thought, or command will issue.

During REM dreaming the editorial services of the thalamus may be employed, for the most part, with material that originates within the brain itself. The thalamus is part of a memory circuit, and far forward in the temporal lobes other structures believed to be crucial in memory also exhibit intense activity during REM sleep. One signal of activity is a rhythm that emanates from the hippocampus, the theta rhythm. It appears during orienting and anxiety as well as dreaming, states in which the individual seems to be immersed in his own feelings and memories, and is least able to incorporate a great deal of outside information. The characteristic theta rhythm has been interpreted by some scientists to mean a kind of closed-circuit activity in memory structures, and this frontal region of the brain may be providing out of its storage files the welter of memories that are transformed into dreams by the cortex.

Impulses can travel with lightning speed from the hippocampal area to another region, the septum, which is involved in emotional behavior. From there they may enter the integrating regions that usually create conscious perception. The insane quality of dreams—as well as the hallucinations of the truly insane—may be explained by the fact that the thalamus is intensely excited and influencing the cortex with communiqués, making consciousness possible—at a time when many normal inhibitions appear to be removed from perceptual regions of the brain. The normal inhibitions of waking are removed, during REM sleep, from the very brain centers that ordinarily mediate waking perception.

There is another attribute of dreaming that may be illuminated by looking at the brain itself. Insofar as dreams express our basic instincts, the uncaged beast within each civilized person, their impulses may filter up to the editorial desks from even deeper and more archaic regions. The thalamus may have to cope with a heavy influx of crude material from the hypothalamus below. The hypothalamus is almost a primitive brain unto itself. It regulates heart rate, blood pressure, indirectly adjusts blood sugar level, appetite, the release of adrenal hormones, body temperature, thirst, sexual behavior—and in its most raw form, emotion. The emotions we feel and recognize in others do not proceed directly from this archaic brain center, but come to the surface only after they have been many times modified and regulated by other brain centers above. Under special circumstances, however, an exhausted child or an adult who is breaking down under prolonged stress may finally give vent to "animal" rage. Emotion is what we experience when some imbalance within requires adjustment—as in the instant when a sudden shot scares us. The scare must be primarily blamed upon the hypothalamus, which causes adrenalin to flow, speeds the heartbeat and respiration, and causes all those events that we feel as fright. Similarly, when body chemistry dictates want of food, brain signals send us on a hungry search for a meal. In part, because hormonal rhythms dictate we may go in search of sex. These raw "feelings" impelling us along the roads of survival have many of their regulations in the hypothalamus.

During REM sleep the hypothalamus—warmer and more active—may be commanding the adrenals to produce their steroid hormones, causing erections, and indirectly feeding commands into the domains of the body so that we see changes in respiration, heart rate, blood pressure, capillary dilation, in a manner so contrasting with quiet sleep that it looks like a show of fear and violence. Presumably, contacts with the thalamus feed in some of this raw material, detached from life's purposes and meanings, so that it becomes part of the editorial package to the cortex, a part of the dream.

A dozen years ago, we might have observed the recurrent agitation of vivid dreaming and inferred that the body was reacting to the inward images of the mind. Today, it is quite as possible to take the opposite view—that dreams are manufactured by certain physiological cycles that are independent of the individual's history, although in detail they are undoubtedly molded by his personal experience, the memories, the character of his brain and his personality. We have begun to see that many activities that go along with the dream process arise in the physical structure, the timing, and the chemistry of the entire body. It happens each night in a predictable rhythm. Where does this rhythm start? What brain regions release certain systems from their usual controls, and perpetrate a dreaming frenzy in the sleeping person?

REM dreaming can be provoked by electrical stimulation within many brain structures, almost always subsequent to quiet sleep. There may, indeed, be means by which the cortical regions could perpetrate REM periods, by which a person could command himself to enter a REM state, not merely to dream. On the whole, the usual daily rhythm of REM dreaming appears to emanate from the lowest portion of the brain, that archaic center of the brain stem known as the pontine reticular formation, or the pons. It is from this region that the unusual brain-wave rhythms accompanying rapid eye movements can be stimulated readily. The importance of the brain stem to the manifestations of the REM interval is plausible. We see that the basic REM rhythm exists in animals such as the rat or opossum that has little brain to brag of. During the development of the nervous system in the embryo, the first little blob of brain tissue to form out of the spinal cord is the brain stem. Premature infants exhibit particularly dominant proportions of REM sleep. Studies of infant sleep, directed by Arthur Parmelee at UCLA, suggest that the rate at which REM sleep declines in the normal infant may indeed imply the growth and development of connections in the brain stem and higher regions.

Long before any of this information had been obtained, a young French physiologist, Michel Jouvet, with his colleagues in Lyon, had focused on the mechanism of REM sleep in cats. They also looked for clues in accident victims whose autopsies showed damage in the brain stem. These people often survived their catastrophes, living for several months in a strange state, occasionally sleeping for brief spells, showing some muscular activity, but when the brain stem was damaged they had no EEGs resembling the REM interval. Other accident victims had damage in the cortex. Although they often survived for several years in a terrible state, unable to see, to hear, to respond to directions—staring vacantly day after day, with no EEG signs of slow-wave sleep—they did have short intervals of REM sleep patterns. Jouvet and his associates speculated that REM states required the function of the brain stem, whose activity must ascend and affect the cortex.

Using cats as their subjects, they performed precise operations, imitating the effects seen in accident victims. If they decorticated a cat, it slept only in the flaccid-limbed state of REMs. However, when they destroyed a tiny spot in the pontine reticular formation of the brain stem, the cat no longer showed REM sleep. On other occasions they would send electric pulses into the pons, whereupon the cat would promptly fall from waking or deep sleep into a REM state, and at this time the characteristic excitements could be recorded from the visual system and the eyes.

Study upon study refined their location of the trigger nucleus to a particular group of cells within the pons. Here, too, they discovered a nucleus that had been called caeruleus, for its mysterious blue spots, and which was capable of inhibiting the spinal muscles. This seemed a likely switch for the flaccid tone of the REM dreamer, for muscle tone was turned off only when this nucleus became active. When they deliberately damaged this infinitesimal structure, they did not abolish the other characteristics of REM sleep. Now, however, the dreaming cat would no longer lie in a placid languor. It moved. It grimaced. It occasionally acted as if in a rage, agitated and insane—the moving dreamer.

The experiments of Jouvet and his cohorts would fill several volumes. They worked by a process of elimination and induction, stimulating or destroying one region of the brain and then another. So long as they left a particular region of the pons intact, the signs of the basic REM rhythm persisted. This is not to infer that dreaming as such remained, although the particular beat accompanying the REM dream state remained. Occasionally, a misfortunate infant is born without a cortex, anencephalic, and this brain-stem creature, who must be kept alive artificially, shows signs resembling the REM state during its few days on earth.

The demonstrable importance of the brain stem in the dream state of REMs does not establish that this brain area is the sole origin and governor. Since brain processes are bioelectric and biochemical, the alternation of sleep and REM dreaming is not like the product of good plumbing—an alternation of hot and cold water from separate taps. There is considerable scientific debate over the precise role of the brain stem and extent to which other brain areas participate in igniting the REM state. Opposing theories suggest that the REM state may be instigated in a variety of ways, just as sleep may be evoked variously by boredom as well as by fatigue. The cerebral cortex appears to exert its influence on dreaming, as laboratory subjects have shown when they aborted REM periods or learned to awaken at their onset. Emotions influence the dreaming period. The particular chemical balance of the brain bears its impact. During stress, fever, mental illness, abnormal REM patterns often occur. The brain responds to a confluence of factors, and the REM interval as we have seen it may represent the harmony of separable cycles that normally occur together.

Whatever the resonances from many brain systems, the physiological hurricane of the REM state does not occur at random but in a relatively clocklike manner. Presumably it wells up from certain repeated body processes, most likely from some part of the body's many metabolisms, body clocks that call out the tempo. A decision to nap or an inability to sleep because of anxiety is merely a modification on the general cycle of day and night. So with dreaming. Probably repeated metabolic cycles, renewing dormant activities in body and brain, set the tempo. The brain stem as an intermediary between body and brain is a plausible location for the trigger, but what ignites the brain-stem activity?

Chemical studies, performed mainly in cats, have shown that a natural body substance, acetylcholine, can be touched to many brain areas and cause sleep, then REM dreaming, but the REM state will not occur instantaneously. Noradrenalin, which produces arousal when injected into many regions in the cat brain also can produce REM sleep. Injections of noradrenalin into the brain stem have generated REM sleep, and injection into the thalamus also have caused REM sleep.

The vigorous internal state of the dreamer, his alacrity, his brain's responses to light, sound, or touch, and his neural excitement, all suggest a link between the REM state and arousal. The location of apparent triggering mechanisms in the pontine reticular formation and the stimulation of REM states by noradrenalin suggest that some component of this weird state may be related to the brain's pervasive system for causing alertness and arousal.

We have not yet unraveled the chemistry of dreaming, but we can expect to discover an underlying chemistry of metabolic cycles. This expectation has been emphasized by a startling group of experiments, largely conducted by William C. Dement, starting back in the 1950's. They were known originally as dream deprivation studies. When Dement began to observe that REM dreaming was a clocklike nightly phenomenon, he wondered what would happen if a person were allowed to sleep yet prevented from having these dream periods. The first results seemed to indicate that dreams were essential to mental health and that their excision from sleep would wreak psychological havoc. Today, with what we know about the physiology of REM intervals, the long and arduous dream deprivation studies make important good sense. When REM periods are excerpted from a person's nightly repertoire—experimentally, by drugs, surgery, alcohol, or sickness—a pervasive chain of physiological processes is prevented. Dreaming of various sorts occurs in other sleep throughout the night, but the frenzied neural activity and glandular outpourings of the REM state are not merely dream images. Whatever validity may abide in psychiatric theories about the need for dreaming, the need for REM periods is not explained by these formulations.

Dement's first studies were conducted with psychiatrist Charles Fisher at Mt. Sinai Hospital in New York City, at a time when the REM interval was a great unknown, perhaps a lost Atlantis. At that time nobody could guess what would happen to a person who was deprived of his nightly orgy. Initially, a group of screened volunteers were observed through several nights of sleep for baseline recordings, and then on five consecutive nights, awakened whenever the desynchronized brain wave pattern and eye movements began. As it happens, this was an inefficient method, which only excised about 65 percent of the total REM time. Even so, there were dramatic effects. The volunteers began "attempting" to dream more often. During the day they said they were concentrating poorly, and some reported an unfounded sense of uneasiness, anxiety. A few began to overeat, and one person quit the study after several days in what appeared to be a panic. Most dramatic, however, was the sleep that followed deprivation. When permitted to sleep without interruption, the REM periods happened thick and fast. For several nights subjects appeared to be making up the lost dream time. It appeared that an individual might have something like a normal quota, a certain amount of time, to spend in the stormy condition of REMs. Perhaps a chemical was accumulating in the nervous system. Perhaps prolonged deprivation would produce psychosis. The penalties of dream loss were as uncharted as the effects of weightlessness, and the next studies proceeded with great caution.

Dement, then a young father with small children, built an EEG laboratory adjacent to his New York apartment in order to maintain contact with his family throughout the grueling vigils. Continuous night monitoring required the stubbornness, the strength, of a mule. Night after night it took unflagging attention, split-second reflexes—to catch a dream, spot equipment failure, and maintain a program that had to be continuous or else a fiasco. Longer deprivation periods were tried; yet Dement and Fisher were always ready to terminate any study at the first signs of damage.

In selecting among volunteers, they tried to choose people who did not look vulnerable, people whose interviews and psychiatric tests would not indicate instability. A healthy prospect was the volunteer for whom challenge and payment ($20 a day) were the main incentives. One such man underwent twelve nights of uninterrupted baseline recording, and sixteen nights of REM deprivation. He took tests of perceptual speed, of tracking agility, memory, mental acumen. He took projective tests such as the Rorschach, which allow the person to freely project his own biases and visions. Images were flashed for an instant on a screen and he was asked what he saw. Flashes of light were aimed at his closed eyelids, and he would describe the lingering aftereffect in his mind's eye. Psychological changes are hard to trap, and the experimenters hoped they would detect changes in perception and outlook by these tests, which were administered before and intermittently throughout the deprivation experiment.

At first the REM deprivation seemed easy, but by the sixth day the volunteer was complaining of apathy and fatigue. He began sitting before his television set or puttering around all day. He was becoming extremely difficult to awaken. By the ninth night, as he was aroused more and more often from attempts to resume REM dreaming, he vented his irritability on Dement. Now he was tired by day, unable to concentrate. He would forget what he was saying in conversation, could barely listen to others, and no longer trusted himself to drive his car. At this point, the experimenters had to be positive that he was not taking naps: he was asked to punch a watchman's clock every fifteen minutes. During the final days, an observer who was also a personal friend attended him continuously. The observer noted that he was avoiding mental activity and drifting through his days, repeating stories he had already told, and occasionally trying to escape surveillance. The topic of homosexuality had now become a major interest.

Nevertheless, during interviews with Fisher the subject insisted that he felt fine. He presented the typical problem in evaluating behavior change. However rotten a person may feel at home, he can usually mobilize himself to give a good show for an hour. If the volunteer did not readily admit changes in himself, they were still revealed on the tests. In the days before the REM deprivation, flickering lights on his eyelids had caused him to visualize geometric patterns. However, as his REM loss continued, he began seeing elaborate images after the same flickering lights. They were almost hallucinations. A face loomed out of the darkness. A piece of furniture snapped to bite him. Man-eating plants grew before his eyes, and there were suckling animals. After sixteen nights of deprivation these grotesque visions had supplanted the geometric patterns evoked by the same neutral, flickering lights. Whatever the volunteer admitted on interviews, it was clear from the tests that a distinct transformation had occurred, and this happened in spite of the fact that his REM deprivation had not been absolute.

Several years later, at Stanford University, Dement began a cautious program to deprive subjects of all REM sleep for sixteen nights. Techniques had been developed to sound an alarm at the very onset of the dream period, before rapid eye movements appeared. After eight nights of this treatment his first subject became immune to almost any form of awakening—and had to be physically wrestled into wakefulness. Once awakened, however, he would lapse almost instantly into a REM state. Dement had to repeat the procedure every few seconds, and it was impossible to deprive the young man of further REM sleep without obliterating all sleep.

The next volunteer received amphetamines which suppressed REM periods and made it possible to deprive him for fifteen nights. At that point however, the experiment had to be stopped in the best interests of the volunteer. On the fourteenth day he had shown a remarkable change in personality. He had been a rather taciturn, compunctious, reliable young man. Suddenly he was a blue-streak talker, impulsive, almost irresponsible. The subject himself remarked that he felt uncommonly carefree and uninhibited, not a whit concerned with what other people thought of him. He wanted to go to sexy nightclubs, and refused to buy drinks until the waitress was forced to kick him out. When he was expelled from a nightclub he was amazed at his own lack of embarrassment. The transformation was dramatic, yet after one night of uninterrupted sleep he reverted to his normal self. The next young man also lasted sixteen nights of deprivation without incurring sleep loss, but at this point he too displayed an alarming change which took the form of an unwarranted suspiciousness bordering on what psychiatrists might call paranoid. He thought his friends were disparaging him and the experimenter insidiously trying to trick him. Yet after a single night of recovery sleep, he, too, returned to his usual personality and remarked that he no longer felt suspicious of people. On the nights that followed their deprivation both subjects indulged in an incredible amount of REM dreaming, until they appeared to have made up for their loss. Despite the intensity of their dreaming, as exhibited on EEGs, they nevertheless experienced the first night of recovery as a deep oblivion from which they remembered no dreams in the morning.

Their compensatory orgy of dreaming, and sudden personality change, suggested that REM deprivation might have prevented the release of some regularly accumulating body chemical. Perhaps it had reached the point where its potency was causing serious emotional and behavioral changes. The possibility that deprivation of REMs might ultimately cause brain damage made it seem unwise to pursue the exploration with human subjects. External factors, such as the strain and self-consciousness a person might feel under continuous observation, also are hard to eliminate with human volunteers.

Cats were a more likely group to study in the next step. They, and other animals, had shown the same compensation after REM deprivation. Of course animal personality changes are hard to detect. Jouvet has observed that cats deprived of REM periods for seventeen days or more, begin to look like tired sad cats. Some of these animals were picked out by visitors to the Lyon laboratory even a year after their deprivation, for they were subdued and unaggressive.

It is not easy to deprive a cat of REM sleep. One ingenious method employs a stone or bucket, set in a bath of cold water. The stone is ample space for a cat to sleep in a crouched position, but if he were to lose muscle tone at the beginning of REM sleep, he would topple into the cold water. Cats also have been placed on treadmills so that they had to keep moving or fall into water. They managed to catch microsleeps on the treadmill, but not REM sleep, and this procedure would ready them for a schedule of prolonged sleep in a recording cage. Then they could be awakened whenever their REM signals appeared on the script of the polygraph machine. It may sound easy.

Imagine four cages and two researchers in a small recording room. Within no time, it resembles a juggling act. One animal or another is always beginning to dream—often two at once. As time goes on, the REM periods happen faster and the cats begin to resist awakening. No automatic alarm system will work. They have to be picked up and forced to stand on their paws. Two researchers scarcely have time to turn their heads to the EEG script before reaching into the cages and lifting, shaking, cajoling two absolutely limp cats, simultaneously. Trying to deprive a cat of REM periods without confusing the issue by introducing undue external stresses becomes a very difficult procedure—especially for long periods of 20 to 70 days. In the end the poor bedeviled experimental creature has obtained what most house pets cannot maneuver, constant human attention and handling around the clock. Films of dream deprivation among the felines have the frenetic quality of W. C. Fields movies. An onlooker might wonder how any research staff could have the stamina to persist through a month or more of perpetual motion. Still, the procedure has produced some remarkable insights.

By pressing cats to ever-longer periods of deprivation, Dement and Jouvet hoped to discover what chemical buildup might occur and what damage it might cause in the brain. Judging by the criterion of behavior alone, Dement had felt that 30 to 70 days of REM deprivation had unexpectedly mild effects. The cats did begin to act somewhat peculiarly. They seemed uncontrollably hungry if kept from eating. Some of the males showed indiscriminate hypersexual behavior, and would mount anesthetized or even dead cats. This is unthinkable for a normal tomcat. They were restless and intense, exhibiting what Dement described as exaggerated drive behavior. Were a human being to show so little control over his instinctive impulses, he would, of course, be locked up in the security ward of a mental hospital.

Another discovery, even more curious, had never been observed with people, for they could not be dream-deprived long enough. The animals seemed to reach a limit after which they no longer compensated for further loss of REM sleep. Jouvet and Dement, independently, found that the orgy of dreaming on recovery was no greater after 70 days of REM deprivation than after about 30 days. The animals seemed to reimburse about 60 percent of their lost dream periods, but no more. If REM deprivation had been causing a buildup of some natural chemical, what happened to this accumulation after 30 days?

The scientists postulated that REM periods must be triggered by a chemical accumulated by a regular metabolic cycle. Ordinarily, perhaps this chemical was consumed in the process of REM sleep, or converted to another form. Presumably it accumulated during REM deprivation, up to a certain point. Then, they conjectured, it might reach such a concentration that it would begin to pass through the usually impermeable membranes of the brain-blood barrier and leak out of the nervous system. Like a fine cotton cloth that is quite water-repellent in a drizzle yet ineffective against a downpour, the membrane barriers between blood and brain also change in "porousness" when chemicals pass certain peaks of concentration. If an accumulating dream chemical actually existed it might eventually pass the limit of concentration and leak out of the nervous system.

Dement and his associate, Peter Henry, arranged to test this theory. In a cat's brain they implanted a hollow catheter into one of the ventricles that holds spinal fluid. They did this to several pairs of cats. One cat of each pair was deprived of REM sleep for about 30 days. The other was placed on a regular sleep schedule so that its normal REM time could be measured. When the deprived animal began to exhibit behavioral changes, spinal fluid was drawn from its brain catheter and injected into the same spot in the brain of the rested animal. The receiver showed a slight increase in REM sleep, precisely what should have happened according to the theory.

The theory and experiment may sound straightforward, but the actual procedure was delicate and touchy. Quite a few cats had to be discarded from the study because their reaction to the injection was fever. Still, the initial study suggested that a chemical process was triggering the periodic REM state, and that the chemical had been accumulating in the cats who were not allowed to "dream." Surely the prevention of the REM state seemed to intensify some change in brain chemistry.

Was this accumulating chemical noradrenalin or a member of this family of stimulant hormones? Adrenergic compounds have been used to heighten the excitability of certain brain systems, to cause arousal, to trigger REM intervals and, in high doses, to generate hallucinations. The evidence is yet too skimpy for a definite statement that REM dreaming comes from an adrenergic period in the brain. Moreover, we have not discovered how the prevailing REM chemistry arises, and what body manufacturing cycles suffuse the brain with stimulants. Nevertheless, the evidence begins to make sense of the widely observed relationships between REM deprivation, often coming from sleep disturbance, and mental illness. Addicts, alcoholics, and many people who suffer sleep disorders also suffer from REM loss, a curtailment that can last months or years. Clinical records begin to indicate that REM suppression occurs at certain stages of mental illness; and this deprivation may alter brain chemistry and thereby change brain function.

Altered brain function has been measured in cats. When a cat hears a click, his EEG response normally takes a particular form, but this will change if the animal's brain has been "poisoned" in any way. James Dewson, III, has performed this test at Stanford University. He compared the EEG responses of cats before, during, and after REM deprivation. During deprivation the cat's brain reacted in an exaggerated way as if unduly excitable. Yet, after the animal had been allowed to sleep freely and compensate, he again showed his normal EEG response.

Dement and his colleagues were interested in this EEG response, but they had expected to see more dramatic surface changes in the behavior of the dream-deprived cats. Dement openly admitted that he was disappointed. Yet he and his team were taking those small and inconspicuous steps toward what may be a very important revelation. Their work was beginning to expose the general excitability of the dream-deprived brain—perhaps thereby explaining what the dream period does to help preserve our sanity, our balance, and health. Dement noticed that his REM-deprived animals did more than just lapse into an orgy of REM dreaming afterward. They had unusually intense REM periods. Their eyes moved a great deal and furiously. Their whiskers and limbs twitched in violent spasms. He took the brain temperature of a cat during its normal REM period, and compared it with the brain temperature during REM periods after deprivation. The cat's brain had become unusually "hot" in the REM periods that followed deprivation, and it seemed that deprivation must have enhanced brain metabolism. At about this time, Harry Cohen, a postdoctoral Fellow working with the team, accidentally shocked a REM-deprived animal. Normally the cat would not have reacted badly, but this creature went into convulsions. The dream-deprived brain looked exceedingly excitable.

The next step was obvious. Cohen and Dement deprived a group of rats of REM sleep for four to five days. Now, a very slight electric shock into the ear would send the rat into convulsions. A far more intense shock was needed to convulse the control rats. It was dramatic evidence of the mounting excitability of the central nervous system. Even more dramatic was the effect of the convulsive shock. The shocked rats did not compensate for their REM loss as usual; they spent much less of their subsequent sleep in REM intervals. On the other hand, rats who had been REM-deprived quite as long, but who received no shock, showed their usual quota of REM sleep during recovery from deprivation.

Did electroconvulsive shock perform some of the discharge of the REM state? Was this a clue to the success of electroshock therapy with a variety of patients—agitated psychotics, depressives, psychopaths?

The Stanford research team began to examine the nightlong sleep patterns of patients, before and after electroshock therapy. In their preliminary studies they noticed that there was less REM sleep after shock than there had been before. This was only a first look at the effects of shock treatment and not conclusive. Nonetheless, Dement, Gulevich and Zarcone seem to have uncovered an important fact of life. Dream-deprived animals exhibited undue brain excitement, making them abnormally susceptible to electroshock, and the shock itself seemed to have accomplished some of the release usually performed by the REM phase of sleep. This groundwork may inspire American scientists with a rationale for taking a new look at electrotherapies used in England, Germany, and Russia.

Hundreds of Soviet clinics are reported to be using a particularly mild form of electrotherapy. Unfortunately, for historical reasons it goes under the misnomer of "electrosleep." The instrument used is an Electroson, which translates "Electrosleep," yet many people do not fall asleep during the treatment, and sleep does not seem to be essential to the efficacy of the therapy. It is certainly not, as sometimes proclaimed, a magical instrument for producing the equivalent of a night's sleep in two hours. It is hardly a certain means of producing sleep. Perhaps it should be called an electric tranquilizer. After Electroson treatment, people with sleep disturbances will, however, show a marked improvement in their nightly sleep. Reports emphasize that patients emerge from this therapy feeling fresh and alert—not dazed as are patients of mild shock therapy. They apparently act as they would after a deep night's sleep.

Electrodes on the head and behind the ears on the neck send pulses to the brain that are generally imperceptible to the patient. These are rectangular waves, delivered in a manner that is known as an interference current. Although the pulses that go through the skin are very weak, they are carefully timed so that they effect an increased amplitude inside the brain, establishing a beat. In greater strength, the method is being explored as a form of portable, safe, and instantaneous anesthesia, suitable for the battlefield or for space.

Few American scientists have seriously experimented with the Electroson technique. In 1963, Sigmund Forster and his associates at New York Downstate Medical Center administered treatments to about 100 people. Only half of them fell asleep although they all showed decreases in heart rate, blood pressure, and respiration, and many emerged feeling calm and refreshed. A number of patients with muscle spasms also obtained relief. At the time, the instrument was advertised as a means of inducing sleep, and its results disappointed quite a few people. American scientists have had many reasons for skepticism. Much of the Soviet literature seems vague and sketchy by our scientific standards. Serious journals in this country demand the presentation of data and methods in a form that will allow others to judge the work and replicate it. Moreover, a few American scientists have concluded that the effects of the Electroson must be largely due to suggestion, for an EEG study with implanted animals revealed no signs that current was entering the brain. Recently, however, a German research team led by H. E. Von Diemath has tested the instrument on a patient with electrodes implanted in the thalamus prior to neurosurgery. Their EEG studies in human beings and other studies of animals indicated that the electrical currents were, indeed, entering the brain and brain stem as intended.

Some of the American scientists' incredulity must be inspired by the use of the Electroson as an almost universal remedy. Treatments have been given to patients with an unbelievable gamut of ailments—schizophrenic symptoms, depression, hysteria, ulcers, muscular spasms, pregnancy toxemia, eczema, and hypertension. According to report Electroson treatment has been used in relaxation training with cosmonauts in order to diminish emotionality and fatigue and gird the men to face stress. An American might think it bizarre to counter tension and remedy eczema with the same treatment applied to a hallucinating psychotic or a child with St. Vitus's dance. In the view of many Soviet scientists, however, these ailments all reflect malfunction in the central nervous system, perhaps an imbalance in the brain's systems of excitation and inhibition.

Surely, one would not blame all these heterogeneous miseries upon a lack of REM sleep, yet an inadequate release of the brain excitement might afflict each individual in his own vulnerable spot. REM sleep appears to reduce this brain excitement. William Dement has suggested that a REM-increasing drug might benefit certain psychotics, narcoleptics, and drug addicts in the throes of withdrawal. LSD has the property of enhancing REM sleep. Moreover, it has been tried among alcoholics in rehabilitation clinics, and these anxious REM-deprived people have experienced a pronounced relief from anxiety and tension. Their relief bears some slight family resemblance to the reactions of patients after various forms of electrotherapy.

Recent models of the Electroson, interestingly enough, have been designed to focus their electrical energy upon the reticular formation, perhaps triggering a low-level discharge within the brain structures associated with REM dreaming. If this electrically stimulated condition were to accomplish a reduction in brain excitement, like that of REM sleep, the nightlong EEG records after treatment should show a decline in REM dreaming similar to that found by the Stanford team in patients after electroshock. The effect of the Electroson does not seem to be sleep but possibly discharge of brain excitement, perhaps acting in the manner of convulsive shock to the REM-deprived rat. Ten years ago it would have seemed improbable that studies of nightly dream patterns might lead toward an explanation of electrotherapy and its mysterious successes with the mentally ill. At that time, dreams and body chemistry seemed widely separate. Nobody would have sought clues to the circadian rhythm in dream periods.

Today, Soviet scientists are said to be conducting extensive studies of the effect of the Electroson upon all body systems and the circadian cycle of sleep and waking. After giving Electroson treatment for anesthesia, they have found interesting chemical changes—resembling those of the REM condition. Treatment produces a release of adrenal steroids and an increase in brain catecholamines, those brain chemicals so crucial to lifting depression. This may explain why patients seem refreshed and cheerful after treatment. Drugs designed to fight depression appear to work by increasing the available supply of brain amines, while those drugs that generate depression also depress REM dreaming. The brain chemistry of mood and the REM cycle appear to be interknit. We have used REM sleep, its frequency, timing, duration, and intensity, as an index to mental and emotional conditions in a somewhat blind fashion. Still, long before the chemistry of dreaming can be deciphered, the properties of the REM state seem to be a fruitful signpost of well-being or disruption in the cycles of the central nervous system.

As physiological evidence pours in from around the world, our picture of the dream cycle will undoubtedly be modified. The discovery of this recurrent dream period and a few of its physical properties now appears to be a momentous one. It has provided a fundamental step in understanding all manner of nervous disorders, from eczema to psychosis, from asthma to emotional upheaval. It appears to contain a kind of built-in shock therapy, a loosing of controls, a discharge of periodically mounting waves of nervous excitement and chemical change that are probably required by body and mind for a multitude of purposes. Researches during the next decade may account for the metabolism that triggers and clocks our dream periods.

Everything that has been discovered about the REM state augments its basic riddle. Why does this recurrent fever of activity possess all mammals in their sleep, bearing them into lunatic visions, agitating their body systems even to the point of peril? Nature is notorious for economy. In the history of medical science we have been wrong whenever we thought a part of the body to be a mere accessory, as we once believed of cartilage in the ear and glial cells in the brain. We were wrong to think bones merely structural, and to presume that vestigial nuisance, the appendix, was merely a hangover from more primitive life functions. We have always found these parts of our tissue served subtle but essential purposes. Surely, the complex and pervasive REM cycle must also balance and regulate essential elements for survival. What are they? Why did mammals evolve this way?

Scientists vary in their opinions. Quite a few have theorized that the primary biological role of the REM phase occurs in the embryo during the development of the infant brain. Life is motion. A forming brain must be in constant action. Perhaps this primitive rhythm, beginning at a time when the brain is merely a brain stem, provides a fundamental rhythm into which later survival activity will be interlocked. Long before birth, in the dark waters of the womb, the human embryo begins exercising his survival apparatus, kicking, sucking his thumb, grimacing. After birth the infant spends most of his existence asleep. As Howard Roffwarg first pointed out, about half of his sleep extends this exercise, his practice in the motions and perhaps the sensations that will later be necessary for him to express his instincts. His eyes move, he gropes, smiles, has erections, pants, grunts, kicks. In later infancy and childhood, he will spend less time asleep, and less of his sleep in this frenzy. His motor activity will diminish. Perhaps the REM period will express, in his body and mental images, the drive excitements that he will be prohibited from expressing by day. In addition, perhaps, it will enable him to maintain a needed balance of hormones, and will discharge the products of the body's relentless chain of chemical cycles, otherwise discharged by daily activity.

Many conjectures about the purpose of the REM state are plausible. Yet they are not answers and the purpose of the dream state remains a mystery. New postulates are voiced each year and one of these very tentative speculations is now reappearing in a slightly different form. If a biological tide, a discharge of excitement in the brain's centers of drive, rises and ebbs roughly every 90 minutes during sleep, could we also see it by day? Is this "dream period" we see so clearly in the quiescence of nightly sleep a lifelong clock, continually charging and recharging our drive centers? Is this a basic motor for our motivation, causing the lazy animal to get up from his rest before his stomach pains begin and search for food, urging the male to search out a mate—a system that periodically jolts us into alertness, pushing us to exert ourselves to survive?

There is no such cycle known during waking life, but perhaps it is merely obscured by life's many activities, finding outlets in eating, talking, smoking, muscular action, sexual behavior, emoting. If a rhythm gave rising and falling vitality to these activities one might observe it under special circumstances. Stanley Friedman and Charles Fisher of Mt. Sinai Hospital in New York City have observed ten normal people while they spent a day in isolation in a denlike hospital room where they could read light fiction and were amply supplied with a refrigerator full of foods and beer, and with cigarettes. Friedman was interested in watching for signs of oral drive. Before the experiment began he gave a numerical rating to every edible—8 points for a can of beer, 3 points for a cigarette, 8 points for a sandwich, and so on. Throughout the day an observer was stationed behind a two-way mirror, recording each time a person put something into his mouth. The volunteers left an unbelievable record. All but two of them showed a rising and falling intensity of eating, drinking, or smoking that cycled at about 80 to 120 minutes. Hunger contractions in the stomach, incidentally, do not occur in this rhythm. They start between 2½ to 4½ hours after a meal. This rhythm suggested a cycle of excitement in appetite regions of the brain at intervals that may not have a bearing on the REM rhythm but were certainly very close.

The only two subjects who did not show this pattern were both single women who did not know the examiner and whose daylong observations took place on a holiday when this region of the hospital was deserted. Body rhythms are not rigid, of course, and can be altered by emotions. Similar variations have been seen in sleep laboratories when anxious or self-conscious subjects showed an irregular REM pattern on their first nights, or after some jarring event. Further studies of isolation may reveal whether the drive to eat, cycles of alertness, indeed all that we call basic motivation, show a REM-like rhythm. This possibility has remained almost unexplored. Indeed, scientists are just starting to examine dream-deprived subjects in daytime to see whether they exhibit heightened, cyclical expressions of drive. Dement has suggested that when people get little sleep and their brains may be excited from REM loss, they may become more driving and ambitious if they happen to channel their drive in a socially acceptable fashion. We do not know whether direct discharge of drive activity in sexual orgasm influences the REM cycle of brain excitement. Our ignorance on this point, and many relevant questions about human sexual behavior, stems merely from taboos on such research.

Freud and many others, with different phrasing, have asserted that man's neuroses and psychosomatic illnesses are entangled with the way he has learned to repress and channel basic drive impulses. REM intervals at night appear to offer a biological upsurgence and discharge of drive pressures, and dream-deprived people and animals have shown some loss of control over their waking behavior. The relationship between man's psychological well-being, his handling of basic drives, and his dreams gave impetus to the intensive study of dreaming that began in the mid 1950's when the REM cycle was first explored. Now, indeed, dreaming as we recall it, enjoy it, and analyze it may prove to be a side product, an epiphenomenon and not the goal of the REM cycle at all. It may be the product of an excited visual system and cortical centers working at high pitch on the only material available to them—memories, thoughts, feelings.

Dreams perform no less an important exorcism of our psychological needs because they result from physical organization. The style of behavior we term personality, the habits we call character, the sensitivity or intensity of experience, the creative inventiveness, emerge from rhythmic physical processes. By the methods of physical science we can hope to understand the process, the tidal motion of our biology that generates the physiological background of REM dreaming. The experience of the mind, evanescent and bizarre, is no less unique and magnificent, no less essential to the spirit because it is formed in physiological events—yet the dream itself, and its meanings to the dreamer, cannot be analyzed by physical methods.

X

THE MEANINGS OF DREAMS

IN 1911, a policeman's wife dreamed that someone had broken into her house. She called out for a policeman but he had gone up several steps into a church, behind which stood a hill capped by a thick wood. The bearded policeman was accompanied by two tramps wearing aprons. Using this example in *The Interpretation of Dreams*, Sigmund Freud offered a paradigm to suggest its hidden meaning. The church was the female genital, the steps a symbol of copulation, the hill a Venus's mound, surmounted by the wood, or pubic hair. Freud's brilliant compendium of case histories and theory revolutionized the treatment of psychological ills, for he saw in dreams the clues to the individual's unconscious. There lay the expressions of primary instincts, the symbols of unrecognized fears and wishes. However innocuous or bewildering, the drama had a meaning. The real meaning of the dream, if it could be unveiled at all, required the kind of guided personal search into its associations that is the basis for psychoanalysis. Almost no modern person is untouched by this theory, yet as Freud's writings were successively abbreviated and restated in popular form, they were mistakenly used as a simple lexicon by which any dream, out of context, could be understood. Most people yearn for some shorter route than psychoanalysis, some quick and simple formula that will disentangle their dreams.

The search for meaning might be called one of man's intellectual and emotional instincts. Throughout history he has pursued the meaning of dreams, usually relying upon some outside person, priest or oracle. Are dreams departures of the soul as the primitive Fiji Islander imagined, or are they portents of reality? The Chester Beatty Papyrus in the British Museum, a document almost 4,000 years old, contains the instructions whereby an ancient Egyptian could know that his dream of a gliding moon signified grace with his god, but a dream of distant crowds meant impending death. There was faith in dreams as portents and their transparence to the interpreter. A pharaoh's haunting dream might place on the interpreter the burden of state decisions. Joseph's interpretation of the fat kine and the lean led to an economic strategy in Egypt that was comparable in magnitude with a modern five-year plan. The Greeks used oracles to prophesy from dreams, and also dream rites to heal the sick. The Iroquois understood dreams as commands to be followed. During the twelfth to sixteenth centuries, Western Europeans lived in fear of an international conspiracy of witches and demons that could invade human thralls in their dreams. The Inquisition judges used their handbook, the *Malleus Maleficarum* (*Hammer for Witches*) to interpret dreams in a period when they could mean burning at the stake. Dreams and their meanings have been influential in the world's religions. Bertrand Russell once asked whether there was a difference between the statement "An angel visited me last night," and "I dreamed I saw an angel last night." The interpretation of dreams has wielded power in human history. Early Talmudic rabbis said, "A dream that is not understood is like a letter that is not opened."

The Romantic era gave dreams a new importance. They were the fire wheels of imagination. They inspired great poetry. They gave Robert Louis Stevenson the plots for his fiction. Frederich Kekule, the organic chemist, made the important discovery of the structure of the benzene ring in a dream of a snake eating its tail. They reveal a man's own mind to himself. Still, people are lured by the romantic appeal that dreams transcend them, even into the supernatural, lending clairvoyance. Historians repeatedly write that Abraham Lincoln was deluged with crackpot letters; Lincoln knew that threats on his life might not be staved off indefinitely. Yet it is part of our dearest legend that Lincoln's dream of his death was a prediction of his actual assassination.

The yearning for instantaneous and spectacular interpretations of dreams must be widespread. Today, at any large newsstand one can purchase a 25-cent dream book that contains remnants of the ancient Egyptian papyri, indiscriminately mixed with brief excerpts from Freudian paradigms. The numbers gambler may discover that his dream of peanuts means that he should bet on number 345. The introspective reader may find that his dream of guns reveals an undue preoccupation with masculine virility. A dozen or so dream books on the market offer this odd mixture of ancient omens, oracles, prophecy, diagnoses, and psychological advice—a sample of man's attempts throughout the ages to understand his dreams.

Since the 1900's, when Freud's theory was first promulgated, psychoanalysts, psychiatrists, and psychotherapists have become our chief interpreters of dreams. Dreams were mirrors of the dreamer, not god-sent visions nor forecasts of external reality. In ancient times a chill of foreboding might have spread through the family if a youngest son dreamed that his father walked around carrying his head on a plate; but after 1900 it was more likely to be seen as a castration wish. A dream of plunging into water suggested the relief of pain to a Babylonian, but a Freudian interpretation might have suggested a fantasy of birth. In the shorthand of colloquial speech, Freudian interpretation endowed dreams with the forces of primary and often repressed instincts. Freud's more mystical contemporary Carl Gustav Jung saw in dreams a self-transcendence that expressed the collective nature of humankind. Erich Fromm has observed that dreaming man can be irrational and beastly, and also unusually wise and sensitive.

None of the great theorists saw dreams as any one kind of event. The theories derived from long experience with patients, from hearing their dreams, the emotions the dreams evoked, and the patients' train of associated memories. Freud, still the dominant dream theorist, was a neurophysiologist by training and a complex thinker. The oversimplification of his theory has created a popular myth that dream events can be equated with symbolic meanings independent of the dreamer, and that universal and cultural symbols are so uniformly imbedded in men that any dream may be understood *in vacuo*.

The patent foolishness of such an endeavor, like the patent foolishness of the dream books, can be demonstrated in any living room. One need only turn on a televised movie for a minute and watch a single film clip. What does it mean? A young man rises from the sofa and shoots an entering stranger. Without the context of the story, how is anybody to decide whether this was murder, an act of self-defense, panic, justice, or revenge? The psychiatrist is in a similar quandary when somebody tells him an isolated dream and asks its meaning. An honest analyst is not likely to venture a curbstone opinion, for he must know the person and his associations. Even then his chances of full understanding are about fifty-fifty.

Have a dozen years of laboratory dream research given us a shorter route to dream interpretation? Have they altered the psychoanalytic theories about the meanings of dreams? The analysis of literally truckloads of dream stories, and the use of laboratory methods lend no hope that there will ever be a quick formula for understanding dreams, but they are beginning to modify our notions about the nature of dreaming. There are a few analysts who resist the incursion of laboratory findings upon theories delineated by Freud. As one analyst has said, "There is no dream beyond the dream Freud described in his early work. I simply question the findings of the laboratory." In his mind the sole avenue to the heart of a dream is the long probing of morning recollections by a trained analyst, according to his discipline. On rare occasion laboratory experimenters, familiar with the biases of psychoanalysis, have gone to the other extreme. "Now that we are able to examine what is more nearly the raw material of the theories, their failures are becoming obvious."

In point of fact, both methods contain discernible biases. The psychiatric patient or analysand from whom theories have been derived is not a representative sample of the population. Nor, indeed, is the laboratory a normal place to sleep. The rarity of nightmares and noctural emissions in the laboratory indicates that the experimenters may be able to tap many more dreams than the psychiatrist, but that the psychiatrist may hear about certain kinds of dreams that do not occur in the laboratory. If a person's rapport with his psychiatrist will affect his degree of candor, a subject's rapport with the experimenter is in the same respect very influential. Experimenters cannot force candor, but they can watch certain physiological changes from the outside, and some of these are being correlated with specific kinds of dreams and feelings. The best example, perhaps, is a male subject's lack of erection, or detumescence, during a rapid-eye-movement dream. Charles Fisher's researches strongly suggest that these signs almost always indicate an anxious or aggressive dream. Whatever the subject describes, these negative emotions are almost invariably imbedded in the dream. Today, as the psychiatric and laboratory methods of dream study are used simultaneously, we may hope to see the differences more clearly, and modify our conception of the actual dream.

The dreams from which theories have arisen have not been dreams, of course, but memories. There is no way of checking dream reports against dreams. However embroidered and shaped, however censored and skewed, we have only human recall to work with. Quite a number of psychiatrists have been interested in seeing how the dreams reported in the laboratory match with dreams reported to the analyst. Roy Whitman of the University of Cincinnati Medical School found, in a study of two patients, that there were some dreams told to the experimenter that were withheld from the analyst, and the reverse was also true. Some of the dreams told the analyst were not mentioned to the experimenter. The male patient told only the psychiatrist certain hostile and sexual dreams about the experimenter, but he told the experimenter about homosexual scenes that he did not tell the psychiatrist in the morning. The woman withheld from the experimenter dreams which implied that she knew more than he did and was seductive toward him, but she withheld from the psychiatrist seventeen dream scenes about the relationship of psychiatrists and patients, and also her sexual dreams.

Neither the psychiatrist nor the laboratory experimenter can be quite sure that they are recording exactly what a person remembers. The dream is filtered through inevitable shyness, self-consciousness, fear of judgment, and even deliberately distorted. Calvin Hall and his associates at the Institute for Dream Research in Miami, Florida, have tried to eliminate the sterile hospital aura from their dream laboratory. It is located in a frame house, offering as homey an atmosphere as possible. Even so, when monitored records of laboratory awakenings were compared with written reports by the same volunteers as they recalled dreams in their own homes, the dream narratives were strikingly different. Laboratory reports were long and incoherent, and less intense than the highly organized dream reports from home. Perhaps volunteers were self-conscious about their intensity when they talked directly with the experimenter, and perhaps the rules of the waking mind prevailed as they worked over their reports at home, so that they came out in the manner of short stories. In another laboratory, the problem of deliberate censorship and distortion was enunciated with touching candor when the volunteer told the experimenter, "All the way over here, I worried about what would happen if I dreamt certain things—if it got too hairy, you know. I made up this story, already to use it in case—but I'm glad I didn't have to use it." Even if the individual were to report his dreams with dispassionate truthfulness, the laboratory technician knowns that his subject is not quite so free in his actual dreams as he might be at home.

Edward Wolpert at the University of Chicago Medical School has recalled a striking example of the manner in which a sleeping person can control his own dreams for self-protection. The volunteer was one of Wolpert's first experimental subjects, a sophisticated young man who had just previously finished a psychoanalysis. He began with some reservations about the sleep study, doubting that the researchers could actually pinpoint his dream periods, and on the other hand, fearing that if they did he might disclose too much about himself. His analysis made him hypersensitive to the interpretations one might put upon a dream and he did not intend to spill his guts in public. For three hours in the laboratory he tossed and turned, unable to fall asleep. Then finally he drifted off and his first REM period soon followed. It was an elaborate and vivid dream. As he related the events he began to feel psychologically naked, and embarrassed about the meanings of the dream. He went back to sleep, and for the rest of the night, each time a REM interval appeared on the EEG script, it lasted only a minute or two and then ceased before anybody could awaken him. In the morning when he awakened, the researchers asked him if he remembered his aborted dreams. He did. He had dreamed that a television set had been switched on. He let it play for a little while and then got up and shut it off. The screen went blank.

Judging from thousands of laboratory nights it is obvious that dreams recalled in the morning comprise only a tiny fraction of the nightly fare. By repeatedly awakening volunteers in all phases of sleep, experimenters have demonstrated that the majority of vivid, memorable episodes occur within the rapid-eye-movement periods, and that everyone has four or five of these intervals a night, occupying about an hour and a half of their sleep. Some people enjoy vivid dreams as they are falling asleep, and others have reported remarkable dramas when awakened from the quiescent stages of slow-wave slumber. Even the most prolific dream recallers emerge from the night with but a small portion of this experience in mind. Our general notion about dream content and the meanings of dreams would appear to be based upon REM dreams, and probably upon particular ones, at that. Although a person may occasionally awaken from a dream in the midst of the night, he is more likely to recall dreaming as he wakes up in the morning, and it may be this last REM period that we have been referring to as dreaming in general.

Not all the dreams of the night are alike, nor do people seem to dream alike. David Foulkes and Gerald Vogel have confirmed in a University of Chicago study that many people slip into sleep along a sluice of reveries and vague thoughts. In an extension of this study at the University of Wyoming, Foulkes and his associates have tracked some individual differences in the dreams of sleep onset. Some people dream so vividly that it might be hard to distinguish these border-state dreams from REM experiences, yet other people do not dream as they drift off to sleep. According to a variety of psychological tests the volunteers in the study appeared to segregate by personality characteristics too. The people who reported dreaming as they drifted into sleep seemed to be less constricted and anxious than those who apparently indulged in no fantasy as they lapsed into sleep.

Early dreams appear to be somewhat harder to remember than the dreams later in the night. Arthur Shapiro, internist and sleep researcher at Downstate Medical Center in Brooklyn, has summed up what appears to be a trend in nightlong dream studies. The early REM periods are somewhat colorless, mundane, and thoughtlike; the later REM dreams exude more vigor and imagery. Indeed, toward the end of the night even the thoughts and fragments reported between REM intervals take on some of the coloration and vividness of REM episodes. Laboratory volunteers have themselves commented that the first dreams of the night did not make a firm impression on their memories. The frustrated experimenter, in addition, may be left listening to the yawn of his dreaming subject who has slipped back to sleep in mid-recital, and when reawakened recalls nothing of his dream.

The issue of memory has been nettlesome to sophisticated analysts as they have tried to theorize about the rules governing content. At the same time, while therapists may be interested, the validity of patients' dream reports is not essential for their use in analysis. Dreams as used in therapy are like a vague sketch that must be fleshed out with trains of personal associations and memories. It is this process, not so much the dream, that is crucial. For theorists, however, the problem of memory and distortion remains an issue. Ernest G. Schachtel, expressing a common sentiment, has sadly remarked that few dreams are recalled upon awakening, and that these are fragmented and transformed very rapidly. Freud said: ". . . the forgetting of dreams depends far more upon the resistance than upon the fact stressed by the authorities that the waking and sleeping states are alien to each other." Dreams were not so much forgotten as repressed because their contents were too disturbing to be consciously confronted. A few people adamantly believe that repression is the sole cause of poor memory for dreams, but laboratory studies have indicated that the forgetting of dreams may be more complicated than that.

During the first years of laboratory dream research at the University of Chicago, William C. Dement and Nathaniel Kleitman observed that the incidence of dream recall dropped sharply after the ending of the REM period. Edward Wolpert and Harry Trosman, also in this laboratory, began awakening volunteers at various intervals after REM periods. When awakened directly from REM dreaming, the volunteers remembered their experiences, but if several minutes had elapsed after the close of the REM period it was gone like the trace of the evanescent neutrino. Again and again the laboratory researchers almost literally watched dreams evaporate. A subject who had slipped away in the midst of reciting a dream, and who was rewakened, might say, "I remember being woken, but I don't remember what it was about. . . ." The sleepy subject makes an effort to unscramble his thoughts and the English words to describe them, and the experimenter, now several minutes too late to affix the dream details, has watched them slip into the bog of the forgotten. The particular stage of sleep and the timing of awakening appear to influence the recall of dreams. But the memory problem is knottier than that. Everyone knows that people differ in their ability to recall dreams.

Ten years ago it was possible for a person who rejoiced in his plentiful morning memories to pity the impoverished soul who said, "I never dream." Such people have been observed in the laboratory, passing through the usual number of REM intervals, and when awakened, have often exclaimed, "Oh—so *that's* a dream!" Why do some people habitually remember their dreams and others fail to recall anything? Psychoanalytic patients have high incentive, and often begin to remember more dreaming. Another aspect of memory may be attention. Introspective people seem to recall dreaming more easily than people who rarely contemplate their own emotions and thoughts.

If the time of awakening is important, the speed of awakening appears to influence dream memory in the person who usually does not recall dreams. Since questions about dream recall lie at the vortex of research into the nature of dream content, they have become the focus of a concerted study by a large research team at New York Downstate Medical Center. Donald Goodenough and Arthur Shapiro have been directing various aspects of the research. When they compared people who rarely remembered dreaming at home with people who called themselves dreamers, they found a number of factors at play. The volunteers with poor dream memory, if awakened very abruptly during a REM episode, would recall more details than they would if awakened slowly. If they were awakened gradually as they might awaken at home, they were apt to say they had been thinking rather than dreaming, even though they were drawn out of a REM state.

On a first sorting, there seemed to be at least three explanations for the inability to recall dreams. At home, of course, a person's alarm clock might awaken him outside of the REM interval or he might awaken too gradually. He might, of course, be repressing unpleasant memories. On the other hand, the laboratory studies indicated that some of these nonrecallers might be physiologically somewhat different from the recallers. Some volunteers who awakened from REM sleep feeling they had been in a dreamless oblivion gave physiological signs of dreaming in a deeper state of sleep than others. It took a real blast to awaken them and when they did awaken, it was a slow process. Other subjects, when awakened from a REM episode, would assert that they had been awake and thinking. They may have been in a physiological state of sleep very near the threshold of waking. Occasionally, however, what they would label as waking thought might reasonably cause incredulity in the experimenter. Some of these dialogues between the experimenter in the monitoring room and the sleepy volunteer in his darkened bedroom have a charming humor:

"I was awake and thinking of going over to a candy machine. I began to put the dime into the machine, and more dimes—3 more came out in the front, so I took the dime back out and put it in again and 3 more dimes came to the front. I did this 4 or 5 times. Then I put the dime almost all the way in and all of a sudden this pile of pennies came flowing out, an endless stream practically. I put the pennies in my pocket. This soda machine was in the classroom. I asked the teacher if she minded and she said no. I just sat and put the pennies in. This classroom was what you call a student seminar which they have at college. It seems the machine was built over an oil well and there were two bubbling wells in there."

"You say you were awake and thinking this?"

"Yes. It's very hard to tell whether you're awake or sleeping. I thought I was awake."

"Any more details?"

"I didn't want to share the pennies with anybody so I asked a girl if I could borrow her hat and I was going to pour everything in. Except it seems the hat was made of some sort of rubber and I couldn't pour it in because there was no room—it came all the way up to the top. It was a white hat."

It may seem implausible that this fellow thought he was awake and thinking yet many people who typically claimed to be awake when aroused from REM intervals seemed to be in unusual contact with the outside world. They tended to awaken easily, and to show less than usual eye movement during their REM dreams. It appeared that they might be dreaming in a lighter than usual stage of sleep. They often gave terse dream reports and said the memory was rapidly fading.

There are, however, instances in which a person awakened will say that he was dreaming but he cannot remember what. Sometimes the Downstate team has noticed that these REM intervals look particularly intense by physiological measures, yet the volunteer says his dream content has crumbled away or that his mind is a blank. These have looked like instances of repression, and the team has been studying the phenomenon by presenting subjects with very stressful films and neutral films on alternate nights before sleep. After a stress film there are more instances than after a neutral film in which a person fails to recall a dream. Sometimes the repression does not seem to take the form of total memory failure but of a kind of dissociation of feeling. One man, for example, had seen a medical film on the birth of a baby just before sleep. During his first REM interval his respiration was notably wild, yet his reported dream of hammering studs into a two-by-four was relatively unemotional. On his next awakening, however, he said that there had been something else in his mind. "I found the word 'murder' in the back of my mind."

Repression is common enough in waking life. It is rather easier to pinpoint during waking than sleep, for there are witnesses to events, whereas no outsider can enter the brain to share a dream. The Downstate approach to the problem has been to obtain many nights of dreams from people who ordinarily recall with ease, and spot those memory failures that occur on nights when they have been subjected to stress. Unconscious repression, time of awakening, speed of awakening, and physiology may not be the only factors determining our recall of dreams.

Of course, forgetting spares our minds from a clutter that might interfere with the events and thoughts at the center of our focus. Focused attention and action necessitates eliminating all distractions. In our daily lives we do not recall most of our dreams, but then we do not remember every reverie, monologue, or thought we composed in the shower each morning. During waking activity our "poor memory" protects our concentration, for we do not have access to the detailed memories that appear to be available in dreams.

The magnitude and richness of this lifetime memory hoard, which seems to lie outside of conscious retrieval yet landscapes and populates our dreams, has been suggested occasionally under hypnosis. Just as an indication of the amount our brains manage to store, Warren McCulloch gave this example to a Cybernetics conference in 1952.

> We tried this sort of trick. We took master bricklayers who laid face brick and had them recall the seventh brick in the row—in a given year. They were able to recall any one such brick—thirty or forty items at the most. That was a brick that had been through their hands some ten years before.
>
> These things are verified by checking the bricks. They are master bricklayers. That means they are laying face bricks. That means that even ten years later you can go to that row and look at the brick.
>
> The kinds of things men remember are that in the lower left-hand corner, about an inch up and two inches over, is a purple stone which doesn't occur in any other brick that they laid in that whole wall. . . . The pebble may be about a millimeter in diameter. . . .

One member of the conference inquired how a man could possibly remember thirty such features on one brick, to which

McCulloch replied, "Oh, they do." In fine detail the unnoteworthy features of our surroundings seem to be physically filed away within the brain, and we may reasonably assume that these billions of "inconsequential" memories form part of the raw material of our dreams.

We are, of course, the authors of our dreams—as Erich Fromm has phrased it, playwrights drawing upon a vast store of materials. They are created out of our emotions, cultural values, and perceptions, and also our biology, our chemistry, our inherited physical structure. These factors also appear to influence our recall of dreams, a recall that appears to be chancy and imperfect. The complex issue of dream memory can be explored and defined by new methods today, as theorists seek to discover or confirm the psychodynamic rules that may dictate the significance of dream content and, indeed, the nature of dream content.

Laboratory methods are allowing us to re-examine some of the old mythology about the nature of dreams. Do they happen in a flash or in real time? Louis Ferdinand Alfred Maury, an ingenious nineteenth-century empiricist, had himself tickled, scorched and sprinkled in order to see how it affected dreaming. His famous dream of the French Revolution has been repeatedly cited as the evidence that dreams occur in the space of an eyeblink. It was an elaborate dream that culminated in his own beheading. As he was taken to the block and felt the guillotine sever his head from his body he awakened in fright. The headboard of his bed had fallen on his neck. Maury concluded that the entire dream occurred between the instant of impact and moment of awakening, and never considered the alternative explanation that the collapsing headboard just happened to coincide with the beheading situation in his dream. Although this dream was reported ten years after it happened, and the alternative explanation was never offered, many people believed that Maury had demonstrated the instantaneousness of dreams. Unfortunately, a great deal of our historical evidence about the nature of dreams is similarly anecdotal. As in clairvoyance, the positive coincidence of prediction and real event is likely to be remembered and offered as proof, but the many negative instances are forgotten. Many dogmatic opinions about dreams have been inspired by a relatively few coincidences.

Laboratory studies now suggest that most dreams probably take place in real time, although "flash" dreams can occur. Foulkes and his associates have obtained reports of very rapid dreams that seem to occur in scenes without intervening continuity, like a series of rapidly flashed photographs. Kleitman, Dement, and Wolpert long ago revealed that the preponderance of our REM dreams probably unfold at about the rate it would take to live out the sequence in waking life. One early subject recalled this scene:

> "I was standing by the record player . . . listening to some music, and intending to go home. The doorbell rang and she [a girl friend] asked me if I would answer it. I hesitated for a moment and . . . it rang again."

The experimenter's finger had accidentally slipped and he had sounded the arousing bell twice, about three or four seconds apart. When the subject was later asked to act out the dream, it took about three seconds. This procedure has been repeated in a number of ways, confirming that dream events often—perhaps usually—take place in ordinary time.

Another myth about dreams has been the notion that they are almost always in black and white, and that the person who dreams in color must be intensely emotional and is exhibiting certain vagaries of personality. Edwin Kahn, William Dement, Charles Fisher, and Joseph E. Barmack studied 38 subjects, whom they awakened from dreams. Apparently, most people pay little attention to color and would not mention it unless asked. If a volunteer never offered a color description, a member of the experimental team would probe. One subject mentioned that she saw a bar of soap in the bathtub with the baby. When later asked what the soap looked like she said, "Like any bar of soap looks. It was round, it was pink, and the baby was playing with it in the bathtub." Another subject mentioned a dream that included girls in bright red bikinis. When the experimenter later asked how he knew the bikinis were red, he replied, "How did I know? I saw them. They were red." Out of the 87 dreams tapped in this study only 15 contained no particular reference to color. The old myth about colorless dreams may simply indicate that people do not mention qualities they take for granted. It should not be surprising that the problems of deciphering the nature of dreams from the reports of dreamers are at least as difficult as discovering what transpired in an accident from the testimony of witnesses.

A very old theory about dreaming suggested that dreams were caused, and assuredly influenced, by sensory stimulation from outside or within the body. The nineteenth-century experimenters had themselves tickled and scorched during sleep, but they had no means of gaining access to all their dreams. Surely, throughout a dreamer's self-immersion air continues to circulate around his head, there are sounds, lights may go on or off, and innumerable events occur within his body. Freud postulated that the dream protects a person from awakening by incorporating these outside events. Today, of course, we are acutely conscious of statistics, and would more likely speculate that this happens in a certain percentage of dreams. Dreams may, indeed, wake a person up. Gemini astronaut Gordon Cooper related an interesting nightmare to Dr. Howard Minners of NASA after his eight-day voyage around earth. While in space he dreamed that he had failed to perform one of his tasks in the spaceship. The dream awakened him, whereupon he checked the instruments, and found that he had actually done his assigned task before he fell asleep.

In their early experiments, Dement and Wolpert systematically waited until their subject had entered a REM interval. Then they would sound a humming tone, flash a light, or spray the person's face with cool water, subsequently awakening him to hear what he dreamed. About 25 percent of the time the dreams bore the obvious impact of the stimuli. After noise people said, "There was a plane flying overhead," or "There was a noise like Niagara Falls." Other experimenters have applied heat or cold to dreaming subjects, and obtained references to temperature in about 25 percent of the dreams. It should not be surprising that external stimuli do not show a direct impact 100 percent of the time. Indeed, neurophysiologists have shown us that the dreaming brain, while in some ways as responsive as the waking brain, tends to censor external distractions as it does when a person is focusing his attention upon a difficult problem.

Similarly, thirst, hunger, a need to urinate, and other bodily states produce a noticeable impact upon only a certain fraction of our dreams. Freud ate anchovies and reported dreaming that he drank water, but we will never know what other dreams he dreamed that night. Dement and Wolpert found references to drinking in about 30 percent of the dreams of their thirsty subjects in one study. Edwin Bokert at New York University added a Machiavellian fillip to enhance thirst in his 18 subjects. They were deprived of food and liquid for 8 to 9 hours and presented with a highly spiced meal upon arrival in the laboratory. At least one of their dreams referred to thirst. On one night, in addition, a tape recorder played during sleep, repeating the phrase "a cool delicious drink of water." Interestingly enough, this suggestion was incorporated into dreams, directly. Also, the number of dreams about liquids increased and the subjects who dreamed of gratifying their thirst drank less in the morning than did the subjects who dreamed that they were frustrated. These people were thirstier when they awakened, a first tentative laboratory confirmation of Freud's theory that dreams may satisfy drives and wishes.

There have been a number of attempts to discover how drugs may influence dream content. Several venturesome experimenters have slugged themselves with alcohol before bedtime, with various antidepressant or tranquilizing drugs—and found no perceptible trend in their own subsequent REM reports.

Since drugs that alter mood or perception presumably act upon the dreaming brain, it is reasonable to expect that they cast some hue or inclination into dreams, but such trends undoubtedly require more than a casual screening of a few nights' dreams. Roy Whitman and his associates at the Cincinnati College of Medicine have detected a trend toward aggressive dreams under the influence of the antidepressant imipramine.

The characteristic nightmares of the alcoholic may reflect a state of toxicity. Milton Gross and his associates at Downstate Medical Center in Brooklyn have heard a vast number of these alcoholic nightmares. Typically, the dreamer is in a truck on a collapsing bridge, or being chased by a cop, shot and borne away dying in an ambulance; he is stomping on screaming hordes of rats; watching doctors dissect living animals, or waiting to be beaten with chains. In general these sick gentlemen arrive at the hospital in a state of hunger, dehydration, and some animal discomfort.

Their dreams appear to reflect this bodily state. One man, in withdrawal, who dreamed of pulling the plug out of a bathtub and continually hallucinated water on the floor, soon thereafter went to the urinal in considerable need. Another bunched up his bedsheet and tossed it onto the floor in his sleep. When he awakened he explained that he had tossed out some spoiled frankfurters. Several men in withdrawal spent their dreaming periods chewing, salivating, making the gestures of someone who is ravenously finding, preparing, and eating food.

Messages from the body, do, indeed, seem to penetrate the dreaming mind. A preliminary study of a large group of nurses suggests that women may often have anticipation dreams, dreams of waiting for a bus or train, before the onset of menstruation. On the first day or two of menstruation, however, the dreams may be fantasies of destruction. This is only a tentative conclusion, from a study by Robert Van deCastle at the Institute for Dream Research in Miami. Members of the Institute have postulated that a careful screening of dream content might permit early detection of physical ailments whose pains or symptoms have been overlooked during waking. The difficulty in establishing correspondence between body symptoms and dream content will be considerable. It is indeed difficult to establish correlations between concrete and clear-cut life events and dreams in order to confirm some of the major points of dream interpretation theories.

Perhaps the best established, out of all the factors that influence our dreams, is the role of events in the preceding day. Freud long ago elaborated the hypothesis that dreams were ignited and molded around this day's residue, and this current experience would begin to evoke associations and memorable childhood events. Laboratory records have supported this hypothesis to a remarkable extent. An initial demonstration was made by Paul P. Verdone at the National Institutes of Health. He found that the early dreams in the night tend to surround current happenings in a somewhat more bland and vague fashion than later dreams. As the night wears on and the dreamer's temperature drops to its daily low point, the dreams seem to recede toward past events while also becoming more intense and vivid. As the temperature begins to rise before waking, there is some indication that dreams also move again toward the events of the present. This trend has been observed in numerous laboratories. Not all protocols are alike, yet the unwinding skein of night memory can be exemplified by this transcript:

1st Awakening:	"I'm trying to remember if I was dreaming or not. I was thinking in terms of the job—a ten-car train that had to get moved from the shop—thinking where I would put it. . . ."
2nd Awakening:	"I was thinking of getting those cars I mentioned—what to do with this train that was getting released from the shop and these ten extra cars. . . ."
3rd Awakening:	"This time I finally started dreaming—I was sitting at a desk in the office where I work, figuring out what I was going to do with these cars. . . ."

4th Awakening: "Seems I was in a little vegetable stand in downtown Manhattan. I'd been looking for a place to park—to do my shopping . . . a block away I saw this stand where the merchandise sits out on the sidewalk. . . . The proprietor handed me two or three pieces of fresh, crisp lettuce from a nice head and asked me to take it inside to wash it off—he had three kids sitting there and he was going to give it to them to pacify them. . . . The guy inside was going to put it into a bag—he misunderstood—and the proprietor called out: 'Hey, Eddy, this lettuce is for the kids. . . .' "

5th Awakening: "Seems I was sitting in the living room in this house, when a dump truck came up with this pile of sand. Seems the people were planning to use it for a brick wall or something. It was a woman with the dump truck. She dumped it out front and we stood out there passing the time of day—saying the kids were going to have the time of their lives, and people were going to track sand all over their carpets. . . . She was a woman in white coveralls, with her hair tied up in a scarf. . . . We were laughing and joking. . . ."

Many of the later dreams could be mistaken for descriptions of reality, they are so richly detailed and so natural. Nobody has suggested a physiological reason for the increasing vividness of fantasy, but the progression away from the immediate present fits with the speculations of some neurophysiologists. Dreaming, they feel, is a kind of filing procedure within memory stations in the brain. It occurs in sleep when there is a lull in the flood of incoming information, a time when the day's events can be recycled for proper filing by drawing out the memory folders of the past and linking present with past according to some hierarchy of importance, association, similarity of emotion. Presumably the new information will be filed in a number of forms so that there is a cross index for recalling pertinent events.

The impact of the day's residue has inspired empiricists, even in Freud's time, to try to create a direct impact upon dreams by deliberately generating some of that residue. Posthypnotic suggestions were used to encourage subjects to dream of specific happenings, and in the morning their dream memories were sifted for traces of the suggestion. Johann Stoyva of Langley Porter Neuropsychiatric Institute in San Francisco and Charles Tart at the Laboratory of Hypnosis Research of Stanford University have used laboratory methods to demonstrate that hypnotic suggestions do crop up in dreams. Stoyva found a curious side effect among his best subjects. Those who would dream of climbing a tree or close facsimile, upon direction, would also seem to cut down on their REM time, yet the less suggestible subjects, who resisted intervention in their dream content, continued to show as much REM dreaming as before. Tart found that hypnotic subjects could be instructed to awaken themselves before or after REM periods. Moreover, one fellow could be instructed to dream all night and would thereupon increase his REM time by 20 percent.

As people have begun to use a variety of techniques to influence dream content, a crucial question has remained at the heart of their endeavor: How does one know when a dream reflects laboratory manipulations? If dreams did no more than parrot reality they would not be difficult to interpret, but their meanings are often hidden in symbols. Some are believed to be common to large cultural groups, some possibly universal, but many cannot be deciphered excepting by questioning the dreamer, who himself holds the key. The search for the relation between dream symbols and real events might be likened to the anthropologist's work in a newly discovered tribe. He must determine how the strange sounds uttered by tribesmen compose words, and then what objects the words refer to, and finally how the language is organized by grammar and syntax.

An early and well-known program was devised by psychoanalyst Charles Fisher of Mt. Sinai Hospital in New York. He demonstrated that subliminal images—slides flashed before the viewer for only 1/100th or 1/200th of a second—would make an impression even though they were not consciously perceived. In a number of experiments with patients and physicians, Fisher would flash a slide, ask his subject to draw a picture of what he had seen, and then report his dreams in the morning. Since this predated the advent of EEG awakenings, his yield of dreams was small, but the technique seemed to work. One bedtime stimulus, for example, was a slide showing a vase in lines bold enough to be seen by a person with normal vision; however, in very faint outline there was a swastika emblazoned on the vase. The slide was flashed for a split second, only once. In the morning one young man remembered a dream that began, "I was in a totalitarian prison camp . . ."

P. W. Wood at the University of North Carolina has, in a sense, done the opposite. Instead of supplying a small and localized stimulus, he has removed stimulation by taking over the entire daytime environment of his subjects. His five volunteers were young college graduates who spent five nights in the laboratory. Their second day was lived out in total isolation, perhaps simulating the environment of monotony and loneliness of the aging invalid, prisoner, or future man in space. Wood found that people spent 60 percent more time in REM dreaming after isolation. Although their dreams were longer they exhibited less rapid eye movement than usual, hinting that they might be less intense. The day of experimental isolation was inactive, and the subsequent dreams were inactive. On the other hand, the dreams suggested a kind of wish fulfillment, for they were very sociable, dreams of groups standing around talking, as if to compensate for the previous day empty of human companionship.

The impact of the environment on dreams has been witnessed repeatedly in laboratories, where subjects have reported long dreams about the laboratory and experimenters. Donald Goodenough heard a dramatic instance of a laboratory dream that the subject, when awakened, did not recall. He had been sitting in the control room when the sleeping subject suddenly began to broadcast an unusually coherent dream conversation. The tape recorder was turned on as the man proceeded to answer standardized questions of a post-dream interview: "Quiet? Uh, no. Jittery? No, I wasn't jittery. Placid? No, I wouldn't say so. . . ." It was a replica of a conversation held on many occasions with Dr. Goodenough following awakening from a dream. Dreams of the laboratory are not always such literal translations of the actual procedures as this one appeared to have been.

David Foulkes and Allan Rechtschaffen examined the effects of two bedtime television programs on a number of subjects and found that the different effects of the two films could be seen in the qualities of the subsequent dreams, rather than a mimicking of events. Their procedure may interest parents, who have watched children spend a transfixed hour before the television screen, watching the favorite bedtime program of monsters or crime or conspiracy. The films used in the laboratory were network shows, one a violent Western with some vicious scenes of brutality, the other a romantic comedy about a female con artist. Actual elements from the two programs were rarely apparent in the dream content, but the team found that the dream narratives differed in a striking fashion. Dreams following the violent Western were more vivid, imaginative, more intense than the dreams following the comedy.

More perceptible effects are being obtained by Herman Witkin, Donald Goodenough, and a sizable research team at Downstate Medical Center in Brooklyn. The emphasis of this mammoth project differs from the television studies. Since dreams do not simply mirror reality, researchers are looking beneath the surface to see how a person's dreams transfigure his experience, and how people cope with stress in dreams. This group has collected a number of bedtime films, powerful enough to affect the strongest stomach. The usual television fare, despite its violence, seems to make little impression on sophisticated viewers. The films seen by volunteers in this study may be neutral travelogues on some occasions, but on others they may be close-ups of gruesome automobile accidents, a traffic safety polemic prepared by highway police. Goodenough has remarked on this film, "I went out the next day and bought safety belts and new tires for my car." There have been medical training films, among them one showing the birth of a baby in detail. Another is a famous anthropological documentary taken among Australian aborigines as they perform, in the desert dirt with sharpened stones, a painful rite of subincision on young boys.

After seeing these stress films the subjects have seemed to take longer to fall asleep and often begin dreaming earlier than usual. On these nights, the experimenter more frequently hears when he awakens his subject from a rapid-eye-movement period, "I was dreaming—but I can't remember anything." If this memory failure is what we mean by repression, the forgetting of the unpleasant, the stress films appear to encourage it. The analysis of these dreams is being attacked for effects than can be summarized numerically and also by a psychological evaluation. Psychoanalyst Helen B. Lewis has been collaborating with psychologist Witkin to assess the emotionality of the dreams and the fashion by which they incorporate, transmute, and restructure elements from the films. Internist Arthur Shapiro has been following the physiological patterns that accompany the dreams. The difficulty in the project can be illustrated by the fact that the traffic film that caused Goodenough to go out and buy safety belts and tires nevertheless failed to make any straightforward appearance in the dreams of subjects who had seen it. This was not to say that the film made no impact, for by other criteria the dream narratives reveal qualitative reactions hinting that the stress films have a huge wallop.

Unlike the volunteers of many sleep studies, the Downstate subjects come from all walks of life. There have been factory workers, bakers, subway dispatchers, telephone engineers, airline mechanics, students, writers, and other professionals. Quite a few have been night workers who report to the laboratory after leaving the job. This makes the dream laboratory on top of the large modern hospital a 24-hour operation. The films are projected for the volunteer while he is comfortably settled in bed, already decorated with electrodes. Then the lights go out, and he will be awakened from each REM period. After he has described his dream over the intercom system, a slide will be projected onto the wall before his bed. It is a chart of adverbs and adjectives, a matrix he can follow in defining the emotions he felt during his dream. Did it make him feel jittery, placid, kindly or fearful? The experimenter, checking off the responses to this chart, will now be able to categorize some of the overt reactions. How does this matrix of feelings change as the night progresses? How do the dream feelings compare with those evoked by the film? Some people have persistently shown the emotions inspired by the film even though their seemingly innocuous dreams bore no obvious relationship to the movie they had seen. The categories of dream feelings as they are graphed over many laboratory nights may reveal some but not all of the film's impact.

The same film means different things to each subject. In morning discussions, one man puzzles about the anthropological film, wondering what those natives were doing. Another is mainly horrified by the filth and unsanitary surgical conditions. Another emphasizes the excruciating pain and marvels that the initiates could dance around after surgery with none of the usual marks of suffering. In his fourth REM period one man dreams:

> "I'm back to that native business again. . . . Let me see, what the heck was I doing? I guess it was on the outskirts of a uh native village. I, uh, was supposed to go someplace with the chief I guess. . . ."

Such explicit references are rare. Another man dreams of a crash and a smoky form like a turtle arising from it. Could this reflect the grayed quality of the old film and the shape of the kneeling men on whose backs the boy initiate lies during surgery? After seeing the birth film, with its close-ups of the baby's bloody expulsion from the womb, a young man dreams of a volcano erupting and red-hot lava pouring down its sides. Only the morning interviews and subsequent biographical interviews begin to show that moments on the film struck off reverberations, and however innocuous the dream, the echoes often travel as in a long tunnel, back to some intense childhood associations.

To an extent that is frequently overlooked in theories of dream interpretation, Witkin and Lewis are finding that people transfigure the films and reality in a characteristic and personal style. One young man, for instance, who consistently reversed reality in dreams, remarked on the bloody gloves of the obstetrician in the birth film—and then proceeded to dream of girls in a park in dim light. The girls all wore long white gloves, and one might say the dream had cleaned up the mess. In a study of the dreams at sleep onset, in which subjects were asked to keep talking after the film until they were asleep, some people exhibited an unusual incorporation from the films and also open reveries about the laboratory and experimenters. These are people who depend heavily upon their surroundings for self-definition. Witkin and Lewis have used a number of tests. If placed in a tilted room and told to straighten his body, will the subject line up with the tilted room or with gravity? People who line up with the tilt of the room and adjust to their surroundings on analogous tests seem more prone than others to incorporate the films into their reveries. Whether or not dreams express instincts and gratify wishes, the individual has a characteristic manner of handling wishes and instincts in dreams as in life. Too quick a generalization about a dreamer's symbols may overlook important meanings. Following the subincision film, for instance, one might expect that dreams of castration and apprehension would be frequent. One man dreamed that he was abducted by gangsters in a car and was going to be exterminated. To him, however, the word "exterminate" had a special meaning. He had commented about the film that it appeared to be a circumcision but the natives did not look Jewish. In his dream recollection he was thinking about the extermination of the Jews. Thus the stress film seems to act like a fuse, igniting in different individuals diverse trains of association.

The dream, like an iceberg, shows on the surface only the barest glimmer of the reality that preceded it. Below lie most of the meanings, and it is clear that the correlation between dream symbol and real events and feelings is a subtle one. If one is inclined to generalize too easily about the meanings of symbols, an individual's very special association adds another hue. Even when the laboratory reality is a truly gruesome film, the experimenters are aware that its impact may be muted by many hidden variables. A man may come to the laboratory after an argument with his boss or his wife. Sifting out and sorting these various influences cannot be accomplished quickly. Laboratory studies of dream content are very young, and while they have suggested modifications of our traditional interpretations, they have not yet contributed a new theory.

Years before the dream hunters had electronic equipment or any means of predictably awakening people in dreams, Calvin Hall founded the Institute for Dream Research in Miami, Florida. He was asking very similar questions about the nature of dreams, and the rules they employ to represent the reality of the dreamer, but he used a very different method. He went about his assay in a manner similar to that of the sociologist, polling opinions and surveying population behaviors. By amassing a staggering number of dream reports, and assaying them statistically, Hall was able to see that certain kinds of dream content typified certain groups of people. Among the 30,000 dream reports in his files, about 5,000 were collected from other cultures, Nigerians, Mexicans, Peruvians, from citizens in other countries and members of tribes. Hall and his associates would select items that recurred in dreams and classify them, the dramatis personae, the settings, objects, predominant emotions. How frequently did particular events occur in the voluntarily remembered dreams of a large group? In 7,000 dreams they discerned a difference between dreams of men and women. Men tended to dream about men generally, but women dreamed about equally of men and women. A thousand dreams from college students, when put to analysis, suggested that young adults are frequently fearful. In about two out of five there were sequences of fear, often of being pursued. A similar assay implied that every dream of good luck was counterbalanced by seven dreams of misfortune, and that the dreamer more often felt himself a victim of circumstance than a beneficiary.

The natural language of the brain is often said to be symbolic, and it need not abide by the artificial logic by which we are educated as we mature. If dreams speak our hearts in a symbolic language, are some symbols universal to all humankind? Are some cultural symbols identifiable throughout a nation? Do these symbols really mean the same things in the dreams of different people? Freud revolutionized our attitudes toward dreams by emphasizing that they had symbolic meaning, that they were communications to ourselves.

The quests of the last decade in dream laboratories seem to confirm that dreams must be as rich in language and meaning as everyday life and behavior. Their contents reflect influence from multifarious sources, and on close inspection may eventually prove diagnostic. Thomas Detre of Yale Medical School, in exploring the relationship between sleep disturbances and mental illness, has the impression that we may find characteristic trends in dreams. Very depressed people who are entering a suicidal stage, for instance, report peculiar nightmares that are often uniquely empty of people and actions, dreams of natural scenes, a desolate rocky beach, a mountain crest, a plateau conveying an ominous and isolated sensation. Certain recurrent nightmares among children have been suggestive of temporal lobe abnormalities.

A child's nightmare differs in its force from an adult's. Sometimes, without ever awakening, a terrified youngster will continue screaming for his mother although seated on her lap and embraced. Dreams are not mere figments of imagination to children. Young children have eidetic imagery, and can count the buttons on a remembered shirt. Dreams have a similarly direct quality. While attempting to study his son's dreaming, Joe Kamiya got the boy to sleep in his laboratory at Langley Porter Neuropsychiatric Institute in San Francisco. He would awaken the child after some minutes of REM activity and ask if he had been dreaming. The boy invariably answered, "No." However, when his father rephrased the question and asked, "What were you doing just now?" the child would say, "Oh, I was playing with a tire out on the back porch. . . ."

At what point in life do dreams begin? The strong physiological markers of the REM cycle have been detected in infants ten weeks premature, occupying about 80 percent of sleep. Studies of Arthur Parmelee and his associates at UCLA have been adding to the evidence that this percentage shows a predictable decline. Indeed, the rate of decline has been thought to be a possible sign of brain maturation, suggesting that infant sleep patterns may provide an index of normal or abnormal development at a time when the infant does little but sleep, and there is not much other behavior to evaluate. By about two years, the vigorous sucking, kicking and waving of fists has subsided, and the REM phase has dropped to 30 percent or less of the child's sleep time. It declines to about 20 to 24 percent during the next few years and throughout early adulthood, appearing to decline somewhat after age forty-five, and dropping until in some aged persons REM sleep occupies only 13 percent of sleep time. Infant animals also show an enormous proportion of REM sleep that begins to diminish soon after birth. Judging from the work of Parmelee and others, this REM state evolves in the womb. Is the infant in the womb dreaming as he sucks his thumb and gives his mother perceptible kicks?

The starting age of dreaming depends in part upon our definition of dreams. Even in the womb there is presumably sensation. A newborn infant feels changes in temperature, the satisfaction of hunger, the discomfort of cramped position, the solace of being held or rocked. An infant's nightmare might be the diffuse memory of hungrily sucking while being held uncomfortably, the frustration of an instinctive need. Visual dreams would not seem likely in the womb or for some time after birth, but the congenitally blind dream without vision. The blind and deaf, who live in a changeless dark silence, also dream. One such patient at Albert Einstein Hospital in New York had never heard of the concept of a dream when questioned by an interpreter, but she recalled that a pet bird had died and weeks later she awakened in inconsolable sorrow having re-experienced the shock of reaching into the bird's cage and finding his lifeless body.

Helen Keller, who was deprived of sight, hearing, and smell by an attack of scarlet fever before she was two years old, managed to learn through language to replace this sensory world. She wrote a great deal about her dreams, commenting that she dreamed little before Miss Annie Sullivan became her tutor. Her dreams had been purely physical, inchoate, instinctive.

> . . . something was always falling suddenly and heavily, and at times my nurse seemed to punish me for my unkind treatment of her in the daytime. . . . I would awake with a start or struggle, frantically to escape my tormentor. I was very fond of bananas and one night I dreamed I found a long string of them . . . all peeled and deliciously ripe, and all I had to do was stand under the string and eat. . . .

Later she was able to see, in her dreams, with her mind alone.

> Once in a dream I held in my hand a pearl. I have no memory-vision of a real pearl. The one I saw in my dream must, therefore, have been a creation of my imagination. It was a smooth, exquisitely moulded crystal . . . dew and fire, the velvety green of moss, the soft whiteness of lilies. . . .

Dreams may start before speech or clear vision. For some period in the womb and early infancy the REM state appears to provide the baby's most active exercise in what are to become the motions of survival—sucking, kicking, erections. This may be a biological exercise required to establish the expression of instinctual drives, helping the infant to develop sucking strength, genital sensation, muscular reflexes, the first exercise of his apparatus for survival. His memories of sensation may, indeed, recur in sleep. From the point of view of the analyst, as Charles Fisher has aptly stated, this activity hardly seems to constitute dreaming until outside influences come to bear upon the evolving personality. At some unspecified day in infancy, sensory perception is sufficiently clear so that impressions from outside can begin to generate coherent internal experience. The rudiments of diffuse dreaming, sensory change, may begin back in the dark waters of the womb, but this is hardly what most of us call dreaming.

The early REM activity of the infant, the movements, the grimaces, the erections, are the first manifestations of the instinctive behavior around which childhood education centers. The first disciplines of the infant and child focus upon the control of instincts. Niceties of civilization demand that adults not urinate whenever and wherever they feel the urge, not instantly satisfy hunger, and the punishment for directly following sexual impulses is usually severe. These are the basic impulses that Freud saw emerging in dream forms. Surely, drive centers would seem to be somewhat charged during REM intervals, and it is interesting that humans and animals deprived of REM sleep for long periods begin to show a loss of waking control over their impulses. Dreams, on the other hand, do not often reflect these impulses straightforwardly, and this fact led Freud and dream researchers since his time to examine the symbolic language of the sleeping mind.

Raul Hernandez-Peón has represented the Freudian theory of dreams as symbolic release of repressed wishes and instincts in the language of neurophysiology, suggesting that we may someday see anatomical reasons why the state of sleep represses thoughts and the punished wishes of childhood. Perhaps, again, viewing our growing library of dreams, we may begin to see in what percentage of our dreams these points of theory hold. Not all dreams protect sleep, or fulfill wishes, or exhibit a covert form of repressed behavior. Sometimes dreams seem to follow a sequence and develop a theme. Sometimes memory fails. Dream researchers are not seeking a single formula to describe all dreams, and indeed in the laboratory they must analyze far more than merely dreams. The experimenter at the controls hears the voice on the intercom system, and he detects a style in the yawns, the pauses, sudden inflections, reticences, the timbre of the speaking voice. Several nights of dream recollections amplify the subject's personal qualities. Interviews begin to relate dream fragments to his life and feelings. The experimenter sees him dressed and awake, and also sleepily arising in the morning. As in the psychiatric clinic or analyst's office, the dream itself is but the first strand in a web of associations and memories gravitating about certain points. The meaning lies within the person, and all that he has become in the history that has molded him, and which he bears within his brain.

XI

UNCONSCIOUS LEARNING

EVERY week the newspapers report small and sometimes spurious accounts of things that are not supposed to happen—human marvels. In the 1920's, many Yogis submitted themselves to live burials in earth, with or without coffins. There was a sleepless saint in a northeast province of India said to have lived 25 years in a cave in a continuous state of ecstatic contemplation. In the 1930's there was word of a motherly old woman in a Bengal jungle who rarely slept and never ate. More recently a young physicist in Massachusetts was said to be sending Morse code messages with his brain waves. A San Francisco doctor reported that deeply anesthetized surgical patients were later repeating the conversations their surgeons had held over them in the operating room while they were supposedly unconscious. An Arkansas psychologist was visited by a patient who could, on demand, cause his hands to pour out sweat. Singular feats of bodily control and mental discipline have marked certain individuals as almost superhuman, throughout history. They could ignore pain, sleep on demand, suffer scarification or danger in the manner of heroes. Their faculties have been studied to some extent, and they reveal what kinds of minds we are blessed with and what we can learn to make them do.

Yogi feats were studied by two doctors in India. They found

one man who could perspire from the forehead on command. He had spent cold winters in Himalayan caves, alone, unclad, seated on an animal skin meditating, and he had learned to "think hot," raising his skin temperature and heart rate, which he did for the scientists. While wearing instruments, Yogis would stop their hearts. In fact they contracted certain muscles, decreasing blood flow into the heart and making its pulse almost imperceptible, and lowering blood pressure. Yogi training involves intensive exercise in controlled breathing, and during deliberate relaxation they would meditate cross-legged, showing an alpha rhythm like that of the relaxed person before sleep. N. N. Das and H. Gastaut watched the brain waves of Yogis who maintained perfect immobility for hours. As they approached the state of ecstasy or enlightenment, their alpha rhythms became transformed into a pattern resembling REM sleep or intense waking concentration. They were insensible to distraction, pale, immobile, with profound muscular relaxation like that of the REM dreamer. The rigorous Yogi discipline over breathing, posture, and thought may result in a meditation state that performs some of the functions usually required of sleep.

Zen Buddhists also attain enlightenment by long and disciplined meditations, in a sitting position known as the lotus, performed with eyes fixed on a point on the floor. They also practice rhythmic breathing to attain an indistractible inner state, and have been known to meditate for hours at a time, and for days in a row to have no sleep. The Zen meditator may look asleep, although in fact he is balanced delicately between instant alertness and relaxed serenity. According to a Japanese EEG study, the Zen meditator is also in a sustained state of alpha rhythm. The brain waves make an even train of about 9 to 12 per second. It is a peculiar state, for it occurs in relaxation before sleep, occasionally in sleep on the threshold of waking—and intermittently during waking—yet it seems to signify neither active waking, nor sleep.

Several years ago Joe Kamiya at Langley Porter Neuropsychiatric Institute in San Francisco began a program of studies to discover whether ordinary people could "feel" the alpha state and control it. While studying dreams he had noticed that volunteers were notoriously inept at describing their internal sensations and experiences. Medical doctors are plagued by patients' inability to describe and localize symptoms. Internal experience is not readily shared. The ability to communicate feelings develops slowly. Indeed, most people never learn to discriminate between levels of consciousness and English does not have a vocabulary to describe them. People enter alpha states many times a day, before drowsing off to sleep, in moments of rest—yet few people could identify the sensation.

As naïve volunteers in the laboratory learned to identify their alpha rhythm, the experimenter saw a process analogous to watching a child who first learns to point to his tummy when it hurts, instead of merely crying, and finally uses words to describe the pain. The subjects—nurses, students, housewives, and technicians—lay in the laboratory bedroom, with eyes closed. Sporadically they heard a bell ring. All they had to do was to guess whether it rang for the alpha state or for other levels of consciousness. Kamiya, who was watching their EEG record, immediately announced whether they were right or wrong. They would then rest for a spell until the bell rang again. After several sessions they were guessing correctly most of the time. To the slight incredulity of Kamiya, one of them very rapidly became 100 percent accurate.

The next instruction was more subtle. This time the volunteer was to sense his own condition and speak up. Without any bell, he was to say "yes" when he was in alpha, and "no" when he was not. Again the volunteers were astonishingly accurate. The experimenters wondered if their subjects had somehow learned how to control the alpha rhythm. They asked the subject to turn on his alpha waves when the bell rang once, and turn them off when the bell rang twice. The results left no doubt that the volunteers had learned control.

An electrical filter was attached to the EEG machine, in a further step. It was set to the individual's particular alpha-wave frequency, and the moment alpha began, a switch would flip automatically to ring a bell. The subject's brain-wave rhythm now controlled the bell, and he was asked, "Would you please keep that bell from ringing." The subjects did: they suppressed the brain waves.

None of these people had ever "felt" this state before. They did not even have a name for it. How did they learn to sense a background rhythm in the brain and control it? When asked, some volunteers said that alpha was a pleasant, serene feeling, a condition empty of visual imagery. When they wanted to turn it off they imagined visual things, seeing a headline, or a face. Interestingly enough, the volunteers said it took effort to drive away the alpha state. Once they learned to sustain it they began ignoring outside distractions, and hardly noticed the very bell they were instructed to silence. Not every subject became adept to the same degree, but Kamiya was satisfied that all could attain a high level of skill with a little more practice. Some subjects in a later study even learned to control the frequency of their alpha rhythm. The electroencephalograph, ordinarily an instrument of detection, had been used successfully for teaching, by giving feedback. In a few sessions, volunteers had learned to identify and control an ineluctable state that often takes years of training, according to Zen Buddhist reports.

The meaning of this peculiar state is unknown, yet people generally agree about its vacant, pleasurable serenity. The Zen dévot enters a meditation alpha state in order to awaken inner perception in a manner that can be destroyed by intellectual effort or logic. Kamiya's subjects found they could suppress the alpha rhythm by attempting to do mental arithmetic, although a few people have been known to do correct computation while maintaining alpha. In Zen practice, sustained meditation should finally lead to an experience of enlightenment, a union with the unconscious, or as some have described it, an illumination of one's physical self in unity with all nature. It is said to resemble the paradise of children, inspiring wonder at each detail of nature, the fragile sensation of an eyeblink, the veil of sunlight on a leaf.

It is a state that may have therapeutic properties, and might benefit tense people with psychosomatic complaints, if they could learn to induce this serenity at will. Like Yogic meditation, it appears to be restful. An American housewife who meditated for five days without sleep at a Zen retreat was closely observed by a psychiatrist for effects of sleep loss. She showed none of the visual distortions or confusions that might normally occur after five days without sleep. If anything, she was refreshed.

Another group of studies suggests additional factors that seem to influence control over the alpha state. As Kamiya pursued his studies of purposeful introspection, a theoretical physicist in Bedford, Massachusetts, was studying alpha waves for a different reason. Edmond Dewan of the Air Force Cambridge Research Laboratories was studying the mathematical properties of brainwave oscillations, and the alpha rhythm seemed a good one to analyze. First he had to produce a sample and sustain it.

Dewan rigged up a filter for his own alpha frequency which sounded a buzzer whenever the alpha appeared. Soon, like many others before him, he found that he could turn alpha on and off at will. He could even send Morse code messages, if he took his time. He allowed about 40 seconds for each letter, sending alpha bursts as dots, and pauses between as dashes. It was slow, but the messages were perfect. He controlled his alpha rhythm as others had, inducing it by closing his eyes and avoiding mental imagery, and opening his eyes to shut it off. The reliability of his control caused him to ask how he facilitated a continuous alpha rhythm. Dewan kept asking himself how he performed this feat. He noticed that his alpha increased, for the buzzer sounded a great deal, whenever he rolled his eyes upward beneath the closed lids. "I don't understand the connection," he said, "but maybe with my eyes turned up I relax more."

In England, meanwhile, another alpha experiment was pointing to a relationship between eye position and the background rhythm of the brain. T. Mulholland and C. R. Evans also found that the alpha state could be enhanced by rolling the eyes upward. The alpha was enhanced whether the eyes were open or closed, whether the person had seen a uniform or patterned image. Traditionally, it has been believed that visual imagery was not consonant with an alpha state. Mulholland and Evans flashed a bright image before the eyes of their volunteers. The flash causes an afterimage that lingers for about 30 seconds after the eyes are closed. Now, with this afterimage, their subjects closed their eyes and rolled them upward—and there was alpha rhythm. Perhaps muscle movements of the eyes and subtle contractions of the lenses do alter the background rhythm of the cerebral cortex. It has been said that the eyes are the windows to the soul, reflecting intense feeling and attention, absorbing information more rapidly than any other sense organ, and perhaps more than that. We may use them, quite unconsciously, to alter the rhythm and the attentiveness of our highest brain centers.

Throughout our waking lives we continuously send and receive information according to stringent laws of which we are totally unaware. We are not even aware of the complexity of our motor system, but stand, walk, sit, without knowing which of our 639 muscles to tense and which to relax. Most of us are unable to control our eye movements consciously, and could not describe our eye movements to another person. Yet the eyes of an attentive person are moving incessantly, as are the eyes of the REM dreamer, similarly darting in sudden bursts. A number of scientists feel that the motor system of the eyes may help to regulate attention. When a person says that he has used mental powers to propel himself into an alpha state, or a trance, he may be saying that he has adopted a subtle frame of mind and also performed a delicate manipulation of muscles without conscious awareness. Undoubtedly, some people will be disappointed if we discover that special effects of concentration and willpower are in part a subtle command of muscular controls.

For practical purposes it is a happy prospect. Once precise muscular movements are defined they can be taught. They may offer cues helping people to induce alpha states in moments of tension and perhaps to aid them in falling asleep.

Studies of alpha rhythms may supply pieces in a very important puzzle, the relationship between the eyes and the fundamental background rhythms of the brain. Sleep exhibits a combination of these rhythms and their effects. Do Yogi and Zen practitioners tolerate sleep loss because they manage to sustain themselves in states we would include as a portion of sleep? From dream studies performed in Philadelphia there are new hints about the relation between eye movements and alpha rhythms during sleep. Eugene Aserinsky of Jefferson Medical College has carefully analyzed the brain waves that occur during dream intervals at moments of rapid eye movements. During these eye-movement bursts, he has found bursts of alpha rhythm. The dreamer is, in some sense, on the verge of waking. Congenitally blind people exhibit lesser eye movements during REM sleep. Interestingly enough, the Russians have noticed that blind people usually exhibit an alpha rhythm that is poor and hard to detect, although deaf people show clear alpha. Animals can be deprived of many sensory organs and portions of the nervous system without showing marked changes in their EEG rhythms, but when the visual system is destroyed the background rhythms of the brain are clearly altered. It would seem that the eyes, and their stimulation to the brain, may perform a regulation of cortical excitement, enhancing or diminishing the rhythms of alertness. The eyes do this more or less at our command. If our eyes could be useful instruments for controlling relaxation or arousal and manipulating events along the nerve tributaries to our bodies, we might learn to exert such controls knowingly by learning what muscles we now unconsciously use.

As people learn to control mental and emotional forces, by whatever tricks, they will also regulate many bodily functions. Anybody can alter his heart rate by thinking a truly alarming thought. The heart will begin to race. People have learned to decrease blood pressure without Yoga discipline. A portion of the nervous system, often said to lie beyond voluntary control, is sovereign over these many vital functions. Perhaps psychosomatic ailments, thought to be caused by malfunction in this part of the nervous system, partly result from an improper if unconscious education. This could happen if brain and body overreact during an event, and continue to overreact so that anything associated with the original feelings and events produces the same intestinal contractions, or increases in blood pressure. An individual may inherit his particular tendency to react in the intestines and develop ulcers, but he has also received physiological education from infancy onward, quite without awareness. Our unconscious education is random, and many scientists have asked whether we can unravel the steps and reverse the training.

For about 40-odd years Soviet scientists have been exploring the way this training might occur, under the name of interoceptive conditioning. They have found, for instance, that a prickle in the lining of the stomach may cause blood vessels in the finger to constrict. If a light is flashed at the time of the prickle, the light soon has the same effect on the blood vessels. By warming the stomach through a swallowed balloon each time a blue light flashed, the finger blood vessels could be made to dilate if the experimenter merely said, "I'm flashing on a blue light." Electric shock would make a person's blood coagulate more rapidly than usual, and soon coagulation would speed up if the researcher said, "I'm going to shock you. It's going to hurt." When the external signal did not always match in the same way with the internal stimulus, people sometimes showed an oscillation in their blood vessels that might be called vascular neurosis. In the course of our lifelong body education, such confusions undoubtedly do happen, perhaps becoming ingrained in the habits of our body parts without our awareness. We learn to anticipate pain, perhaps not very rationally, and our bodies, our very blood, react with a multitude of changes. One may begin to see, in this pattern, how anxiety could cause constipation, and how fear might affect the cardiovascular system.

Some of the Soviet experiments indicate that the body habits grow slowly but, even when trained in the laboratory, they are hard to reverse. A few experiments have used feedback to reverse the normal reaction. When persons could prevent a shock by showing blood vessel dilation instead of constriction, and especially when they could watch the recordings of their physical reactions, they quickly caught on and showed dilation in their arms. Whether they did this by thinking, changes in breathing, or slight muscular action does not matter. They learned to reverse the normal reaction to apprehension of shock. By a similar feedback method, it is said that some ulcer patients in Russia have learned to reduce gastric secretion. Systematic research of this kind might enable us to control some of the damaging habits we unconsciously learn, by making us aware of the way in which our insides react to external events. The essence of this new training is feedback. Soviet cosmonauts, it is said, may see how their blood pressure behaved during a parachute jump from recordings, and in simulated jumps under hypnosis be told to reduce heart rate and blood pressure. It seems likely that people can be taught to control pain, anger, fear and other emotions by learning what happens inside them. Feedback is a powerful teacher. It can guide us into the dark of our own unconsciousness. This method has even taught some people what it is they are doing at night when they sleep.

Several night nurses in New York City were amazed to discover that they could distinguish one phase of sleep from another—while asleep. In 1963, Judith and John Antrobus, working with Charles Fisher, determined to find out whether ordinary people could sense the difference between dreaming and nondreaming sleep. Volunteers slept with a microswitch taped to their forefinger so that a pressure from the finger would close the circuit and make a signal. They were instructed to press the switch twice when dreaming, and five times when asleep without dreams. (On some trials the number of presses were reversed and five signals meant dreaming, a precaution to rule out accidental finger twitches that might be mistaken for signals.)

The volunteers did better at signaling they were dreaming than at notifying the outside world when they were in a deep oblivion. One girl remarked she had been dreaming of pressing the switch, and thought she had failed to signal although she had given three signals that night. Another woke up saying she had dreamed she was an Indian sending smoke signals all night. Judging from the brain-wave record, signaling did not interfere with dreaming. One girl summed up the difficulty of signaling in other sleep: "Nondreaming is nothing—there are no landmarks—nothing to notice." This venture did not divulge how expertly people might discriminate between phases of sleep, yet it hinted strongly that people can become aware of the different feelings of their sleep, while asleep.

Judith Antrobus decided to try awakening subjects and giving them feedback. She and her husband were living in the Riverside Drive apartment once occupied by Dement, which had its own fully equipped sleep laboratory in an anteroom. The atmosphere was homey. The family cat would wander through, a baby was in evidence and another on the way, lending as domestic an aura as any laboratory might capture. Three night nurses came here, when they got off duty. They were invariably exhausted, and had no trouble falling asleep. However, they showed the characteristically disturbed sleep of night workers and occasionally awakened. The payment, $15 a session, compensated for the prospect of being awakened in their night. One Philippine girl happened to be a sensitive, engaging, and ideal subject. Her hospital duty began at midnight, and lasted until 8 A.M. She would eat breakfast, change clothes and then report to the laboratory high over the Hudson River.

She was told that she would be awakened from two kinds of sleep—"A" sleep (which was a REM period) and "B" sleep (which was Stage II, light, spindling sleep). When awakened she was asked to guess: "What type of sleep were you in?" She was told whether she was right or wrong and immediately allowed to fall back asleep. None of the volunteers believed that there were really two distinct kinds of sleep, and even if there were, refused to imagine they could tell them apart. The one nurse who did learn to discriminate perfectly was overwhelmed and perplexed. It was true. There were two kinds of sleep. "I had thought yesterday," she wrote the experimenter, "that it would be hard to distinguish between different types of sleep when one is sleepy . . . but about halfway through . . . I thought there was a pattern being followed." Oddly enough, she described REM sleep as restful and deep, and described Stage II sleep as not very deep. "You are having type A sleep when you have a vivid dream—very clear—like a motion picture . . . a lot of action . . . it takes longer to get out of type A sleep, it lingers." She described type B sleep—Stage II—as restless. One girl called it silent sleep.

Interestingly enough, the three nurses described these stages of sleep very similarly. The difference did not lie in the existence of dreams, for they dreamed in Stage II as well. These dreams were subjectively different in quality, apparently like drowsy fantasy or thought, on the verge of waking. One girl never became adept at discriminating among her phases of sleep, but the nurse from Manila attained a sensitivity that extended beyond the experiment. Occasionally when she awakened, she was aware that she was not in A or B sleep, but yet a third state of consciousness. She was ready to proceed to finer judgments of her sleep, an area of self-learning as uncharted as the bottom of the seas, for which we have no vocabulary, nor absolute definitions on the EEG. In other laboratories some subjects have learned to wake up spontaneously after REM intervals and record their dreams. Although these people usually explain their abilities by mentioning the quality of dreams, and sense of distance and relaxation, they do not mention any of the dramatic physical changes that might serve as cues. Aserinsky's observation that alpha waves accompany the rapid eye movements may, in fact, provide one clue. People who awaken themselves from dreams may learn to seize the right moment, when they have come into an alpha burst and near the threshold of waking. How far can we go? Using the EEG or physical cues, it seems possible that a person could become acquainted with the texture of his own nights, and imagination. An education in nighttime communication with the self has only begun.

In a casual experiment on dream work in the 1950's, William Dement gave two groups of adults a problem to consider for fifteen minutes before going to sleep. He asked them to record their dreams and think about the problem for no more than 15 minutes on arising. The problem itself has a decidedly frustrating elusiveness for adults although young children often solve it within two or three minutes. Very simply, it says: "The letters O,T,T,F,F,S,S* are the first letters of words in a well-known series. Once you add the next letter of the series correctly, you can add an infinite number of letters." Most of the people who reported dreaming at all had, in some way, dreamed about the problem. A few had, indeed, found the answer to the problem in their dreams but failed to recognize it.

Within the vagaries of an intricate mind a wealth of experience and productive thought may be buried in sleep. Many gifted people have solved problems during sleep. John von Neumann, a great mathematician and father of modern computers often wrote theorems in his sleep. Neurophysiologist Warren McCulloch of MIT often solves in sleep problems that evade him by day, and some of these appear as visualizations of great complexity—such as a 6-dimensional Birkoff lattice made of one-ohm resistors. As a young man McCulloch witnessed a dramatic episode of sleep work in a young cousin who visited him at Nantucket Island on a vacation. The boy was about twenty, a talented mathematician. Friends at the National Observatory in Washington wrote him a problem, enclosing a complicated set of data, and asking if they had enough information to compute something. If so, would he solve it.

* One, two, three, four, five, six, seven. . . .

He put the letter aside and went on playing chess, and did that for two or three days, sailing during the day and playing chess all evening. We slept next to each other. In the middle of the night he woke me up fumbling about. With his eyes tight shut he lit a candle, took pencil and paper and sat with his eyes shut and wrote down the solution. Mind you, he had not looked at the data in three days. He wrote the numerical answer first, then the arithmetic leading to that kind of answer, then the general method of solving this kind of problem. He blew out the candle and went to bed without opening his eyes. I got up, looked at what he had done, and hid the paper under the blotter.

Three days later he told me he had the funniest feeling that he solved that problem, but he was unable to recall anything bearing on it. By the end of the fifth day he was fairly sure he had a solution. At that time I asked him to look under the blotter.

To McCulloch this incident seemed to have the earmarks of a somnambulistic trance. Although there were no brain wave recordings to notarize the stage of sleep, the event suggested a quality of mental activity in sleep transcending anything yet demonstrated in the laboratory. On the other hand, it also demonstrated the kind of memory failure that commonly attends sleep events. Gregory Portnoff and his associates at Downstate Medical Center in Brooklyn have awakened volunteers and presented them with words. The volunteers remembered nothing in the morning unless they had been kept awake for quite a long time. However, if they were allowed to slip back into sleep immediately, it appeared to prevent any memory of the word. One can only speculate that some gifted people are so intensely motivated to solve their unsolved problems that they are attuned to relevant thoughts during sleep so that they can transcribe them, or actually awaken for a long period. The cues they employ may indeed be discovered in the laboratory, and even taught by a feedback technique. An individual can benefit from freer access to his own mind and control over his sleep behavior. There are, moreover, practical reasons for discovering what man can do in his sleep. Could he use the time to learn, taking courses? Could he manage to "keep his ear open" on a job?

In more than a dozen laboratory studies volunteers have shown that they could communicate with the outside world while asleep by pressing a switch. They have told experimenters, by signaling, when they began dreaming. They have signaled whenever a particular tone sounded. They have listened to tape-recorded numbers during dreams, and repeated them accurately when awakened ten seconds later. The subjects were by no means alike in their performance, nor perfect, but the effects of training were particularly noticeable during REM sleep. During slow-wave sleep, the deep quiescence of Stages III and IV, people often claimed they heard no signal. Laboratory studies may not have disclosed a fraction of our true capacities yet. It is difficult to whip up enthusiasm for discriminating between two tones all night, and experimenters can only pay small sums for correct responses. Indeed, they have often been more effective when they threatened the subject with harassments, shocks, flashing lights, fire alarms and noxious noises if they failed to press a switch promptly. Still, people can hear significant things in their sleep and can signal. Friends of Norbert Wiener, the mathematical prodigy, used to say that he listened better in sleep than waking. When awake, he was too busy thinking to hear anyone else. He was famous among his scientific colleagues and students for dropping off to sleep in the midst of meetings. "He'd be snoring. He'd snore in your face as you talked, but if you made a mistake he would wake up and correct you." It was, in a way, a compliment to hear Wiener snoring, for it intimated that his mind was absorbing all that was spoken.

Long before we had begun exploring the various properties of the stages of sleep, phenomenal behavior, like Wiener's snoring attention, suggested that man should be able to learn during sleep. In the United States sleep-teaching companies have become a multimillion-dollar business since 1947, when the first venturesome concern offered a pillow-speaker and built-in time clock to play recorded courses at the beginning and end of the purchaser's night of sleep. There are now sleep-teaching offices in almost every major city, promising all kinds of effortless education and personality improvement—anything from French or engineering to subliminal psychotherapy to overcome nail-biting, smoking, or to improve salesmanship, sharpen memory, and cure insomnia. In Kiev, USSR, the Radiotechnical Engineering School has a dormitory classroom where sleeping students are said to be learning English. The glowing stories of witnesses and participants include the so-called scientific rationale for the success of the method.

Sleep learning is a clouded issue. In the mid-1950's two astute young scientists at the Rand Corporation took a close look at the literature and scientific studies that weakly supported claims of improved waking performance after sleep instruction. Charles W. Simon and William Emmons saw room for doubt in the evidence. Perhaps repetition of material during sleep was irrelevant. They ran several EEG studies of their own, and for clarity of definition, said that the person was awake if there was an alpha rhythm on his record. Even using very intelligent volunteers they obtained no evidence that material was recalled if it had been presented during the brain waves of quiet deep sleep. As the alpha rhythm diminished, so did learning, and in the morning the volunteers were no more informed than before. Simon made the important, if overlooked, observation that training may be impossible during deep sleep, yet quite feasible during drowsiness, and many states of consciousness that fall below optimal alertness. We now have some hints that such states may momentarily sprinkle our sleep, albeit very briefly.

A good many rigorous researchers have probed the question: What can we actually learn while asleep? When scientists have taught subjects to discriminate between tones, brain-wave patterns of alertness have appeared after each shock. One might conclude that they were actually learning during these moments of waking. José P. Segundo and his associates at UCLA conditioned cats to flex a paw or miaow in sleep to avoid the shock that accompanied a particular tone of the several played. The cats discriminated among the tones in all phases of sleep, yet whenever the shock tone sounded, their brain waves shifted toward a pattern of alertness. Do we merely apply in sleep what we learn in waking?

In 1965 an Australian scientific team published perhaps the first evidence that simple discrimination might be learned during the slow-wave phase of sleep. The volunteers in the study were given chloralose as a sedative. Like the cats, they were exposed to two tones during sleep, only one of which was accompanied by a shock. Their acquired ability to discriminate between the tones did not seem to stem from a moment of arousal, however, for the EEG showed that they did not even rise up to a lighter sleep when the significant (or shock tone) was played. Nevertheless, when they were later tested during waking, they demonstrated that they knew the shock tone from the neutral tone.

The mystery of possible sleep learning has been deepened by Soviet and American studies. For several years A. Bliznichenko, a linguist and phoneticist at the Institute of Linguistics in the Ukranian Academy of Science, has been studying dormitory classes in English. Translated documents do not tell whether learning actually occurs in sleep although they claim that students with no prior training have learned to speak English in 22 nights, using a vocabulary of 1,000 words. According to Soviet reports, which offer conclusions and case histories rather than data, the nightlong droning of lessons does not impair health or disturb sleep, and several institutes of pedagogy are exploring a combination of subliminal training at night with daytime instruction. It is quite possible that anybody with sufficient ambition and interest could acquire new information just by listening to courses each night as he relaxed and dozed and when he awakened in the morning, and that the sleep interval remains entirely irrelevant to learning. On the other hand, Soviet studies of sleep learning that go back to the 1930's suggest that there is an obscure factor in the ability to learn in sleep far more puzzling than we ever anticipated.

In the 1930's A. M. Svyadoshch found that most people did not perceive speech during sleep, just as most people don't remember what the radio broadcast while they slept. Svyadoshch and his associates trained people to become receptive, coaxing them into a state of self-suggestion resembling autohypnosis. Some people did this more easily than others, and children proved easiest to train because they were already quite suggestible. Soviet experiments on what they call hypnopedia may explain some of the spectacular and unverified successes claimed by sleep-teaching companies. Perhaps a person can indeed learn to speak a little Mandarin Chinese in ten nights—if he happens to possess the peculiar capacities of suggestibility, the capacity to be hypnotized. Soviet children, according to V. N. Kulikov, have been given hypnotic kinds of instructions while asleep, and have learned stories and some Pavlovian psychology during sleep, and have been able to repeat the stories or text information the next day, without knowing where the knowledge came from. They performed quite as well as children who absorbed the same material when awake. None of the theories proposed to explain this odd phenomenon do, in fact, approach any answer, and unfortunately the Soviet studies have made exciting reading without supplying EEGs or a countdown of the data. Nonetheless, it appears that a special group of people who are hypnotically suggestible may be capable of sleep learning.

An American reasearch team at the Institute of the Pennysl-vania General Hospital has been arriving at this conclusion from another direction. Martin Orne, an authority on hypnosis, had been attempting to discover whether relatively unresponsive hypnotic subjects might not become more responsive during sleep. The team compared four highly responsive hypnotic subjects with four whom they considered unresponsive. The volunteers received no hypnotic suggestion before sleep. They settled down, adorned in electrodes, in the laboratory bedroom of the vast wing of the Institute, and the experimenters waited until they were soundly asleep. Then, whenever the brain-wave pattern rose to the irregular configuration of Stage I sleep, the low-voltage pattern of REM dreaming, the experimenter would issue instruction. "Whenever you hear the word 'pillow' your pillow will feel uncomfortable and you will move your pillow." During the deeper stages of sleep a different instruction was spoken: "Whenever you hear the word 'itch' you will scratch your nose."

During these instructions or the subsequent mention of the imperative words unresponsive subjects gave either no reaction whatsoever, or showed signs of waking. The deeply hypnotizable volunteers were strikingly different. If the instruction was spoken during Stage I sleep, they followed the command thereafter without awakening. It was an improbable sight. The experimenter would say: "Itch" and the sleeper would reach up quite as naturally as if his nose itched and scratch it. The experimenter would say "Pillow" and like somebody uncomfortable in sleep, the subject would shift his pillow.

Not only had these hypnotizable people heard and followed instruction, but they remembered the next day. In the morning they were presented with a word association test. "Itch" and "pillow" were inconspicuously slipped into the list. The subjects tended to scratch their noses and mention pillow positions. They seemed unaware of the origins of the associations. More remarkable yet was their behavior on the following night, when they again slept in the laboratory. On this night the instructions were not repeated, but when the cue words were mentioned they continued to scratch their noses and move their pillows. Why does a deeply hypnotizable person follow instructions in sleep? What sets him apart from the "average" person? Does he have some capacity to adjust his mind so that he is unusually receptive?

A deeply suggestible person seems capable of throwing himself into a rapid-eye-movement state when he is instructed to dream. At the University of Pennsylvania Medical School, John Paul Brady and Burton S. Rosner have induced dreaming in subjects by giving them hypnotic suggestion. The people who responded to the suggestions with vivid dreamlike experiences also showed eye movements typical of the REM state. Unhypnotized control subjects who were treated in the same manner often had dreamlike fantasies but never showed the same degree of rapid-eye-movement activity. Ordinarily memory of REM dreams is notably evanescent, and may vanish altogether less than a minute after the rapid eye movements stop, but the hypnotized subjects could be left in a trance for ten minutes after their REMS stopped and they still remembered the dream details clearly when they were awakened. The ability of the responsive hypnotic subject to "switch" on a REM period may suggest that he can manipulate states of consciousness in a manner that most people cannot. Can he voluntarily enter states we think of as involuntary? If we can discover what the suggestible person does with his mind and attention, perhaps the ability can be taught. If a person can acquire a receptivity for sleep instruction by practice—as one can acquire an ear for musical pitch—sleep may become a time for auxiliary education or psychotherapy. People who have taken language lessons under hypnosis describe the experience as uncanny, for the entire world seems to vanish, leaving them relaxed yet totally focused, aware of nothing but the vocabulary of the lesson. We do not yet know what hypnotism is, nor what distinctive physiological signs can identify the trance, but as scientists explore it, they may finally discover the secret mechanisms by which one can enter a relaxed condition in which the mind is fully attentive and focused. Such a state in waking or sleep would seem to be ideal for learning.

An individual's ability to will himself to sleep or manipulate his sleep may also benefit from research in hypnosis. It is very common for a hypnotist to ask his subject to fix his eyes upon an object suspended before him, a light, a windowpane, a lamp shade. Perhaps there is good reason for inducing trance this way. The relaxation experienced by the hypnotic subject may be the result of eye position. It may be related to the fact that raised eyes enhance the calm and relaxed state associated with the alpha rhythm, and this may provide a step in training people to relax themselves and fall asleep at will. Soviet cosmonauts and American astronauts who have cultivated the ability to sleep on command may instinctively use subtle controls over eye muscles and other muscles without being aware of their procedure.

To some extent we have all learned to sleep on command. The command takes the form of lengthy rituals, tooth brushing, bedclothing, good-night kisses, baths. It is the result of training begun in infancy and embellished throughout life. There may be a more direct, more rapid and deliberate method of conditioning sleep. The possibility has been demonstrated with cats. C. D. Clemente and M. B. Sterman at UCLA have used direct electrical stimulation to the forebrain of the cat. The forebrain region may be important in habit formation. A cat might be meandering around his cage when the stimulation began and in a minute or two he would be sound asleep. If given a somewhat higher voltage a cat who was in the process of throttling a live rat would stop his death grip, drop the rat, and retreat drowsily to a corner to curl up and sleep. By pairing a tone to the stimulation, after a few trials the cat could be put to sleep by the sound of the tone itself. The experimental animals did not seem to mind the training, for they would willingly enter the recording cage, and even start purring. The very sound of the tone made them drowsy and they soon exhibited the EEG patterns of sleep. The soporific electric frequency was similar to that of the cat's natural beat during slow-wave sleep. This is interesting, since it has been thought that monotonous stimulation simulating the synchronous brain waves of sleep would be a kind of soporific.

Unfortunately, no comparable instrument for training instant sleep has been developed for people. Electrosleep instruments of the past have not succeeded. Meanwhile, our own diffuse and random lifetime training in sleep induction is too inefficient and inflexible to allow us to sleep on command. A massive survey of family sleep habits has produced no useful clues. However, a study of rats conducted at the University of Florida suggests that the most important factor in determining how long an animal will take to fall asleep is his diurnal periodicity.

People who fall asleep rapidly may be sensitive to changes within their bodies. An individual who notices his decrease in concentration, who feels slightly chilled, and is not coordinating well, may seize the moment and fall asleep readily. Many anecdotal stories indicate that people can feel their optimal times for falling asleep, yet if they ignore the moment and wait too long, they wake up again. Perhaps their bodies pass through a cycle of arousal that would be called REM dreaming, were they asleep. Careful studies must tell us how our body cycles are timed before we will know what cues we should obey in deciding to go to sleep at once. Surely we can improve upon the cumbersome and haphazard sleep habits we casually acquire at home, and every one of us, not only space explorers, is bound to benefit.

Certain people seem to control the process of awakening as well as the knack of swiftly falling asleep. How does one cultivate ease of awakening? Apparently inherited constitution plays some role. Within families a mother and her daughter may grope half-blindly through the first hour of morning, while males of the houschold have leapt out of bed whistling and have already started breakfast. There are larks and owls, and overlaid upon physical heritage are a panoply of emotions and habits. When Wilse Webb and his associates at the University of Florida surveyed the waking habits of some 600 local citizens of all ages they discovered that the vast majority did not awaken of their own accord in the morning. Only a hundred or so awoke spontaneously. Within the whole group fewer than 200 claimed they felt instantly alert, and about 100 asserted that they would fumble around for an hour before feeling thoroughly awake and alive. Surely the amount of sleep obtained, and feelings of happiness or unhappiness can accelerate or impede awakening, but perhaps in addition there are factors of timing that no alarm clock could calculate.

Webb and his team began to assay factors that might determine a person's speed of awakening. In general, laboratory sleep studies have demonstrated that it is difficult to awaken from deep slow-wave sleep, Stage IV, which predominates in the early part of the night. Folklore states that it is hard to awaken a person early in the night, and this may be one reason. On the other hand people have learned to awaken themselves during light Stage II sleep and REM intervals. The paradox of the REM dream period is that people can be very obdurate about resisting sounds, shouts, even shocks, yet if they are motivated may learn to awaken of their own accord in this phase. Moreover, researchers have found that people emerge from this phase of sleep with unusual mental abilities, and will give rich and fluent associations to words surpassing any responses they offer if awakened from other stages of sleep. Since many studies have suggested that the mind regains its faculties more rapidly than the body, Webb's team used a test of simple mental agility and a test measuring strength of handgrip in their study of a group of healthy young men. The tests were given during the daytime, and after awakening from sleep. Just after awakening, handgrip strength showed about a 13 percent drop on the average, and it took the subjects about two minutes to recover normal strength. Mental agility was measured by a simple procedure. The volunteer, when awakened, simply had to press four buttons on a handy illuminated panel beside him. The buttons were numbered in order 1 to 4. However, the subject was instructed to press them in the order indicated by a row of digits above, which might read 2-4-1-3. They had practiced during waking, and their usual proficiency and speed was established when the night tests began. Now the investigators waited for possible answers. Was it better to awaken at one time of night than another? Did a person's mental faculties really return faster from a particular stage of sleep?

After several weeks the data returned a surprising pattern. It did not seem to matter how long the subject had been asleep. Whether he was awakened after an hour, after five hours, or in the morning, the performance pattern was the same. The subjects took a comparatively long time to awaken from Stage IV sleep, but they performed well. They awakened most rapidly from REM sleep, and performed most poorly. Mere speed of awakening, opening eyes and showing an alert EEG record did not indicate that the person was mobilized. Subjects would react promptly to the buzzer or light shock during REM sleep and touch the first button within half a second, yet judging from their errors it took their minds about 30 seconds to become more fully awake. Although the subjects revealed consistent individual differences in their efficiency of arousal, each person's performance was related to his efficiency level on daytime testing, and thus determined by his general ability to do the task at any time. Even though the body, the muscles, may take longer than the mind, the mind would seem to require a certain minimum time to mobilize its waking capacities from any stage of sleep.

This study, like so many others of the last decade, intimates that a person who wants to control his sleep behavior and awakening may achieve greater command and also greater contact with the outside world during periods of rapid-eye-movement sleep, and possibly intermittent spells of light Stage II and Stage I. These would seem to be the moments for awakening oneself most easily. Perhaps detailed studies will show that controlled and swift awakenings coincide with the alpha bursts that intermittently occur, particularly as the dreamer shifts his gaze. The alpha rhythm has been conceived to mean a threshold of arousal, and it may be that the eye movements stimulate the visual brain and encourage arousal. Most of us are still very inept and out of contact with our sleeping selves, but this does not mean we cannot learn control any more than the inability to swim when first tossed into the water means that we cannot learn to swim. The study of man's sleeping capacities has just begun and there are many cues to be learned. People do set mental alarm clocks and awaken themselves. Tired travelers do seem to sense the depth of their sleep enough to open their eyes periodically and see that they are not passing their destination. People do arise to solve problems in the dead of night. Some people follow commands in sleep. As we discover the cues and make them explicit people will learn them as they learn the other skills of self-control and coordination.

Almost all cultures, however primitive, have some ritual that demonstrates a remarkable exercise of self-discipline. A Sabey girl could lie motionless during the puberty rite of female circumcision, when a cowbell on her chest would clang if she flinched. Trance states are learned in some tribes, autohypnotic resistance to pain, or the muscle relaxation that permits a fakir to sit comfortably on a bed of nails. In times past, remarkable self-controls have been acquired by inherent sensitivity, by traditions that contained some empirical wisdom mingled with irrelevancy and outright superstition, a process often requiring years of diffuse and laborious discipline. In Western society, it appears that "mind control" and the so-called remarkable powers may be evolved and disseminated instead from the systematic probings of science.

Our covenant with the timing of our bodies, our self-mastery, is learned haphazardly, if at all. With progressive scientific discovery we may find that these elements can become a national part of child rearing. Quite as modern men find it amazing to encounter a person who is totally oblivious to the psychological factors underlying behavior, future generations may find it curious to encounter a person who cannot relax and sleep, or awaken at will. They may be astonished to encounter someone who cannot tune in on his dreams and night thoughts, exploit his sleeping mentation, and employ tricks of mind and muscle to protect himself against the emotional and physiological reactions that might prove harmful. Even beyond the broad applications of sleep study to psychotherapy and medicine, the research into our many states of consciousness may have benefits of unparalleled magnitude as we learn to understand attention. In studies of dreaming and hypnosis we have already begun to see unexpected clues to man's attention mechanisms. Ultimately, the productivity and perhaps the enjoyment of a life depends upon the extent to which the individual can focus his attention and command concentration. If everyone could be taught how to control and sustain attention, the productivity and richness of life might be expanded tenfold.

XII

WHAT IS SLEEP?

EACH night a tide of invisible changes floods over us. The eyes lose their sight and the mind fills with images. We begin to recede from the exigent world of the present, drifting, sometimes with subtle sensations, in a fragile balance between waking and sleep. The gentle transition may be abruptly reversed if the person lying in darkness imagines for a moment that he hears an ominous footfall in the house. Then, from the outermost layers of the thinking brain communications are instantly showered through his brain and body. His heart races, his blood receives adrenalin, and his muscles tense for action. As silence prevails once again, the soothing warmth and darkness may damp the alarm. But even as he sinks through the feathered layers of reverie, cells in his brain will continue to act as sentinels. Novelty may excite them although they will rapidly grow accustomed to repetition, and so the continuous whirr of the air conditioner goes ignored, but the brain may awaken if the sound suddenly stops. Each night the long journey begins again, down and up the stairs of consciousness, never quite the same on any landing. Functions within the brain seem to shift at each descent and ascent, and unbeknownst to himself, the sleeping person slips into the entire dominion of his life. He may suffer or laugh. He may answer questions put to him, or babble aimlessly. He may rise out of his bed and walk, usually with no subsequent memory of the emotions that caused his sleeping face to contort in fear or to smile bemusedly. What is this metamorphosis we call sleep, and why does it happen?

Primitive man answered, with some charm, that the imprisoned soul had to be emancipated to wander and communicate with the spirit world of night, but early in scientific history clues were sought in the body. In the sixth century B.C. a Greek theorist suggested that sleep was caused when the blood retreated into the veins leaving the anemic brain malnourished. Today we know this is not so, although striking circulatory changes occur in the brain during the stages of sleep, and blood pressure changes in the main neck arteries appear to influence the wakefulness of the brain. Other theorists had supposed sleep to be caused by oxygen starvation in the brain, but we have seen evidence that oxygen consumption continues at a relatively high rate during sleep. Others have hypothesized that muscular activity or other body functions might generate a fatigue substance whose potent hypnotic accumulation would overpower the brain each day. Responsibility for sleep has been accredited to one after another of the body organs and systems. Today we are apt to think that quite a number of them participate in generating sleep, presumably through their direct or indirect effects upon the brain. During the last 25 years scientists have concentrated more attention upon the brain itself, and upon what appear to be two networks of nerve cells that run all the way up the spinal cord and into many brain regions. When touched with electricity or certain chemicals, one of these pathways seems to provoke waking, the other, sleep.

Looking back across the centuries at the tacking course of sleep theories, turning in one direction and then another, a modern person may be struck with their narrowness and naïveté. They were, after all, the creations of scientists, restricted by their instruments and available knowledge, each with a focus of attention, whether it was the formation of dreams or the cardiovascular system, and by the kinds of subjects he studied, whether patients, people in laboratories, or animals. Men gazing through microscopes inevitably see different aspects of nature than do those who rely on telescopes, and until recently it was impossible for a single individual to gain even a faint glimpse of the entirety. The scientists of sleep, in the last decade, have been pioneers in a remarkable transformation occurring in the process of research. On their own initiative they have utilized rapid communications, travel, teamwork, and have pooled their knowledge and skills at all levels. Thus a man studying dream content knows about the shifting volleys of single cells within the sleeping brain, and concurrent changes in the blood and the stomach. This pooling of discovery not only accelerates research, but it gives to every man on earth a totally new perception of his nightly sleep, although we still do not know what sleep is.

Today, when a man falls asleep he realizes that he is not merely losing consciousness for the night. He can anticipate the stations of his route, the fleeting thoughts and dreamlets of his descent into the first stage, perhaps briefly interrupted by a muscle spasm, and then as his brain evinces a new rhythm and his muscles relax further, into the second stage, and with pulse slowing, breathing even, into the depths of quiet slumber that have been denoted by their brain waves as the third and fourth stages of sleep. He will not remain there, but will soon begin to rise upward toward the surface, and roughly an hour and a half from his start, he will be transfigured by a physiological storm and five or ten minutes of vivid dreaming, in that paradoxical state known as Stage I REM. A man will acquire an erection, and a tense person may grind his teeth. The eyes will move, the breath seem uneven, and the dream is likely to contain some of the mundane aspects of the day just departed. Then he enters another descent, and in the unremembered pit of quiet sleep he may sit up, speak, or even rise out of bed to perform strange actions as one in a trance, and then return. Approximately an hour or an hour and a half after the first REM storm, he will have risen again breathing irregularly, into a longer, more intense episode, perhaps less concerned with his daily life. Again, about six hours after falling asleep he will rise, for about twenty minutes or longer, into a yet more vivid entertainment, unleashed from reason and circumstance, in which he is exposed to a curious sample from all he has ever seen or felt. His temperature will be low, his experience vigorous, and he will probably rise once more into this state before he awakens, perhaps with some remnant of the experience, although the night's many previous sequences of dream and thought will have vanished. In the morning, even if he feels he has slipped from the previous day through a shaft of darkness, a modern man knows too much about the night's progression and his sleeping capacities to consider sleep a transient death.

We have not adequately explained why this stillness overtakes each man and creature within the circle of a day, yet the question has prompted researchers that promise to touch all our lives. Evolutionary thinkers remind us that primitive cell life probably depended upon solar energy and was attuned to daylight for survival, and that our more complex ocean ancestors incorporated the rhythms of the sea and moon. Some scientists have postulated that man's circadian rhythm of sleep and waking may be a residue of these lunar and solar cycles, and that our timing is dictated by a kind of timer within the brain. Others suppose that we ourselves are the clock, and that the daily rhythm may be the result of innumerable cycles within the body. Although light and dark impinge upon it, something like a 24-hour rhythm appears to abide in our flesh, persisting in men who have lived in deep caves or in constant light. Body organs and metabolisms fluctuate in a daily tempo as do symptoms of illness. When a jet traveler lengthens his day by several hours, his body will go out of phase with his schedule, and he will feel the discord. If he continues to stay out of phase for long stretches, he may begin to develop symptoms like those of some stewardesses or pilots. Even a complete reversal of day and night can detract from a person's well-being, and night workers often have disturbed sleep and psychological problems.

We have begun to acknowledge the importance of hidden laws of periodicity within ourselves, a timed gearing of our body functions that we override at some unknown risk, and which we may also learn to exploit for personal benefit. An individual can learn to recognize his daily fluctations of temperature, to exert himself during peaks of alertness and sleep during his nadir period. Are there optimal hours for particular kinds of activity, muscular or mental, and for specific medical treatments? Can we discover how light and darkness, strong emotion, food, and other factors may influence and perhaps reset our body clocks? At no prior time in history were we equipped to ask these questions with so great a hope of obtaining answers. The answers we presently have are bound to disappoint some people, for they indicate human limits, and many modern men would like to sleep at their convenience, perhaps twice a week rather than every night. Still others would gladly accept a substitute, if there were one, for sleep.

Ironically, in an era when people would like to eradicate sleep, laboratory scientists have performed that experiment, only to dramatize the dangers of sleep loss and accent the importance of regular nightly sleep. When totally deprived of sleep for several days, a person follows a predictable course of deterioration. He may seem astute, yet unreliable at his job. We now know that he may perform erratically because he suffers from brief spells of sleep on his feet. He may show a certain mental laziness, and an undue susceptibility to certain quantities of alcohol, or the temperature of a room. His concentration diminishes. Slowly, strange sensations invade him, visual illusions, then hallucinations and a transitory psychosis. Mentally ill persons, epileptics, narcoleptics and others are vulnerable to loss of sleep, and while the young appear to have greater tolerance, they too eventually follow the same course. So, in some respects, do monkeys. Protracted sleeplessness appears to interfere with the body's energy metabolism, and even after 48 hours of wakefulness there has been evidence of altered body chemistry, indicating that we may generate substances in stress whose effects on the brain are unknown. Nobody is positive that we escape without permanent neural damage from simple loss of sleep. Although it is rare for people to altogether skip sleep, many people habitually shortchange themselves. By sleeping four hours a night instead of the usual eight or seven, a person has altered his usual progression through the EEG stages of sleep, and the proportion of time he will spend in each stage. Reduced sleep is not a miniature of the full night, and thus the quality of rest may be quite different. In the early 1950's we had not fully realized that the logistics of sleep were as crucial as food and sanitation, for we did not yet know how seriously sleep loss could influence a man's mind. Sleep is a state for which we have no drug substitute, nor are we likely to have one until we have deciphered all that it does for us.

Only a decade ago an entirely new dimension was injected into our concept of sleep when scientists discovered that each night is punctuated by regular periods of body change and rapid-eye-movement dreaming. Never in history were so many dream memories collected for study as in the subsequent years, although the importance of the discovery extended well beyond the ability to capture dreams. Mammals all showed the signs of this cycle and it was prominent in newborn babies, bearing on closer inspection the lineaments of a major body cycle related to drives and metabolisms as well as dreams. During this particular phase of sleep vigorous transformations seize the body. Temperature rises in drive centers within the brain, there is a pronounced increase in cerebral blood flow, certain muscles suddenly grow flaccid, and unusual brain-wave patterns emanate from deep within. Imperturbable and limp as the dreamer may appear, his brain responds in the manner of a waking brain during moments of intense concentration. It is during these periods that some medical crises are thought to arise. For example, ulcer patients secrete abnormal amounts of gastric juices. Whatever the role of the dream, this phase of sleep appears to be discharging an accumulated excitement. When animals or people have been deprived of REM sleep they later compensated with orgies of REM dreaming. Some people have exhibited little behavioral change after sustained dream deprivation while others have seemed to lose their usual self-controls. Dream-deprived animals have proven surprisingly vulnerable to slight electric shocks. Does this mean that without REM dreaming there is a mounting excitability in the central nervous system? If so, we may begin to understand the increasing aberrations among drug addicts, alcoholics, and mentally ill people who suffer a prolonged reduction in their nightly dream periods as a consequence of their illness or drugs. It may begin to explain some of the bizarre consequences of sleep loss, and indeed, some of the irritabilities and symptoms we show when we have slept poorly.

We have only begun to learn what people mean when they say they do not sleep restfully or well, or when they say they sleep soundly. Physiological differences between good and poor sleepers are being written out in brain-wave patterns, in heart rates and temperatures, as well as in attitudes and psychosomatic complaints. The differences are indeed measurable. People who complain of poor sleep have appeared to sleep in a state that is physiologically closer to waking than that of people who sleep soundly. Poor sleepers have shown temperature curves that did not decline so low at night nor rise so early in the morning, hinting that their bodies might not quite follow the usual 24-hour rhythm. They have shown an unusually small amount of REM sleep, a more nervous and disturbed frame of mind, and indeed, in the laboratory, they have obtained less sleep than their sound-sleeping counterparts. Perhaps these are people who need more sleep, and one must wonder why they differ, whether their peculiarities are genetically inherited, or the marks of early training and life circumstance. Will our intensive studies of infant sleep display the first signs of the poor sleeper, who may be unduly sensitive to his environment and to neurosis? Will these infant sleep patterns help us forecast retardation or behavior abnormalities in the early months of life when preventive action can be most beneficial? We have just recently discovered that we can study the sleep of an adult or an infant and learn a good deal about the individual. The slumber of the night manifests the broad range of individual differences we so acutely perceive during daytime.

Therapies for sleep problems have been complicated by our new discoveries, and now rest uneasily upon questions born of greater knowledge. We have seen that alcohol, barbiturates, tranquilizers, do not induce sleep in the manner of the healthy body. They alter the usual pattern of nightly sleep, generally reducing the rapid-eye-movement phase. Stimulants such as amphetamines also have this effect, and yet many of the people who rely upon these drugs already seem to suffer from a diminution of REM sleep.

If this decade of research had accomplished no more, it did a great service by making the risks of self-medication very tangible and comprehensible. Stimulant drugs will not compensate for sleep loss nor poor sleep, and indeed may impair sleep. Sedatives do not merely induce sleep, and indeed people who suffer from a transient insomnia are ill advised to take several drinks and then sleeping pills, particularly if they are over fifty. In combination the drug effects are enhanced, and the doses a person may consider moderate can even prove fatal.

Even more important than a systematic definition of drug effects is the gradual revelation that poor sleep and insomnia arise from a multitude of causes. Sedatives are ineffective against the insomnia of the manic, and barbiturates can exacerbate the symptoms of a person on the brink of psychosis. We have been impelled to look behind the mask of persistent sleep disorders for specific origins, for sleep abnormalities are often the harbingers of mental illness. True, some insomniacs may claim they are awake all night because they sleep lightly or even dream they are awake, but when a person persistently fails to sleep, only a doctor can determine what drug will give him rest, for a sedative may not be of any help. The same sedative that soothes one patient may drive a depressive into deeper despair, allow a psychotic to sleep while intensifying his symptoms, and leave a manic insomniac quite sleepless. On the other hand, a compound that provides rest for a depressed person would be likely to keep a normal person awake. The chemical that remedies a sleep disorder depends upon the chemistry of the specific cause of sleeplessness.

Sedation is no longer the straightforward problem it was thirty years ago when we knew less, for now we can see a multitude of questions nesting under the single complaint of disturbed sleep. By studying the specific ailment and the actions of each drug, we have begun the work that may permit us to tailor drugs to need. At this point we realize that many different kinds of sleep may be built into a sleeping pill. We may need to provide alcoholics, drug addicts, or psychotics with compounds to enhance REM sleep at one phase of illness, and with drugs to enhance deep Stage IV sleep at another stage. Our still rather scanty knowledge of drug effects does not tell us how to design drugs that compensate for the particular sleep phases that are diminished in illness, but has emphasized the fact that sleeping pills do not induce normal sleep.

Quite a number of scientists have begun to ask how the body chemistry produces sleep, and this avenue of research is likely to burgeon in the decade to come. The biochemistry of sleep is, today, almost a virgin territory. Researchers have hinted that the body generates a number of hypnotic substances, each prevailing under the appropriate circumstances. Ammonia concentrations during liver disease cause one kind of sleepiness. Sex hormones apparently can act as sedatives. We do not yet know how many special soporifics exist in the body, or how they put us to sleep. Perhaps most of them are intermediaries, working through master brain chemicals, which in turn trigger sleep-inducing cells in the brain. Surely, even at this early date, we have begun to see links between certain brain chemicals, our moods, and the efficiency and restfulness of our sleep. As this research unfolds we may at last acquire sedatives that mollify specific sleep abnormalities, inducing not just somnolence, but refreshing sleep.

While sleep studies have led inward into the difficulties of biochemistry, they have also led us to some of the wilder shores of human behavior and consciousness, for they have rediscovered in a scientific fashion some of the remarkable capacities of the human mind. During defined stages of sleep people have discriminated between sounds in the laboratory, listened to information and repeated it upon awakening, communicated by signals with the outside world, followed commands, and even learned to sense, while asleep, their shifting levels of consciousness. Within the laboratory they have learned to sense and control that state of internal relaxation from which we see the alpha rhythm on the EEG. They learned to turn it on and off at will and even to control the frequency of their brain waves. Quite a few researchers have shown us that our bodies accidentally learn reactions to anxiety or pain, but recent work on brain-wave control also suggests we could learn to cultivate techniques that counteract tension and its penalties.

We are beginning to explore the muscle movements or respiration that may be used in executing commands over our bodies. In a systematic fashion we have begun to ask what factors would permit us to fall asleep and awaken at will, reduce our blood pressures, our gastric secretions, permitting individuals to employ their own preventive remedies by disciplines of mind. Although most of our attempts at sleep teaching have proven negative, hypnotizable persons have shown an ability to execute commands during a particular phase of sleep, and scientists are now trying to discover the properties that distinguish these people and their particular attentiveness.

The study of sleep may help us to find out what characterizes attention, and how such focus is attained in sleep and waking. Can we wakefully enjoy the vivid experiences and the power of concentration we exhibit during REM dreaming? Quite a few modern people seek expanded consciousness from drugs, yet the visions and intensities they unfetter would seem to be based upon the brain's store of incredibly detailed memories, and fleeting emotions in the mind's constellation that compose our nightly dreams. Every night the sleeping person experiences some psychedelic limitlessness that is pursued by the drug taker. Can we acquire cues of entry so that each of us can plunge within and retrieve into conscious memory what is already there? The sleeping mind may have many attributes that we could wish to exploit during our waking life.

With implosive force, this era of sleep research has broken through conceptual barriers that obscured both the importance and nature of sleep. It has produced for us a sizable bounty of practical applications, and of questions that could not have been asked a decade earlier. We are still left with the oldest question of all: What is sleep? We cannot answer it. Perhaps we have learned that it is the wrong question. Physicists used to ask: What is an atom? At first they seemed to find only mass and charge. Then powerful instruments revealed a host of transient particles, obeying subtle forces, spinning in different directions. Each discovery revealed a more mysterious constellation. So with sleep.

Each discovery leads inward. Ultimately we face profound questions about the composition and function of the central nervous system. These questions about sleep are being pursued in neurophysiological and chemical studies that could be alluded to only fleetingly in this book. A massive literature of technical studies underlies our reconsideration of the nature of sleep, and influences the work of psychologists and doctors as they study behavior. Almost all of these foundation researches are conducted in laboratories by procedures that would be unfamiliar to laymen, indeed by scientists whose names are not generally known, and whose contributions rarely appear in the popular press. There is a certain irony in this inconspicuousness. Human studies are often publicized because they are easily understood and contain some inherent drama, but neither intelligibility nor drama indicate the importance of research.

Discoveries prompted by human sleep inevitably raise questions about what is happening underneath the skin, and while the answers might not be comprehensible to most people, they are indeed being found by an army of biologically oriented scientists. Quietly, in their laboratories, these men are probing the atoms of sleep. They too are involved in the incidental dramas of science, and in relationships with the laboratory animals on whom much of the work is done. These may be chimpanzees with whom they play during leisure moments, monkeys, dogs, cats that they tend and coddle for several years, coming to know them better and sometimes more fondly than their own house pets. Animals, like human beings, must not feel disturbed or pained if scientists are to observe the complicated transactions of their brains. Their mute signals of mood or relaxation are as much a part of laboratory concern as are the anxieties of human volunteers, but this aspect of laboratory life is rarely reported.

Animal research has been crucial to the understanding of sleep, and close contact and communication between psychologists, psychiatrists and the biological scientists has facilitated an extraordinary rate of progress. We can watch a sleep-starved person enact hallucinations, describe his illusions and sensations. We can test his performance and make surface measurements of his bodily changes, and we may infer that his chemistry has changed by examining his excretions. But we can never look inside his brain to see whether cells have been damaged or to chemically analyze brain tissue and see in what manner it may have changed. Animal studies thus remain an indispensable counterpart in the study of ourselves. From them we may discover the physical mechanisms that underlie our subjective experiences, perceptions, and mental capacities.

In a decade our concept of sleep has been revolutionized, and we have started to close the gap between our sleeping and waking lives, discovering how the creature of night is related to his daytime self, how the quality of sleep relates to behavior. Each discovery impels us to probe more deeply into the physical laws that determine our states of being. Like a stone dropped into water, widening circles at the surface reflect growing knowledge and practical benefits, but do not show the ever-deeper plunge of biological research into the mechanisms of consciousness. Within another decade there may burst upon us answers to some of our basic questions about what sleep does for us, and its chemical nature, and how the brain rotates its duties during our many successive states. If sleep research has inspired great excitement during the last ten or so years, it is now clear that this was only the beginning.

BIBLIOGRAPHY

General References:

Akert, K., Bally, C., and Schade, J. P. (eds.), *Progress in Brain Research—Sleep Mechanisms*. Vol. 18, American Elsevier, New York, 1965.

Fair, C. M., *The Physical Foundations of the Psyche*. Wesleyan University Press, 1963.

Kleitman, N., *Sleep and Wakefulness* (Rev. Ed.). University of Chicago Press, 1963.

Murray, E., *Sleep, Dreams and Arousal*. Appleton-Century-Crofts, 1965.

Oswald, I., *Sleeping and Waking*. American Elsevier, New York, 1962.

Wolstenholme, G. E. W., and O'Connor, M. (eds.), *The Nature of Sleep*. Little Brown, Boston, 1960.

Neurophysiologie des Etats de Sommeil, No. 127. Editions du Centre National de la Recherche Scientifique, Paris, 1965.

Sleep and Altered States of Consciousness. Association for Research in Nervous and Mental Disease (45th Annual Meeting). In press.

Current Research on Sleep and Dreams. U. S. Dept. of Health, Education, and Welfare, U. S. Public Health Service, National Institute of Mental Health, Bethesda, Maryland, 1965.

CHAPTER I

References for the general reader:

Giles, Luray, *Sleep*. Bobbs-Merrill, 1938.

Rosenteur, Phyllis, *Morpheus and Me*. Funk & Wagnalls, 1957.

Additional References:

Aubert, V., and White, H., Sleep: A Sociological Interpretation. *Acta Sociologica* 4: Fasc. 2,3, 1959.

Frankl, V. E., *Man's Search for Meaning* (From Death-Camp to Existentialism). Beacon Press, 1962.

Harms, E. (ed.), *Problems of Sleep and Dreams in Children*. International Series of Monographs on Child Psychiatry, Vol. 2, Macmillan, New York, 1964.

Kanner, L., *Child Psychiatry*. Charles C. Thomas, 1960.

Parmelee, A. H., Sleep Patterns in Infancy. *Acta Paediatrica* 50: 150-170, 1961.
Runes, D. B. (ed.), *The Diary and Sundry Observations of Thomas Alva Edison.* The Philosophical Library, 1948.
Shneidman, E. S., Suicide, Sleep, and Death. *J. Consult. Psychol.,* Vol. 28, April, 1964.
Shneidman, E. S., Sleep and Self-Destruction: A Phenomenological Approach. In Shneidman, E. S. (ed.), *Essays in Self Destruction.* Holt, Rinehart & Winston, 1965.

CHAPTER II

References for the General Reader:

Berrill, N. J., Living Clocks. *Atlantic Monthly,* December 1963.
Cloudsley-Thompson, J. L., *Rhythmic Behavior in Animal Physiology and Behavior.* Academic Press, 1961.
Galton, L., The Best Time to Work. *New York Times Magazine,* November 5, 1961.
Reinberg, A., and Ghata, J., *Biological Rhythms.* Walker & Co., New York, 1964.

Additional References:

Alluisi, E. A., Chiles, W. D., Hall, T. J., and Hawkes, G. R., Human Group Performance During Confinement. Aero-space Medical Research Laboratories, TDR—63-87.
Arduini, A., and Pinneo, L. R., The Tonic Activity of the Lateral Geniculate Nucleus in Dark and Light Adaptation. *Arch. Ital. Biol.* 101: 493-507, 1963.
Arduini, A., and Pinneo, L. R., The Effects of Flicker and Steady Illumination on the Activity of the Cat Visual System. *Arch. Ital. Biol.* 101: 508-529, 1963.
Arduini, A., and Hirao, T., EEG Synchronization Elicited by Light on the Midpontine Pretrigeminal. *Arch. Ital. Biol.* 98: 275, 1960.
Aschoff, J., Circadian Rhythms in Man. *Science* 148, June 11, 1965.
Biological Clocks. Cold Spring Harbor Symposia on Quantitative Biology, Vol. xxv, The Biological Laboratory, Cold Spring Harbor, L.I., New York, 1960.
Denisova, V. G., The Training of Soviet Cosmonauts. TT: 64-510109, JPRS: 26, 762, U. S. Department of Commerce Joint Publications Research Service, 1964. Clearinghouse for Federal Scientific and Technical Information, Springfield, Va.
Fairbain, D., Man and the Machine. *Interline Reporter,* May 15, 1965.
Gjessing, L. R., Studies of Periodic Catatonia (I. Blood Levels of Protein-Bound Iodine and Urinary Excretion of Vanillyl-Mandelic Acid in Relation to Clinical Course. II. The Urinary Excretion of Phenolic Amines and Acids with and Without Loads of Different Drugs). *J. Psychiat. Research.,* Vol. 2, Pergamon Press, London, 1964.
Halberg, F., and Howard, R. B., Twenty-four Hour Periodicity and Experimental Medicine, *Post Graduate Medicine* 24: 349-358, 1958.
Ivanov, D. I., Malkin, V. B., Popkov, V. L., Popova, Ye. O., and Chernyakov, I. N., Automatic Analysis of Diurnal Periodic Changes in Human EEG Rhythms. In *Problems of Space Biology,* Vol. 4: 642-645, Izd.-vo, Nauka, Moscow, 1965. Clearinghouse for Federal Scientific and Technical Information, Springfield, Va.
Lavernhe, J., Lafontaine, E., and Laplane, R., An Investigation on the Subjective Effects of Time Changes on Flying Staff in Civil Aviation. Air France, 1965.
Lindsley, D. F., Wendt, R. H., Fugett, R., Lindsley, D. B., and Adey, W. R.,

Diurnal Activity Cycles in Monkeys under Prolonged Visual Pattern Deprivation. *J. Comp. Physiol. Psych.* 55: 633-640, 1962.

Lisk, R. D., and Kranswischer, L. R., Light: Evidence for Its Direct Effect on Hypothalamic Neurons. *Science* 146: 272-273, 1964.

Lomov, B. F. (ed.), *Problems of Engineering Psychology,* May, 1965. NASA TT F-312, National Aeronautics and Space Administration, N 65-24370, Clearinghouse for Federal Scientific and Technical Information, Springfield, Va.

Metz, B., Scharf, G., and Gridel, F., Psychophysiological Effects of Sleep Deprivation. 16th International Congress in Psychology, Bonn, Germany, 1960.

Passey, G. E., Alluisi, E. A., and Chiles, W. D., Use of the Experimental Method for Evaluations of Performance in Multi-man Systems. Aerospace Medical Research Laboratories Memorandum, 1964.

Pizzarello, D. J., Isaak, D., Chua, K. E., and Rhyne, A. L., Circadian Rhythmicity in the Sensitivity of Two Strains of Mice to Whole-body Radiation. *Science* 145: 286-291, 1964.

Ray, J. T., Martin, O. E., and Alluisi, E. A., *Human Performance as a Function of the Work-Rest Cycle.* National Academy of Sciences, National Research Council, No. 882, 1961.

Richter, C. P., *Biological Clocks in Medicine and Psychiatry.* Charles C. Thomas, 1965.

Sisakyan, N. M., and Yazdovskii, V. I. (eds.), *First Group Flight into Outer Space—August 11–15, 1962.* TT-64-31567. JPRS 25, 272, U. S. Department of Commerce, Office of Technical Services, Joint Publications Research Service, Clearinghouse for Federal Scientific and Technical Information, Springfield, Va.

Weiss, T., and Roldan, E., Comparative Study of Sleep Cycles in Rodents. *Experientia* 20: 280-281, 1964.

Wolf, W. (ed.), *Rhythmic Functions in the Living System.* Annals of the New York Academy of Sciences, Vol. 98, Art. 4, October, 1962.

CHAPTER III

Reference for the General Reader:

Lessing, L., Sleep. *Fortune,* June, 1964.

Additional References:

Adey, W. R., Kado, R. T., Didio, J., and Schindler, W. J., Impedance Changes in Cerebral Tissue Accompanying a Learned Discriminative Performance in the Cat. *Exp. Neurol.* 7: 259-281, 1963.

Adey, W. R., and Walter, D. O., Applications of Phase Detection and Averaging Techniques in Computer Analysis of EEG Records in the Cat. *Exp. Neurol.* 7: 186-209, 1963.

Agnew, H., Webb, W. B., and Williams, R. L., The Effect of Stage 4 Sleep Deprivation. *EEG clin. Neurophysiol.* 17: 68-70, 1964.

Albe-Fessard, D., Massion J., Hall, R., and Rosenblith, W., Modifications au Cours de la Veille et du Sommeil des Valeurs Moyennes de Reponses Nerveuses Centrales Induites par des Stimulations Somatiques Chez le Chat Libre. *C. R. Acad. Sci. Paris* 25: 258, Jan. 6, 1964.

Anliker, J., Variations in Alpha Voltage of the EEG and Time Perception. *Science* 140: 1307-1309, 1963.

Aserinsky, E., and Kleitman, N., Two Types of Ocular Motility Occurring in Sleep. *J. Appl. Physiol.* 8: 1-10, 1955.

Aserinsky, E., and Kleitman, N., Regularly Occurring Periods of Eye Motility and Concomitant Phenomena During Sleep. *Science* 118: 273-274, 1953.

Brazier, M. A. B. (ed.), Computer Processing of EEG. *EEG Journal Suppl.*, 1963.

Brazier, M. A. B., The Electrical Fields at the Surface of the Head During Sleep. *EEG. clin. Neurophysiol.* 1 (2): 195-205, May, 1949.

Cohen, H. D., Shapiro, A., and Goodenough, D. R., The EEG During Stage 4 Sleep Talking. Association for the Psychophysiological Study of Sleep, Washington, D. C., 1965.

Dement, W. C., and Kleitman, N., Cyclic Variations in EEG During Sleep, and Their Relations to Eye Movements, Body Motility, and Dreaming. *EEG. clin. Neurophysiol.* 9: 673-690, 1957.

Foulkes, D., and Vogel, G., Mental Activity at Sleep Onset. *J. Abnorm. Psychol.* 70: 231-243, 1965.

Foulkes, D., Spear, P. S., and Symonds, J. D., Individual Differences in Mental Activity at Sleep Onset. *J. Abnorm. Psychol.* 70: 231-243, 1965.

Goff, W. R., Rosner, B. S., and Allison, T., Distribution of Cerebral Somatosensory Evoked Responses in Normal Man. *EEG clin. Neurophysiol.* 14: 697-713, 1962.

Goodenough, D. R., Cyclical Fluctuations in Sleep Depth and Eye-Movement Activity During the Course of Natural Sleep. *Canad. Psychiat. J.* 8: 406-408, 1963.

Hawkins, D. R., Puryear, H. B., Wallace, C. D., Deal, W. B., and Thomas, E. S., Basal Skin Resistance During Sleep and Dreaming. *Science* 136: 321-322, 1962.

Jacobson, A., Kales, A., Lehmann, D., and Hoedemaker, F. S., Muscle Tonus in Human Subjects During Sleep and Dreaming. *Exp. Neurol.* 10: 418-424, 1964.

Jacobson, A., Kales, A., Zweizig, J. R., and Kales, J., Special EEG and EMG Techniques for Sleep Research. *Am. J. EEG Tech.*, Vol. 5, 1965.

Kamiya, J., Behavioral, Subjective, and Physiological Aspects of Drowsiness and Sleep. In Fiske, D. W., and Maddi, S. R. (eds.), *Functions of Varied Experience*. Homewood: Dorsey, 1961.

Konecci, E. B., and Shiner, A. J., Uses of Telemetry in Space. In Caceras, C. A. (ed.), *Biomedical Telemetry*. Academic Press, 1965.

Liberson, W. T., and Liberson, C. W., EEG, Reaction Time, Eye Movements, Respiration, and Mental Content During Drowsiness. Association for the Psychophysiological Study of Sleep, Washington, D. C., 1965.

Liberson, W. T., Electroencephalography. *Am. J. Psychiat.* 121, 1965.

MacWilliams, J. A., Blood Pressure and Heart Action in Sleep and Dreams. *Brit. Med. J.* 2: 1196-1200, 1923.

Maron, L., Rechtschaffen, A., and Wolpert, E. A., The Sleep Cycle During Napping. *Arch. Gen. Psychiat.* 11: 503-508, 1964.

Rechtschaffen, A., Goodenough, D. R., and Shapiro, A., Patterns of Sleep Talking. *Arch. Gen. Psychiat.* 7: 418-426, 1962.

Rosenblith, W. A., (ed.), *Processing Neuroelectric Data*. Massachusetts Institute of Technology Press, Cambridge, 1960.

Rosner, B. S., Goff, W. R., and Allison, T., Cerebral Electrical Responses to External Stimuli. In Glasser, G. H. (ed.), *EEG and Behavior*. Basic Books, New York, 1963.

Weitzman, E. D., and Kremen, H., Auditory Evoked Responses During Different Stages of Sleep in Man. *EEG clin. Neurophysiol.* 18: 65-70, 1965.

Weitzman, E. D., Kripke, D. F., Pollak, C., and Dominguez, J., Cyclic Activity in Sleep of Macaca Mulatta. *Arch. Neurol.* 12, May, 1965.

Williams, H. L., Tepas, D. I., and Morlock, H. C., Evoked Responses to Clicks and Electroencephalographic Stages of Sleep in Man. *Science* 138: 685-686, 1962.

CHAPTER IV

References for the General Reader:

Biderman, A. D., and Zimmer, H. (eds.), *The Manipulation of Human Behavior.* John Wiley & Sons, 1961.

Clarke, A. C., Sleep No More. *Holiday,* December, 1958.

McCann, H. W., The Strange World of Sleepless People. *Science Digest,* February, 1962.

Newman, A. S., Sleep and the Soldier. *Army,* October, 1963.

Williams, H. L., Sleep Starvation and You. *Army Information Digest,* June, 1964.

Additional References:

Ax, A., and Luby, E. D., Autonomic Responses to Sleep Deprivation. *Arch. Gen. Psychiat.* 4: 55-59, 1961.

Bennett, D. R., Mattson, R. H., Ziter, F. A., *et al.,* Sleep Deprivation: Neurological and Electroencephalographic Effects. *Aerospace Medicine,* September, 1964.

Berger, R. J., and Oswald, I., Effects of Sleep Deprivation on Behavior, Subsequent Sleep, and Dreaming. *J. Ment. Sci.* 108: 457-465, 1962.

Combat Fatigue Lasts. *Science News Letter,* May 29, 1965.

Johnson, L., Slye, E., and Dement, W., EEG and Autonomic Activity During and After Prolonged Sleep Deprivation. *Psychosomatic Medicine* 27: 415-423, 1965.

Kiyano, S., Kawamoto, T., Sakakura, H., and Iwama, K., Effects of Sleep Deprivation upon the Paradoxical Phase of Sleep in Cats. *EEG. clin. Neurophysiol.* 19: 34-40, 1965.

Koranyi, E. K., and Lehman, H. E., Experimental Sleep Deprivation in Schizophrenic Patients. *Arch. Gen. Psychiat.* 2: 534-544, 1960.

Kornfield, D. S., Zimberg, S., and Malm, J. R., Psychiatric Complications of Open-Heart Surgery. *New Eng. J. Med.* 273: 287, 1965.

Loveland, N. T., and Williams, H. L., Adding, Sleep Loss, and Body Temperature. *Percept. Mot. Skills* 16: 923-929, 1963.

Luby, E. D., Frohman, C. E., Grisell, J. L., Lenzo, J. E., and Gottlieb, J. S., Sleep Deprivation: Effects on Behavior, Thinking, Motor Performance, and Biological Energy Transfer Systems. *Psychosom. Med.* 22: 182-192, 1960.

Luby, E. D., Grisell, J. L., Frohman, C. E., Lees, H., Cohen, B. D., and Gottlieb, J. S., Biochemical, Psychological, and Behavioral Responses to Sleep Deprivation. *Ann. New York Acad. Sci.* 96: 71-78, 1961.

Mahurin, W., *Honest John.* G. P. Putnam's Sons, 1962.

Mandell, A. J., Kolar, E. J., and Sabbat, I., Starvation, Sleep Deprivation and the Stress Responsive Indole Substance. *Rec. Adv. Biol. Psychiat.* 6: 96-104, 1964.

Mandell, A. J., Slater, G., Mersol, I., and Geertsma, R. H., Stress-Responsive Indole Substance. *Arch. Gen. Psychiat.* 9:89-95, 1963.

Marshall, S. L. A., *Night Drop.* Little Brown, Boston, 1962.

McKenzie, R. B., Hartman, B., and Graveline, B. E., An Exploratory Study of

Sleep Characteristics in a Hypodynamic Environment. Brooks Air Force Base, School of Aviation Medicine, Texas, 1960.

Morris, G. O., and Singer, M. T., Sleep deprivation. *Arch. Gen. Psychiat.* 5: 453, 1961.

Murawski, B. J., and Crabbe, J., Effect of Sleep Deprivation on Plasma 17-Hydroxycorticosteroids. *J. Appl. Physiol.* 15: 280-282, 1960.

Murray, E., Schein, E. H., Erikson, K. T., Hill, W. F., and Cohen, M., The Effects of Sleep Deprivation on Social Behavior. *J. Soc. Psych.* 49: 229, 1959.

Murray, E. J., Williams, H. L., and Lubin, A., Body Temperature and Psychological Ratings During Sleep Deprivation. *J. Exp. Psych.* 56: 271, 1958.

Ross, J. J., Neurological Findings After Prolonged Sleep Deprivation. *Arch. Neurol.* 12: April, 1965.

Schein, E. H., The Effects of Sleep Deprivation on Performance in a Simulated Communication task. *J. Appl. Psych.* 41, 1957.

Tyler, D. B., Psychological Changes During Experimental Sleep Deprivation. *Diseases of the Nervous System* 16: October, 1955.

Webb, W. B., Some Effects of Prolonged Sleep Deprivation on the Hooded Rat. *J. Physiol. Comp. Psychol.* 55: 791-793, 1962.

Webb, W. B., Sleep Deprivation: Age and Exhaustion Time in the Rat. *Science* 136: 1122, 1962.

Webb, W. B., and Agnew, H. W., The Results of Continued Partial Sleep Deprivation. Association for the Psychophysiological Study of Sleep, Washington, D. C., 1965.

West, L. J., United States Air Force Prisoners of Chinese Communists. In Methods of Forceful Indoctrination: Observations and Interviews. Group for the Advancement of Psychiatry Symposium, 4: 270-284, 1957.

West, J. L., Janszen, H. H., Lester, B. K., and Cornelisoon, F. S., The Psychosis of Sleep Deprivation. *Ann. New York Acad. Sci.* 96: 66-70, 1962.

Wilkinson, R. T., Effects of up to 60 Hours of Sleep Deprivation on Different Types of Work. *Ergonomics* 7: 175-186, 1964.

Wilkinson, R. T., After Effect of Sleep Deprivation. *J. Exp. Psychol.* 66: 439-444, 1963.

Wilkinson, R. T., Interaction of Noise with Knowledge of Results and Sleep Deprivation. *J. Exp. Psychol.* 66: 332-337, 1963.

Wilkinson, R. T., Sleep Deprivation. In Edholm, O. G., and Bacharach, A. L. (eds.), *The Physiology of Survival.* Academic Press, 1966.

Williams, H. L., Granda, A. M., Jones, R. C., Lubin, A., and Armington, J. C., EEG Frequency and Finger Pulse Volume as Predictors of Reaction Time During Sleep Loss. *EEG. clin. Neurophysiol.* 14: 64-70, 1962.

Williams, H. L., Hammack, J. T., Daly, R. L., Dement, W. C., and Lubin,, A., Responses to Auditory Stimulation, Sleep Loss, and the EEG Stages of Sleep. *EEG. clin. Neurophysiol.* 16: 269-279, 1964.

Williams, H. L., Morris, G. O., Lubin, A., Illusions, Hallucinations, and Sleep Loss. In West, L. J. (ed.), *Hallucinations.* Grune & Stratton, 1962.

Williams, H. L., Lubin, A., and Goodnow, J. J., Impaired Performance with Acute Sleep Loss. *Psych. Monograph* No. 484, Vol. 73, #14, 1959, Am. Psychological Assn. Washington, D. C.

Wolff, H. G., Every Man Has His Breaking Point—The Conduct of Prisoners of War. *Military Medicine* 125, February, 1960.

CHAPTER V

References:

Brown, B., Shryne, J., and Dell, M., Relationship Between Personality-Behavior Characteristics and the Sleep-Dream Cycle in Cats. Association for the Psychophysiological Study of Sleep, Palo Alto, 1964.

Brown, B., and Shryne, J., EEG Theta Activities and Fast Activity Sleep in Cats Related to Behavior Traits. *Neuropsychologia,* 311-326, 1964.

Buresova, O., Bures, J., Fifkova, E., Vinogradova, O., and Weiss, T., Function Significance of Corticohippocampal Connections. *Exper. Neurol.* 6: 161, 1962.

Corazza, Di R., and Parmeggiani, P. L., Desincronizzazione dei Ritmi Bioelettrici dell' Ippocampo. *Arch. Sci. Biol.* 45: 401, 1961.

Feldman, S., Neurophysiological Mechanisms Modifying Afferent Hypothalamus-Hippocampal Conduction. *Exper. Neurol.* 5: 269, 1962.

Grastyan, E., The Hippocampus and Higher Nervous Activity. In Brazier, M. (ed.), *The Central Nervous System and Behavior.* The Josiah Macy Foundation, 1959.

Hammack, J. T., An Experimental Analysis of Behavior During Sleep. Three annual progress reports to the Defense Documentation Center, 1962, 1963, 1964.

Iwata, K., and Snider, R. S., Cerebello-hippocampal Influences on the Electroencephalogram. *EEG. clin. Neurophysiol.* 11: 439, 1959.

Monroe, L. J., Psychological and physiological differences between good and poor sleepers. Unpublished doctoral dissertation, University of Chicago, 1965.

Webb, W. B., and Ades, H., Sleep Tendencies: Effects of Barometric Pressure. *Science* 132: 263, 1964.

Williams, R. L., Agnew, H. W., and Webb, W. B., Sleep Patterns in Young Adults: An EEG Study. *EEG. clin. Neurophysiol.* 17: 376-381, 1964.

Wilson, W. P., and Zung, W. K., Arousal Threshold of Males and Females During Sleep. 10th Annual Conference V.A. Cooperative Studies in Psychiatry, New Orleans, March, 1965.

Zung, W. K., Naylor, T., Gianturco, D., and Wilson, W. P., Computer Simulation of Sleep EEG Patterns Using a Markov Chain Model. In *Recent Advances in Biological Psychiatry,* Vol. VIII, Plenum Press, New York, 1965.

CHAPTER VI

References for the general reader:

Adams, R. D., Sleep and Its Abnormalities. In Harrison, T. R. (ed.), *Principles of Internal Medicine,* Vol. I. McGraw-Hill, 1958.

Brower, B., America's Sleeping Sickness—Staying Awake. *New York Times Magazine,* October 15, 1961.

Kaplan, J., Sleepwalking: Fact, Fallacy, or Fancy? *Today's Health,* September 1960.

Laing, A. M., *The Sleep Book.* Frederick Muller Ltd., London, 1948.

Additional References:

Daly, D. D., and Yoss, R. E., Electroencephalogram in Narcolepsy. *EEG. clin. Neurophysiol.* 9: 109, 1957.

Delange, M., Castan, P., Cadilhac, J., and Passouant, P., Study of Night Sleep

During Centrencephalic and Temporal Epilepsies. *EEG. clin. Neurophysiol.* 14: 777, 1962.

Dement, W. C., Dream Recall and Eye Movements During Sleep in Schizophrenics and Normals. *J. Nerv. Ment. Dis.* 122: 263, 1955.

Dement, W. C., Rechtschaffen, A., and Gulevitch, G., A Polygraphic Study of the Narcoleptic Sleep Attack. *EEG. clin. Neurophysiol.* 17: 608, 1964.

Detre, T., Davis, J., and Spaulding, P., *et al.*, Sleep Disturbance in Mental Patients. Association for the Psychophysiological Study of Sleep, Washington, D. C., 1965.

Deutsch, A., *The Shame of the States.* Harcourt, Brace & World, 1948.

Evarts, E. V., Bental, E., Bihari, B., and Huttenlocher, P., Spontaneous Discharge of Single Neurons During Sleep and Waking. *Science* 135: 726-728, 1962.

Evarts, E. V., Temporal Patterns of Discharge of Pyramidal Track Neurons During Sleep and Waking in the Monkey. *J. Neurophysiol.* 27: 152-171, 1964.

Feinberg, I., Koresko, R. L., Gottleib, F., and Wender, P. H., Sleep Electroencephalographic and Eye-Movement Patterns in Schizophrenic Patients. *Comp. Psychiat.* 5: 44-53, 1964.

Feinberg, I., Koresko, R. L., and Gottleib, F., Further Observations on Electrophysiological Sleep Patterns in Schizophrenics. *Comp. Psychiat.,* Vol. 6, February, 1965.

Feinberg, I., Koresko, R. L., Heller, N., and Steinberg, H. R., Unusually High Dream Time in an Hallucinating Patient. *Am. J. Psychiat.* 121: 10, April, 1965.

Feinberg, I., Koresko, R. L., and Schaffner, R., Sleep Electroencephalographic and Eye Movement Patterns in Patients with Chronic Brain Syndrome. *J. Psychiat. Res.* 3: 11-26, 1965.

Feinberg, I., Lane, M., and Lassen, N. A., Senile Dementia and Cerebral Oxygen Uptake Measured on the Right and Left Sides. *Nature* 188: 962-964, 1960.

Gastaut, H., Batini, C., and Fressy, J., On Epileptic Attacks Recorded During the Night Sleep of Epileptic Children. *EEG. clin. Neurophysiol.* 15: 142, 1963.

Gastaut, H., and Broughton, R. J., Conclusions Concerning the Mechanism of Enuresis Nocturna. *EEG. clin. Neurophysiol.* 16:625, 1964.

Gresham, S. C., Agnew, H. W., and Williams, R. L., The Sleep of Depressed Patients: An EEG and Eye Movement Study. *Arch. Gen. Psychiat.* 13: 503-507, 1965.

Hanretta, A. G., Diagnostic Utilization of Sleep Characteristics. *Texas State J. of Med.* 59, September, 1963.

Hawkins, D. R., Scott, J., and Thrasher, G., Sleep Patterns in Enuretic Children. Association for the Psychophysiological Study of Sleep, Washington, D. C., 1965.

Hartmann, E. L., Verdone, P. P., and Snyder, F., A Longitudinal Study of Sleep and Dream Patterns in Psychiatric Patients. Association for the Psychophysiological Study of Sleep, Palo Alto, 1964.

Hawkins, D. R., Knapp, R., Scott, J., and Thrasher, G., Sleep Studies in Depressed Patients. Association for the Psychophysiological Study of Sleep, Washington, D. C., 1965.

Huttenlocher, P. R., Evoked and Spontaneous Activity in Single Units of Medial Brain Stem During Natural Sleep and Waking. *J. Neurophysiol.* 24: 451-468, 1961.

Jacobson, A., Kales, A., Lehmann, D., and Zweizig, J. R., Somnambulism: All Night EEG Studies. *Science* 148: 975-977, 1965.

Keefe, W. P., Yoss, R. E., Martens, T. G., and Daly, D. D., Ocular Manifestations of Narcolepsy. *Am. J. Ophth.* 49: 953-957, 1960.

Koresko, R. L., Snyder, F., and Feinberg, I., "Dream Time" in Hallucinating and Non-hallucinating Schizophrenic Patients. *Nature* 199: 1118, 1963.

Lassen, N. A., Feinberg, I., and Lane, M. H., Bilateral Studies of Cerebral Oxygen Uptake in Young and Aged Normal Subjects and in Patients with Organic Dementia. *J. Clin. Investigation* 39, March, 1960.

Lester, B. K., and Burch, N. R., Psychophysiological Studies of Sleep in Schizophrenic and Control Subjects. *Am. Psychiat. Assn.* New York, May 5, 1965.

Nixon, O., Pierce, C., Lester, B. K., Mathis, J. L., Narcolepsy, Nocturnal Dream Frequency in Adolescents. *J. Neuropsychiat.* 5: 150-152, 1964.

Oswald, I., Berger, R. J., Jaramillo, R. A., Keddie, K. M. G., Olley, P. D., and Plunkett, G. B., Melancholia and Barbiturates: A Controlled EEG, Body, and Eye-Movement Study of Sleep. *Brit. J. Psychiat.* 109: 66-78, 1963.

Pierce, C. M., Whitman, R., Maas, J. W., and Gay, M. I., Enuresis and Dreaming. *Arch. Gen. Psychiat.* 4: 166-170, 1961.

Rand, R. W., Crandall, P. H., Adey, W. R., Walter, R. D., and Markham, C. H., Electrophysiologic Investigations in Parkinson's Disease and Other Dyskinesias in Man. *Neurology* 12: 754-770, 1962.

Rechtschaffen, A., Wolpert, E. A., Dement, W. C., Mitchell, S. A., and Fisher, C., Nocturnal Sleep of Narcoleptics. *EEG clin. Neurophysiol.* 15: 599-609, 1963.

Reding, G. R., Rubright, W. C., Rechtschaffen, A., and Daniels, R. S., Sleep Pattern of Tooth-Grinding: Its Relationship to Dreaming. *Science* 145: 725, 1964.

Saint-Laurent, J., Batini, C., Broughton, P., and Gastaut, H., A Polygraphic Study of Nocturnal Enuresis in the Epileptic Child. *EEG clin. Neurophysiol.* 15: 904, 1963.

Schwartz, B. A., Guilbaud, G., and Fischgold, H., Single and Multiple Spikes in the Night Sleep of Epileptics. *EEG clin. Neurophysiol.* 16: 56-67, 1964.

Sours, J. A., *et al.*, Somnambulism. Its Critical Significance and Dynamic Meaning in Late Adolescence and Adulthood. *Arch. Gen. Psychiat.* 9: October, 1963.

Yoss, R. E., and Daly, D. D., Hereditary Aspects of Narcolepsy. *Trans. Amer. Neurol. Assn.*, 239-240, 1960.

Yoss, R. E., and Daly, D. D., Narcolepsy in Children. *Pediatrics* 25: 1025-1033, 1960.

Zung, W. K., Wilson, W. P., and Dodson, W. E., Effect of Depressive Disorders on Sleep EEG Arousal. *Arch. Gen. Psychiat.* 10: 439, 1964.

CHAPTER VII

References for the general reader:

Davidson, B., The Thrill Pill Menace. *The Saturday Evening Post,* December 4, 1965.

Hentoff, N., Profiles, *The New Yorker,* June 26, 1965.

Phipps, J., and Robinson, R., The Growing Menace of "Nice" Drugs. *Good Housekeeping,* September, 1963.

Proceedings, White House Conference on Narcotic and Drug Abuse. Govt. Printing Office, Washington, D. C., 1962.

The Drug Takers. Time-Life, Inc., 1965.
Uhr, L., and Miller, J., *Drugs and Behavior.* John Wiley & Sons, 1960.

Additional References:

Adey, W. R., Bell, F., and Dennis, B. J., Effects of LSD-25, Psyilocybin, and Psilocin on Temporal Lobe EEG Patterns and Learned Behavior in the Cat. *Neurology* 12: 591-602, 1962.

Bessman, S. P., and Skolnik, S. J., Gamma Hydroxybutyrate and Gamma Butyrolactone Concentration in Rat Tissues During Anesthesia. *Science* 143: 1045, 1964.

Chapman, L. F., Walter, R. D., Adey, W. R., Crandal, O. H., Rand, R. W., Brazier, M. A. B., and Markham, C. H., Altered Electrical Activity of Human Hippocampus and Amygdala Induced by LSD-25. *The Physiologist* 5, 1962.

Control of Psychotoxic Drugs. Hearing before the Subcommittee on Health, of the Committee on Labor and Public Welfare, U. S. Senate, 88th Session, on S. 2628. U. S. Government Printing Office, 1964.

Freeman, F. R., Agnew, H. W., and Williams, R. L., An EEG Study of the Effects of Meprobamate on Human Sleep. *Clin. Pharmacol. Ther.* 6: 172-176, 1965.

Giarman, N. J., and Roth, R. H., Differential Estimation of Gamma-Butyrolactone and Gamma-Hydroxybutyric Acid in Rat Blood and Brain. *Science* 145: 583-584, 1964.

Green, W. J., The Effect of LSD on the Sleep-Dream Cycle. *J. Nerv. Ment. Dis.* 140: 417-426, 1965.

Greenberg, R. M., and Pearlman, C., Delirium Tremens and Dream Deprivation. Association for the Psychophysiological Study of Sleep, Palto Alto, 1964.

Gresham, S. C., Webb, W. B., and Williams, R. L., Alcohol and Caffeine: Effects on Inferred Visual Dreaming. *Science* 140: 1226, 1963.

Gross, M. M., Goodenough, D. R., Tobin, M., Halpert, E., Dominick, L., Perlstein, A., Sirota, M., DiBianco, J., Fuller, R., and Kishner, I., Sleep Disturbances and Hallucinations in the Acute Alcoholic Psychosis. Association for the Psychophysiological Study of Sleep, Palto Alto, 1964.

Hobson, J. A., The Effect of LSD on the Sleep Cycle of the Cat. *EEG. clin. Neurophysiol.* 17: 52-56, 1964.

Jouvet, M., Cier, A., Mounier, D., and Valatx, J., Effets du 4-Butyrolactone et du 4-Hydroxybutyrate de Sodium sur l'EEG et le Comportement du Chat. *C. R. Soc. Biol.* 155: 1313, 1961.

Kaufman, E., Roffwarg, H., and Muzio, J., Alterations in the Sleep EEG Configuration of a Drug Addict During Addiction, Withdrawal, and Baseline Nights. Association for the Psychophysiological Study of Sleep, Palo Alto, 1964.

Matsuzaki, M., Takagi, H., and Tokizane, T., Paradoxical Phase of Sleep: Its Artificial Induction in the Cat by Sodium Butyrate. *Science* 146: 1328, 1964.

Mirsky, A. F., and Kornetsky, C., On the Dissimilar Effects of Drugs on the Digit Symbol Substitution and Continuous Performance Tests: A Review and Preliminary Integration of Behavioral and Physiological Evidence. *Psychopharmacologica* 5: 161-177, 1964.

Muzio, J., Roffwarg, H., and Kaufman, R., Alteration in the Young Adult Human Sleep EEG Configuration Resulting from d-LSD-25. Association for the Psychophysiological Study of Sleep, Palo Alto, 1964.

Rechtschaffen, A., and Maron, L., The Effect of Amphetamine on the Sleep Cycle. *EEG clin. Neurophysiol.* 16: 433-445, 1964.

CHAPTER VIII

References for the general reader:

Asimov, I., *The Human Brain.* New American Library, Signet Science Library, 1965.

Fisher, A. E., Chemical Stimulation of the Brain. *Scientific American* 210: 60-68, 1964.

Miller, N. E., Chemical Coding of Behavior in the Brain. *Science* 148: 328-338, 1965.

Additional References:

Akert, K., Koella, P., and Hess, R., Jr., Sleep Produced by Electrical Stimulation of the Thalamus. *Am. J. Physiol.* 168: 260-267, 1952.

Bailey, S., Bucci, L., Gosline, E., and Kline, N. S., *et al.*, Comparison of Iproniazid with Other Amine Oxidase Inhibitors, Including W-1544, JB-516, RO4-1018, and RO5-0700. *Am. N. Y. Acad. Sci.* 80: 652, 1959.

Bessman, S. P., and Bessman, A. N., The Cerebral and Peripheral Uptake of Ammonia in Liver Disease with an Hypothesis for the Mechanism of Hepatic Coma. *J. Clin. Investigation* 31: 1, April, 1955.

Bessman, S. P., Amoniagenic Coma, the Chemistry of an Endogenous Intoxication. *Proc. 4th Intnatl. Cong. Biochem.*, Vienna, 1958.

Buchwald, N. A., and Ervin, F. R., Evoked Potentials and Behavior: A Study of Responses to Subcortical Stimulation in the Awake, Unrestrained Animal. *EEG clin. Neurophysiol.* 9, 1957.

Cordeau, J. P., EEG and Behavioral Changes Following Microinjections of Acetylcholine and Adrenaline in the Brain Stem of Cats. Association for the Psychophysiological Study of Sleep, Palo Alto, 1964.

Faure, J., The Paradoxical Phase of Sleep in the Rabbit—Its Neurohumoral Relationship. *EEG clin. Neurophysiol.* 14: 784, 1962.

Favale, E., Loeb, C., Rossi, G. F., and Sacco, G., EEG Synchronization and Behavioral Signs of Sleep Following Low Frequency Stimulation of the Brain Stem Reticular Formation. *Arch. Ital. Biol.* 99: 1-22, 1961.

Hartmann, E. L., Dreaming Sleep and the Menstrual Cycle. Association for the Psychophysiological Study of Sleep. Washington, D. C., 1965.

Hernandez Peon, R., Psychiatric Implication of Neurophysiological Research. *Bulletin of the Menninger Clinic* 28, July 1964.

Hernandez-Peon, R., Central Neuro-Humoral Transmission in Sleep and Wakefulness. In Akert, K., Bally, C., and Schade, J. P. (eds.), *Progress in Brain Research,* Vol. 18, Elsevier, Amsterdam, 1965.

Hernandez-Peon, R., A Cholinergic Hypnogenic Limbic Forebrain-Hindbrain Circuit. *Neurophysiologie des Etats de Sommeil.* Editions du Centre National de la Recherche Scientifique, Paris, 1965.

Hernandez-Peon, R., and Chavez-Ibarra, G., Sleep Induced by Electrical or Chemical Stimulation of the Forebrain. *EEG clin. Neurophysiol.* Supp. 24, 1962.

Hernandez-Peon, R., Limbic Cholinergic Pathways Involved in Sleep and Emotional Behavior. *Exp. Neurol.* 8: 93-111, 1963.

Hernandez-Peon, R., Atropine Blockade Within a Cholinergic Hypnogenic Circuit. *Exp. Neurol.* 8: 20-29, 1963.

Heuser, G., Buchwald, N. A., and Wyers, E. J., The "Caudate-Spindle": Facilitatory and Inhibitory Caudate-Cortical Pathways. *EEG clin. Neurophysiol.* 14: 519-524, 1961.

Hyden, H., and Lange, P. W., Rhythmic Enzyme Changes in Neurons and Glia During Sleep. *Science* 149: 654, 1965.

Kanematsu, S., and Sawyer, C. H., Effects of Intrahypothalamic Implants of Reserpine on Lactation and Pituitary Prolactin in the Rabbit. *Proc. Soc. Exper. Biol. & Med.* 113: 967, 1963.

Kawakami, J., and Sawyer, C. H., Induction of Behavioral and Electroencephalographic Changes in the Rabbit by Hormone Administration or Brain Stimulation. *Endocrinol.* 65: 631-643, 1959.

Kline, N. S., Clinical Experience with Iproniazid. *J. Clin. & Exper. Psychopath.* 19: 2, Suppl. 1, June, 1958.

Kline, N. S., Comprehensive Therapy of Depressions. *J. Neuropsychiat.* Suppl. 1, 15-26, 1961.

Kline, N. S., and Sacks, W., Relief of Depression Within One Day Using an M.A.O. Inhibitor and Intravenous 5-HTP. *J. Psychiat.* 120, September, 1963.

Koella, W. P., Trunca, C. M., and Czicman, J. S., Serotonin: Effect on Recruiting Responses of the Cat. *Life Sci.* 4: 173-181, 1965.

Koella, W. P., and Czicman, J. S., Influence of Serotonin upon Optic Evoked Potentials, EEG, and Blood Pressure of Cat. *Am. J. Physiol.* 204: 873, 1963.

Lloyd, C. W., Effects of Hormones on Brain and CNS Control of Endocrine Function in the Human. *Proc. Second Intnatl. Cong. of Endocrinology,* Symposium 25, Series 83, pp. 591-596, London, 1965.

Mandell, M. P., Mandell, A. J., and Jacobson, A., Biochemical and Neurophysiological Studies of Paradoxical Sleep. In Wortis, J. (ed.), *Recent Advances in Biological Psychiatry,* 7: 115-124, Plenum, N. Y., 1965.

Mandell, A. J., and Mandell, M. P., Biochemical Aspects of Rapid Eye Movement Sleep. *Am. J. Psychiat.* 122: 391-401, 1965.

Matsumoto, J., and Jouvet, M., Effet de Reserpine, DOPA, et 5-HTP sur les Deux Etats de Sommeil. *C. R. Soc. Biol.* 158: 2037, 1964.

Monnier, M., and Hosli, L., Dialysis of Sleep and Waking Factors in Blood of the Rabbit. *Science* 146: 796-797, 1964.

Moruzzi, G., Reticular Influences on the EEG. *EEG clin. Neurophysiol.* 16: 2-17, 1964.

Riser, L., and Levey, J., *et al.,* Influence de la Serotonine et du 5-HTP sur le Sommeil Experimental en Presence ou Non d'Iproniazide. *Rev. Agressologie* 1: 4, 1960.

Rossi, G. F., Sleep Inducing Mechanisms in the Brain Stem. *EEG. clin. Neurophysiol.* Suppl. 24, 113-124, 1963.

Sawyer, C. H., and Kawakami, M., Characteristics of Behavioral and Electroencephalographic After-reactions to Copulation and Vaginal Stimulation in the Female Rabbit. *Endocrinology* 65: 622-630, 1959.

Sawyer, C. H., and Kawakami, M., Interactions Between the Central Nervous System and Hormones Influencing Ovulation. In Villee, C. A. (ed.), *Control of Ovulation.* Pergamon Press, 1961.

Sawyer, C. H., Mechanisms by Which Drugs and Hormones Activate and Block Release of Pituitary Gonadotropins. *Proc. First Intnatl. Pharmacol. Meeting,* Vol. 1, 27-46, Pergamon Press, 1963.

Snyder, S. H., and Axelrod, J., Circadian Rhythm in Pineal Serotonin: Effect of Mono Amine Oxidase Inhibition and Reserpine. *Science* 149: 542, 1965.

Wurtman, R. J., and Axelrod, J., The Pineal Gland. *Scientific American,* July, 1965.

Yamaguchi, N., Ling, G. and Marczynski, T., The Effects of Chemical Stimulation of the Preoptic Region, Nucleus Centralis Medialis, or Brain Stem Reticular Formation with Regard to Sleep and Wakefulness. *Rec. Adv. Biol. Psychiat.* 6: 9-20, 1964.

CHAPTER IX

References for the general reader:

Dement, W. C., An Essay on Dreams: The Role of Physiology in Understanding Their Nature. *New Directions in Psychology* II. Holt, Rinehart & Winston, 1965.

Diamond, E., *The Science of Dreams.* McFadden-Bartell, New York, 1963.

Trillin, C., A Third State of Existence. *The New Yorker,* September 18, 1965.

Additional References:

Adey, W. R., Kado, R. T., and Rhodes, J. M., Sleep: Cortical and Subcortical Recordings in the Chimpanzee. *Science* 141: 932, 1963.

Allison, T., Cortical and Subcortical Evoked Responses to Central Stimuli During Wakefulness and Sleep. *EEG clin. Neurophysiol.* 18: 131-139, 1965.

Amadeo, M., and Gomez, E., Eye Movements and Dreaming in Subjects with Lifelong Blindness. Association for the Psychophysiological Study of Sleep, Palo Alto, 1964.

Armstrong, R. H., Burnap, D., Jacobson, A., Kales, A., Ward, S., and Golden, J., Dreams and Gastric Secretions in Duodenal Ulcer Patients. *The New Physician,* September, 1965.

Aserinsky, E., Brainwave Pattern During the Rapid Eye Movement Period of Sleep. *The Physiologist* 8: 104, 1965.

Aserinsky, E., Periodic Respiratory Pattern Occurring in Conjunction with Eye Movements During Sleep. *Science* 150: 763, 1965.

Austen, B. G., *The Electrophysiology Related to Electrically-Induced Sleep.* Master of Arts Thesis, Ohio State University, 1964.

Baldridge, B. J., Whitman, R. M., and Kramer, M., The Concurrence of Fine Muscle Activity and Rapid Eye Movement Sleep. *Psychosom. Med.* 27: 19-26, 1965.

Batini, C., Moruzzi, G., Palestini, M., Rossi, G. F., and Zanchetti, A., Effects of Complete Pontine Transections on the Sleep-Wakefulness Rhythm: The Midpontine Pretrigeminal Preparation. *Arch. Ital. Biol.* 97: 1-12, 1959.

Baust, W., Berlucchi, G., and Moruzzi, G., Changes in the Auditory Input in Wakefulness and During the Synchronized and Desynchronized Stages of Sleep. *Arch. Ital. Biol.* 102: 657-674, 1964.

Berger, R. J., Tonus of Laryngeal Muscles During Sleep and Dreaming. *Science* 134: 840, 1961.

Berger, R. J., Olley, P., and Oswald, I., The EEG, Eye Movements, and Dreams of the Blind. *Quart. J. Exp. Psychol.* 14: 183, 1962.

Berger, R. J., and Oswald, I., Eye Movements During Active and Passive Dreams. *Science* 137: 601, 1962.

Berlucchi, G., Callosal Activity During Sleep and Wakefullness. Association for the Psychophysiological Study of Sleep, Washington, D. C., 1965.

Berlucchi, G., Moruzzi, G., Salvi, G., and Strata, P., Pupil Behavior and Ocular Movements During Synchronzied and Desynchronized Sleep. *Arch. Ital. Biol.* 102: 230-244, 1964.

Bizzi, E., Pompeiano, O., and Somogyi, I., Vestibular Nuclei: Activity of Single Neurons During Natural Sleep and Wakefulness. *Science* 145: 414, 1964.

Bizzi, E., and Brooks, D. C., Pontine Reticular Formation: Relation to Lateral Geniculate Nucleus During Deep Sleep. *Science* 141: 270, 1963.

Bizzi, E., Discharge Patterns of Lateral Geniculate Neurons During Paradoxical Sleep. Association for the Psychophysiological Study of Sleep, Washington, D. C., 1965.

Brebbia, D. R., and Altshuler, K. Z., Oxygen Consumption Rate and Electroencephalographic Stage of Sleep. *Science* 150: 1621-1623, 1965.

Brooks, D. C., and Bizzi, E., Brain Stem Electrical Activity During Deep Sleep. *Arch. Ital. Biol.* 101: 648, 1963.

Broughton, R. J., Poire, R., and Tassinari, C. A., The Electrodermogram (Tarchanoff Effect) During Sleep. *EEG clin. Neurophysiol.* 18: 661-708, 1965.

Camacho-Evangelista, A., and Reinoso-Suarez, F., Activating and Synchronizing Centers in Cat Brain: EEGs After Lesions. *Science* 146: 268-270, 1964.

Cadilhac, J., Passouant-Fontaine, T., and Passouant, P., L'Organisation des divers Stades du Sommeil chez le Chaton de la Naissance à 45 Jours. *J. Physiol.* 54: 305, 1962.

Candia, O., Favale, E., Guissani, A., and Rossi, G., Blood Pressure During Natural Sleep and During Sleep Induced by Electrical Stimulation of the Brain Stem Reticular Formation. *Arch. Ital. Biol.* 100: 216-233, 1962.

Carli, G., Armengol, V., and Zanchetti, A., EEG Desynchronization During Deep Sleep After Destruction of Midbrain-Limbic Pathways in the Cat. *Science* 140: 677, 1963.

Caspers, H., On Steady Potential Shifts During Various Stages of Sleep. *Neurophysiologie des Etats des Sommeil.* Editions du Centre National de la Recherche Scientifique, Paris, 1965.

Cohen, H. B., and Dement, W. C., Sleep: Changes in Threshold to Electroconvulsive Shock in Rats After Deprivation of "Paradoxical" Phase. *Science* 150, December 3, 1965.

Deckert, G. H., Pursuit Eye Movement in the Absence of a Moving Stimulus. *Science* 143: 1192, 1964.

Delorme, F., Vimont, P., and Jouvet, D., Etude Statistique du Cycle Vielle-Sommeils chez le Chat. *C. R. Soc. Biol.* 158: 2128, 1964.

Dement, W. C., The Occurrence of Low Voltage, Fast EEG Patterns During Behavioral Sleep in the Cat. *EEG clin. Neurophysiol.* 10: 291, 1958.

Dement, W. C., The Effect of Dream Deprivation. *Science* 131: 1705, 1960.

Dement, W. C., Experimental Dream Studies. In Masserman, J. (ed.), *Science and Psychoanalysis* 7: 129-184, Grune & Stratton, 1964.

Dement, W. C., Recent Studies on the Biological Role of Rapid Eye Movement Sleep. *Am. J. Psychiat.* 122: 404, 1965.

Dement, W. C., Greenberg, S., and Klein, R., The Persistence of the REM Deprivation Effect. Association for the Psychophysiological Study of Sleep, Washington, D. C., 1965.

Dewson, J. H., Dement, W. C., Wagener, T., and Nobel, K., A Central-Neural Change Coincident with REM Sleep Deprivation in the Cat. Association for the Psychophysiological Study of Sleep, Washington, D. C., 1965.

Dreyfus-Brisac, C., Samson, D., Blanc, C., and Monod, N., L'Ectro-Encephalogramme de l'Enfant Normal de Moins de 3 Ans. *Etudes Neo-Natales* 7: 143, 1958.

Evarts, E. V., Effects of Sleep and Waking on Spontaneous and Evoked Discharge of Single Units in Visual Cortex. *Fed. Proc.* 19: 828, 1960.

Evarts, E. V., Activity of Neurons in Visual Cortex of the Cat During Sleep with Low Voltage Fast EEG Activity. *J. Neurophysiol.* 25: 812, 1962.

Evarts, E. V., Photically Evoked Responses in Visual Cortex Units During Sleep and Waking. *J. Neurophysiol.* 26: 229, 1963.

Favale, E., Loeb, C., and Manfredi, M., Somatic Evoked Potentials During the Different Phases of Sleep in Cats. *EEG. clin. Neurophysiol.* 15: 917, 1963.

Fisher, C., and Dement, W. C., Studies on the Psychopathology of Sleep and Dreams. *Am. J. Psychiat.* 119: 1160, 1963.

Fisher, C., Gross, J., and Zuch, J., A Cycle of Penile Erections Synchronous with Dreaming (REM) Sleep. *Arch. Gen. Psychiat.* 12: 29, 1965.

Gilbaud, G., and Rosenblith, W., Evolution chez l'Homme Normal, au Cours des differents Stades de Sommeil des Activites Evoquees au Vertex par Diverses Stimulations Sensorielles. *J. de Physiologie* 57, February, 1965.

Gilyarovskiy, V. A., Liventsev, I. M., Segal, Y. Ye. and Kirillova, Z. A., *Electric Sleep: A Clinical-Physiological Investigation.* CSO: 3243-N, JPRS, 2278, U. S. Department of Commerce, Joint Publication Research Service, Clearinghouse for Federal Scientific and Technical Information, Springfield, Va.

Gross, J., Feldman, M., and Fisher, C., Eye Movements During Emergent Stage I EEG in Subjects with Lifelong Blindness. Association for the Psychophysiological Study of Sleep, Washington, D. C., 1965.

Hartmann, E. L., The D-State, *New Engl. J. Med.*, July, 283: 30, 1965.

Henry, P., Cohen, H., Stadel, B., Stulce, J., Ferguson, J., Wagener, T., and Dement, W. C., CSF Transfer from REM Deprived Cats to Nondeprived Recipients. Association for the Psychophysiological Study of Sleep, Washington, D. C., 1965.

Hernandez-Peon, R., O'Flaherty, J. J., and Mazzuchelli-O'Flaherty, A. L., Modifications of Tactile Evoked Potentials at the Spinal Trigeminal Sensory Nucleus During Wakefulness and Sleep. *Exper. Neurol.*, Vol. 13, 1965.

Hernandez-Peon, R., Attention, Sleep, Motivation and Behavior. In Heath, R. (ed.), *The Role of Pleasure in Behavior.* Hoeber-Harper, New York, 1964.

Hobson, J. A., L'activite Electrique Phasique du Cortex et du Thalamus au Cours du Sommeil Desynchronise chez le Chat. *C. R. Soc. Biol.* 158: 2131, 1964.

Hobson, J. A., The Effects of Chronic Brain Stem Lesions on Cortical and Muscular Activity During Sleep and Waking in the Cat. *EEG clin. Neurophysiol.* 19: 41-62, 1965.

Hobson, J. A., Goldfrank, F., and Snyder, F., Respiration and Mental Activity in Sleep. *J. Psychiat. Res.* 3: 79-90, 1965.

Hodes, R., Ocular Phenomena in the Two Stages of Sleep in the Cat. *Exp. Neurol.* 9: 36-42, 1964.

Hodes, R., and Suzuki, J., Comparative Thresholds for Cortico-Spinal and Vestibulo-Spinal Movements, and for Reticular Formation Arousal in the Cat, in Wakefulness, Sleep, and Periods of Rapid Eye Movements. *EEG clin. Neurophysiol.* 18: 239-248, 1965.

Hodes, R., and Dement, W. C. Abolition of Electrically Induced Reflexes (EIR's of II Reflexes) During Rapid Eye Movement Periods of Sleep in Normal Subjects. *EEG clin. Neurophysiol.* 17: December, 1964.

Jeannerod, M., Mouret, J., and Jouvet, M., Etude de la Motricite Oculaire au Cours de la Phase Paradoxale du Sommeil chez le Chat. *EEG clin. Neurophysiol.* 18: 554-566, 1965.

Jouvet, M., Neurophysiology of the States of Sleep. *Physiological Reviews,* in translation.

Jouvet, M., Paradoxical Sleep—A Study of Its Nature and Mechanisms. In Akert, K., Bally, C., and Schade, J. P. (eds.), *Sleep Mechanisms,* Vol. 18. Elsevier, Amsterdam, 1965.

Jouvet, M., Etude de la Dualite des Etats de Sommeil et des Mecanismes de la Phase Paradoxale. In *Aspects Anatomo-fonctionnels de la Physiologie du Sommeil.* C.N.R.S., 1965

Jouvet, M., and Jouvet, D. Le Sommeil et les Reves chez l'Animal. *Psychiatre Animal.* Bibliotheque Neuropsychiatrique de Langue Française, 1964.

Jouvet, M., and Jouvet, D. A Study of the Neurophysiological Mechanisms of Dreaming. *EEG clin. Neurophysiol.,* suppl. 24: 133-156, 1963.

Jouvet, M., Pellin, B., and Mounier, D., Polygraphic Study of the Different Sleep Phases During Chronic Disturbances of Consciousness (Prolonged Comas). *EEG clin. Neurophysiol.* 14: 138, 1962.

Jouvet, M., Recherches sur les Structures Nerveuses et les Mecanisms Responsables des Differentes Phases du Sommeil Physiologique. *Arch. Ital. Biol.* 100: 125-206, 1962.

Jouvet, D., Valatx, J. L., and Jouvet, M., Etude Polygraphique du Sommeil chez l'Agneau. *C. R. Soc. Biol.* 156: 1411-1414, 1962.

Kales, A., Hoedemaker, F. S., Jacobson, A., and Lichtenstein, E. L., Dream Deprivation: An Experimental Reappraisal. *Nature* 204: 1337, 1964.

Karacan, I., Goodenough, D. R., Shapiro, A., and Witkin, H. A., Some Psychological and Physiological Correlates of Penile Erections During Sleep. Association for the Psychophysiological Study of Sleep, Washington, D. C., 1965.

Kawamura, H., and Sawyer, C. H., Elevation in Brain Temperature During Paradoxical Sleep. *Science* 150: 912-913, 1965.

Kawamura, H., and Sawyer, C. H., D. C. Potential Changes in the Rabbit During Slow Wave Sleep, Paradoxical Sleep, and Wakefulness. *Am. J. Physiol.,* December, 1964.

Khazan, N., and Sawyer, C. H., "Rebound" Recovery from Deprivation of Paradoxical Sleep in the Rabbit. *Proc. Soc. Exp. Biol. Med.* 114: 536-539, 1963.

Klein, M., Etude Polygraphique et Phylogenique des Etats de Sommeil. Bosc Freres, Lyon, 1963.

Klein, M., Michel, F., and Jouvet, M., Etude polygraphique des Etats de Sommeil chez les Oiseaux. *C. R. Soc. Biol.* 158: 99-103, 1964.

Kuzin, N. I., Zhukovskiy, V. D., and Sachkov, V. N., The Use of Interference Currents in the Combined Exclusion of Pain in Surgical Operations. NASA TT F- 9346, Clearinghouse for Federal Scientific and Technical Information, Springfield, Va., August, 1965.

Lena, C., and Parmeggiani, P. L., Hippocampal Theta Rhythm and Activated Sleep. *Helv. Physiol. Acta.* 22: 120, 1964.

Liberson, W. T., and Cadilhac, J. G., Electroshock and Rhinencephalic Seizure States. *Confinia Neurol.* 13, 1953.

Lissak, K., Karmos, G., and Grastyan, E., A Peculiar Dreamlike Stage of Sleep in the Cat. *Act. Nerv.* Sup. 4: 347, 1962.

Liventsev, N. M. (ed.), Apparatus for Sinusoidal Impulse Therapy, the SNIM-1, pp. 139-148. In *Electromedical Apparatus,* Icd. Meditsina, Moscow, 1964. In translation. Available in Russian, National Library of Medicine, Bethesda, Md.

MacLean, P. D., and Ploog, D. W., Cerebral Representation of Penile Erection. *J. Neurophysiol.* 25: 29-55, 1962.

MacLean, P. D., Denniston, R. H., and Dua, S., Further Studies on Cerebral Representation of Penile Erection: Caudal Thalamus, Midbrain, and Pons. *J. Neurophysiol.* 26: 273-293, 1963.

MacLean, P. D., New Findings Relevant to the Evolution of Psychosexual Function of the Brain. *J. Nerv. Ment. Dis.* 135: 289-301, 1962.

Manzoni, T., and Parmeggiani, P. L., Hippocampal Control of the Activity of Thalamic Neurones. *Helv. Physiol. Acta.* 22: 28, 1964.

Meier, G. W., and Berger, R. J., The Development of Sleep and Wakefulness Patterns in the Infant Rhesus Monkey. *Exper. Neurol.* 12: 257, 1965.

Michel, F., Rechtschaffen, A., and Vimont-Vicary, P., Activite Electrique de Muscles Oculaires Extrinsiques au Cours du Cycle Vielle-Sommeil. *C. R. Soc. Biol.* 158: 106, 1964.

Mikiten, T. M., Neibyl, P. H., and Hendley, C. D., EEG Desynchronization During Behavioral Sleep Associated with Spike Discharges from the Thalamus of the Cat. *Fed. Proc.* 20: 327, 1960.

Mouret, J., Les Mouvements Oculaires au Cours du Sommeil Paradoxical. J. Tixier and fils, 1964.

Nowlin, J. B., Troyer, W. G., Collins, W. S., Silverman, G., Nichols, C. R., McIntosh, H. D., Estes, E. H., and Bogdonoff, M. D., The Association of Nocturnal Angina Pectoris with Dreaming. *Clin. Research.* 13: 2, April, 1965.

Palestini, M., Pisano, G., Rosadini, G., and Rossi, G. F., Visual Cortical Responses Evoked by Stimulating Lateral Geniculate Body and Optic Radiations in Awake and Sleeping Cats. *Exper. Neurol.*, Jan. 9, 1964.

Parmeggiani, P. L., and Zanocco, G., A Study on the Bio-Electrical Rhythms of Cortical and Subcortical Structures During Activated Sleep. *Arch. Ital. Biol.* 101: 385, 1963.

Parmeggiani, P. L., Hippocampal Theta Rhythm and Neocortical Responses to Photic Stimuli. *Helv. Physiol. Pharm. Acta.* 20: 71, 1962.

Parmelee, A. H., Wenner, W. H., and Schulz, H. R., Infant Sleep Patterns: From Birth to 16 Weeks of Age. *J. Pediat.* 65: 576, 1964.

Parmelee, A. H., and Wenner, W. H., Sleep States in Premature and Full Term Newborn Infants. Association for the Psychophysiological Study of Sleep, Washington, D. C., 1965.

Petsche, H., Stumpf, C., and Gogolak, G., The Significance of the Rabbit's Septum as a Relay Station Between the Midbrain and the Hippocampus. *EEG clin. Neurophysiol.* 14: 202, 1962.

Pierce, C. M., Mathis, J. L., and Jabbour, J. T., Dream Patterns in Narcoleptic and Hydranencephalic Patients. *Am. Psychiat. Assn.*, New York, May, 1965.

Pompeiano, O., The Neurophysiological Bases for Alterations of Muscle Activity During Desynchronized Sleep. In *Sleep and Altered States of Consciousness,* 45th Annual Meeting of the Assn. for Research in Nervous and Mental Disease, New York, December, 1965.

Rechtschaffen, A., Cornwall, P., and Zimmerman, W., Brain Temperature Variations with Paradoxical Sleep in the Cat. Association for the Psychophysiological Study of Sleep, Washington, D. C., 1965.

Reite, M., Rhodes, J. M., Kavan, E., and Adey, W. R., Normal Sleep Patterns in Macaque Monkey. *Arch. Neurol.* 12: 133-144, 1965.

Roffwarg, H. P., Dement, W. C., and Fisher, C., Preliminary Observations on the Sleep-Dream Patterns in Neonates, Infants, Children and Adults. In Harms, E. (ed.), *Problems of Sleep and Dreams in Children.* Pergamon, London, 1963.

Roffwarg, H. P., Dement, W. C., Muzio, J. N., and Fisher, C., Dream Imagery: Relationship to Rapid Eye Movements of Sleep. *Arch. Gen. Psychiat.* 7: 235-258, 1962.

Roffwarg, H. P., Muzio, J. N., and Dement, W. C., Ontogenetic Development of the Human Sleep-Dream Cycle. *Science.* In press.

Roldan, E., Weiss, T., and Fifkova, E., Excitability Changes During the Sleep Cycle of the Rat. *EEG clin. Neurophysiol.* 15: 775-785, 1963.

Rossi, G. F., Favale, E., Hara, T., Giussani, A., and Sacco, G., Researches in the Nervous Mechanisms Underlying Deep Sleep in the Cat. *Arch. Ital. Biol.* 99: 270-292, 1961.

Sampson, H., Deprivation of Dreaming Sleep by Two Methods. *Arch. Gen. Psychiat.* 13, July, 1965.

Scheibel, M. E., and Scheibel, A. B., Some Structuro-Functional Correlates of Development in Young Cats. *EEG clin. Neurophysiol.* Supp. 24, 235, 1963.

Scott, J., Blood Plasma Free Fatty Acid Levels During Sleep. Association for the Psychophysiological Study of Sleep, Palo Alto, 1964.

Segundo, J. P., Moore, G. P., Stensaas, L. J., and Bullock, T. H., Sensitivity of Neurones in Aplysia to Temporal Pattern of Arriving Impulses. *J. Exp. Biol.* 40: 643-667, 1963.

Snyder, F., The New Biology of Dreaming, *Arch. Gen. Psychiat.* 8: 381-391, 1963.

Snyder, F., Progress in the New Biology of Dreaming. *Am. J. Psychiat.* 122: 14: 377-391, 1965.

Snyder, F., The Organismic State Associated with Dreaming. In Greenfield, N. S., and Lewis, W. C. (eds.), *Psychoanalysis and Current Biological Thought.* University of Wisconsin Press, 1965.

Snyder, F., Hobson, J. A., Morrison, D. R., and Goldfrank, F., Changes in Respiration, Heart Rate, and Systolic Blood Pressure in Human Sleep. *J. Appl. Physiol.* 19: 417-422, 1964.

Snyder, F., The REM State in a Living Fossil. Association for the Psychophysiological Study of Sleep, Palo Alto, 1964.

Stoyva, J., Kamiya, J., and Forsyth, R., Observations of Blood Pressure and Heart Rate in the Sleeping Macaca Mulatta. Associaiton for the Psychophysiological Study of Sleep, Washington, D. C., 1965.

Tyler, F. M., Migeon, C., Florentin, A. A., and Samuels, L. T., The Diurnal Variation of 17-Hydroxycorticosteroid Levels in Plasma. *J. Clin. Endocrinol.* 14: 774, 1954.

Valatx, J. L., Jouvet, D., and Jouvet, M., Evolution Electroencephalographique des Differents Etats de Sommeil chez le Chaton. *EEG clin. Neurophysiol.* 17: 218-233, 1964.

Valenstein, E. S., and Valenstein, T., Interaction of Positive and Negative Reinforcing Neural Systems. *Science* 145: 1456-1458, 1964.

Valleala, P., and Evarts, E. V., The Temporal Relation of Unit-Discharge in Visual Cortex and Activity of the Extraocular Muscles During Sleep. Association for the Psychophysiological Study of Sleep, Washington, D. C., 1965.

Vaughan, C. J., The Development and Use of an Operant Technique to Provide Evidence for Visual Imagery in the Rhesus Monkey under "Sensory Deprivation." Unpublished Ph.D. thesis, University of Pittsburgh, 1964.

Walsh, J. T., and Cordeau, J. P., Responsiveness in the Visual System During Various Phases of Sleep and Wakefulness. *Exper. Neurol.* 11:80, 1965.

Weitzman, E. D., Fishbein, W., and Graziani, L., Auditory Evoked Responses

Obtained from Scalp of the Full Term New-born Human During Sleep. *Pediatrics* 35: 458-462, 1965.

Weitzman, E. D., A Note on the EEG and Eye Movements During Behavioral Sleep in Monkeys. *EEG clin. Neurophysiol.* 13: 790, 1961.

Weitzman, E. D., Schaumberg, H., and Fishbein, W., Plasma 17-Hydroxycorticosteroid Levels During Sleep in Man. Association for the Psychophysiological Study of Sleep, Washington, D. C., 1965.

Woods, L. W., Tyce, F. A. J., and Bickford, R. G., Electric Sleep-Producing Devices, an Evaluation Using EEG Monitoring. *Am. J. Psychiat.* 122: 153-158, August, 1965.

Yokota, T., and Fujimori, B., Effects of Brain-Stem Stimulation upon Hippocampal Electrical Activity, Somatomotor Reflexes and Autonomic Functions. *The EEG Journal* 16: 375, 1964.

Zanchetti, A., Electroencephalographic Activation During Sleep After Destruction of the Midbrain-Limbic Pathways in the Cat. Association for the Psychophysiological Study of Sleep, New York, 1963.

CHAPTER X

References for the General Reader:

De La Mare, W., *Behold This Dreamer!* Knopf, New York, 1939.

Hall, C. S., *The Meaning of Dreams.* Dell, New York, 1959.

Hall, C. S., and Van de Castle, R. L., *The Content Analysis of Dreams.* Appleton-Century-Crofts, 1965.

Woods, R. L., *The World of Dreams.* Random House, New York, 1947.

Additional References:

Antrobus, J. S., Dement, W. C., and Fisher, C., Patterns of Dreaming and Dream Recall: EEG Study. *J. Abnorm. Soc. Psychol.* 69: 341, 1964.

Bastos, O., Dream Activity in Depressive States. *Psychiat. Digest.* 26: 8, August, 1965.

Benedek, T., An Investigation of the Sexual Cycle in Women. *Arch. Gen. Psychiat.* 8, April, 1963.

Berger, R. J., Experimental Modification of Dream Content by Meaningful Visual Stimuli. *Brit. J. Psychiat.* 109: 722-740, 1963.

Bertini, M., Lewis, H. B., and Witkin, H. A., Some Preliminary Observations with an Experimental Procedure for the Study of Hypnogogic and Related Phenomena. *Archivio di Psicologia Neurologia e Psichiatria* 25: 492-534, 1964.

Bokert, E., Effects of Thirst and a Meaningfully Related Auditory Stimulus on Dream Reports. Unpublished Ph.D. thesis, New York University, 1965.

Dement, W. C., Kahn, E., and Roffwarg, H. P., The Influence of the Laboratory Situation on the Dreams of the Experimental Subject. *J. Nerv. Ment. Dis.* 140: 119-131, 1965.

Dement, W. C., and Wolpert, E. A., Relationships in the Manifest Content of Dreams Occurring on the Same Night. *J. Nerv. Ment. Dis.* 126: 568, 1958.

Dement, W. C., and Wolpert, E. A., The Relationship of Eye Movement, Body Motility, and External Stimuli to Dream Content. *J. Exp. Psychol.* 55: 543-553, 1958.

Domhoff, B., and Kamiya, J., Problems in Dream Content Study with Objective Indicators. A Comparison of Home and Laboratory Dream Reports. *Arch. Gen. Psychiat.* 11: 519, 1964.

Fisher, C., *Dreaming and Sexuality*. International Universities Press, New York, 1966.

Fisher, C., Psychoanalytic Implications of Recent Research on Sleep and Dreaming. *J. Am. Psychoanal. Assn.*, April, 1965.

Foulkes, D., Dream Reports from Different Stages of Sleep. *J. Abnorm. Soc. Psychol.* 65: 14-25, 1962.

Foulkes, D., Theories of Dream Formation and Recent Studies of Sleep Consciousness. *Psychol. Bull.* 62: 236-247, 1964.

Foulkes, D., and Rechtschaffen, A., Presleep Determinants of Dream Content: The Effects of Two Films. *Percept. Mot. Skills.* 19: 983-1005, 1964.

Freud, S., *The Interpretation of Dreams*. Science Editions, John Wiley & Sons, New York, 1960.

Fromm, E., *The Forgotten Language*. Holt, Rinehart & Winston, 1951.

Goodenough, D. R., Lewis, H. B., Shapiro, A., Jaret, L., and Sleser, I., Dream Reporting Following Abrupt and Gradual Awakenings from Different Types of Sleep. *J. Pers. Soc. Psychol.* 2: 170-179, 1965.

Goodenough, D. R., Shapiro, A., Holden, M., and Steinschriber, L., A Comparison of "Dreamers" and "Nondreamers": Eye Movements, Electroencephalograms, and the Recall of Dreams. *J. Abnorm. Soc. Psychol.* 62: 295-302, 1959.

Hall, C. S., and Van de Castle, R. L., A Comparison of Home and Monitored Dreams. Association for the Psychophysiological Study of Sleep, Palo Alto, 1964.

Hall, C. S., and Domhoff, B., A Ubiquitous Sex Difference in Dreams. *J. Abnorm. Soc. Psychol.* 66: 278, 1963.

Hernandez-Peon, R., A Neurophysiological Model of Dreams and Hallucinations. *J. Nerv. Ment. Dis.*, December, 1965.

Jung, C. G., *Freud and Psychoanalysis*. Vol. 4., *The Collected Works of C. G. Jung*, Pantheon, 1961.

Kahn, E., Dement, W. C., Fisher, C., and Barmack, J., Incidence of Color in Immediately Recalled Dreams. *Science* 137: 1054, 1962.

Karacan, I., The Effect of Exciting Presleep Events on Dream Reporting and Penile Erections During Sleep. Unpublished thesis, Psychiatry Department, State University of New York, Downstate Medical Center, Brooklyn, 1965.

Keller, H., *The World I Live In*. The Century Co., 1936.

Kety, S. S., A Biologist Examines the Mind and Behavior. *Science* 132: 1861, 1960.

Lewin, B. D., *The Psychoanalysis of Elation*. Norton, 1950.

Lewis, H. B., Bertini, M., and Witkin, H. A., Hypnogogic Reverie and Subsequent Dreams. Association for the Psychophysiological Study of Sleep, Palo Alto, 1964.

Monroe, L. J., Rechtschaffen, A., Foulkes, D., and Jensen, J., The Discriminability of REM and NREM Reports. *J. Pers. Soc. Psychol.* In press.

Offenkrantz, W., and Wolpert, E., The Detection of Dreaming in a Congenitally Blind Subject. *J. Nerv. Ment. Dis.* 136: 88-90, 1963.

Offenkrantz, W., and Rechtschaffen, A., Clinical Studies of Sequential Dreams: I. A Patient in Psychotherapy. *Arch. Gen. Psychiat.* 8: 497-508, 1963.

Portnoff, G., Baekland, F., Goodenough, D. R., Karacan, I., and Shapiro, A., The Effect of Sleep on Retention. Association for the Psychophysiological Study of Sleep, Washington, D. C., 1965.

Rechtschaffen, A., and Foulkes, D., The Effect of Visual Stimuli on Dream Content. *Percept. Mot. Skills* 20: 1149-1160, 1965.

Rechtschaffen, A., and Verdone, P., Amount of Dreaming: Effect of Incentive, Adaptation to Laboratory, and Individual Differences. *Percept. Mot. Skills* 19: 947-958, 1964.

Rechtschaffen, A., Verdone, P., and Wheaton, J., Reports of Mental Activity During Sleep. *Canad. Psychiat. Assn. J.* 8: 409-414, 1963.

Rechtschaffen, A., Vogel, G., and Shaikun, G., Interrelatedness of Mental Activity During Sleep. *Arch. Gen. Psychiat.* 9: 536-547, 1963.

Shapiro, A., Goodenough, D. R., and Gryler, R. B., Dream Recall as a Function of Method of Awakening. *Psychosom. Med.* 25: 174-180, 1963.

Shapiro, A., Goodenough, D. R., Biederman, I., and Sleser, I., Dream Recall and the Physiology of Sleep. *J. Appl. Physiol.* 19: 778-783, 1964.

Stoyva, J., Posthypnotically Suggested Dreams and the Sleep Cycle. *Arch. Gen. Psychiat.* 12: 287-294, 1965.

Tart, C. T., Frequency of Dream Recall and Some Personality Measures. *J. Consult. Psychol.* 26: 467, 1962.

Tart, C. T., A Comparison of Suggested Dreams Occurring in Hypnosis and Sleep. *Inter. J. Clin. Exp. Hypnosis* 12: 263-389, 1964.

Tart, C. T., Toward the Experimental Control of Dreaming: A Review of the Literature. *Psych. Bull.*, Vol. 64, August, 1965.

Tauber, E. S., and Green, M. R., *Prelogical Experience.* Basic Books, New York, 1959.

Trosman, H., Rechtschaffen, A., Offenkrantz, W., and Wolpert, E. A., Studies in Psychophysiology of Dreams: IV. Relations Among Dreams in Sequence. *Arch. Gen. Psychiat.* 3: 602-607, 1960.

Verdone, P. P., Variables Related to the Temporal Reference of Manifest Dream Content. *Percept. Mot. Skills* 20: 1253, 1965.

Whitman, R. M., Remembering and Forgetting Dreams in Psychoanalysis. *J. Am. Psychoanal. Assn.* 7: 759-774, 1959.

Whitman, R. M., Ornstein, P., Kramer, M., and Baldridge, B., Hypnotic Conflict Implantation and Dream Formation. Association for the Psychophysiological Study of Sleep, New York, 1963.

Whitman, R. M., Pierce, C., Maas, J., and Baldridge, B., Drugs and Dreams: II. Imipramine and Prochlorperazine. *Comp. Psychiat.* 2: 219-226, 1961.

Whitman, R. M., Pierce, C., Maas, J., and Baldridge, B., The Dreams of the Experimental Subject. *J. Nerv. Ment. Dis.* 134: 431-439, 1962.

Witkin, H. A., and Lewis, H. B., The Relation of Experimentally Induced Presleep Experiences to Dreams: A Report on Methods and Preliminary Findings. *J. Am. Psychoanalyt. Assn.*, October, 1965.

Wood, P. B., Dreaming and Social Isolation. Unpublished Ph.D. Dissertation. University of North Carolina, 1962.

Wolpert, E. A., and Trosman, H., Studies in Psychophysiology of Dreams: I. Experimental Evocation of Sequential Dream Episodes. *Arch. Neurol. Psychiat.* 79: 603-606, 1958.

CHAPTER XI

References for the General Reader:

Brierley, N., *Learn While You Sleep.* Ward Lock & Co. Ltd., London, 1965.

Kasamatsu, A., and Hirai, T., An Electroencephalographic Study of Zazen. In *Zen: The Way to a Happy Life.* Soto Zen Sect, Kasai Publishing and Printing Co., Tokyo, 1963.

Additional References:

Antrobus, J., Discrimination of EEG Sleep Stages I-REM vs. II. Association for the Psychophysiological Study of Sleep, Washington, D. C., 1965.

Antrobus, J. S., Antrobus, J., and Fisher, C., Discrimination of Dreaming and Non-dreaming Sleep. *Arch. Gen. Psychiat.* 12: 395-401, 1965.

Antrobus, J. S., Antrobus, J., and Singer, J. L., Eye Movements Accompanying Daydreaming, Visual Imagery, and Thought Suppression. *J. Abnorm. Soc. Psychol.* 59: 244-252, 1964.

Arduini, A., and Hirao, T., On the Mechanism of the Sleep Pattern Elicited by Acute Visual Deafferentation. *Arch. Ital. Biol.* 97: 140, 1959.

Aserinsky, E., The Brainwave Pattern During the Rapid Eye Movement Period of Sleep. *The Physiologist* 8: 104, 1965.

Beh, H. C., and Barratt, P. E. H., Discrimination and Conditioning During Sleep as Indicated by the Electroencephalogram. *Science* 147: 1470-1471, 1965.

Buendia, N., Sierra, G., Goode, M., and Segundo, J. P., Conditioned and Discriminatory Responses in Wakeful and in Sleeping Cats. *EEG clin. Neurophysiol.* Supp. 24, 199-218, 1963.

Clemente, C. D., Sterman, M. B., and Wyrwicka, W., Forebrain Inhibitory Mechanism: Conditioning of Basal Forebrain Induced EEG Synchronization and Sleep. *Exp. Neurol.* 7, 1963.

Clemente, C. D., and Sterman, M. B., Cortical Synchronization and Sleep Patterns in Acute Restrained and Chronic Behaving Cats Induced by Basal Forebrain Stimulation. *EEG clin. Neurophysiol.* Suppl. 24, 1963.

Cobb, J., Evans, F., Gustafson, L., O'Connell, D. N., Orne, M., and Shor, R., Specific Motor Responses During Sleep to Sleep-Administered Meaningful Suggestion: An Exploratory Investigation. *Percept. Mot. Skills* 20: 629-636, 1965.

Das, N. N., and Gastaut, H., Variations de l'Activité Electrique du Cerveau, du Coeur, et des Muscles Squelettiques au Cours de la Meditation et de l'Extase Yogique. *EEG clin. Neurophysiol.* Suppl. 6: 211, 1957.

Emmons, W. H., and Simon, C. W., The Nonrecall of Material Presented During Sleep. *Am. J. Psychol.* 69: 76-81, 1956.

Evans, F. J., Gustafson, L., O'Connell, D. N., Orne, M. T., and Shor, R. E., Specific Motor Response During Sleep to Sleep-Administered Meaningful Suggestions: Further Explorations. Association for the Psychophysiological Study of Sleep, Washington, D. C., 1965.

Fiss, H., Klein, G. S., and Bokert, E., Waking Fantasies Following Interruption of Two Types of Sleep. *Arch. Gen. Psychiat.* In press.

Granda, A. M., and Hammack, J. T., Operant Behavior During Sleep. *Science* 133: 1485-1486, 1961.

Hammack, J. T., Williams, J. M., Weisberg, P., Brooks, P., and Gerard, M., An Experimental Analysis of Behavior During Sleep. U. S. Army Medical Research and Development Command, 1964, Contract. No. Da-49-193-MD-2180.

Hess, E. H., and Polt, J. M., Pupil Size in Relation to Mental Activity During Simple Problem-Solving. *Science* 140: 1190, 1964.

Izquierdo, I., Wyrwicka, W., Sierra, G., and Segundo, J. P., Establishment of Trace Reflexes During Natural Sleep in the Cat. In Masson et Cie, *Actualites Neurophysiologiques.* In press.

Jeanneret, P. R., and Webb, W. B., Strength of Grip on Arousal from a Full Night's Sleep. *Percept. Mot. Skills* 17: 759, 1963.

Kamiya, J., Conditioned Discrimination of the EEG Alpha Rhythm in Humans. Western Psychological Assn., 1962.

Klausner, S. Z., *The Quest for Self Control.* Free Press, Chicago, 1964.

Konstantinovskii, M., Soviet Research on Teaching During Sleep: Kiev Higher Radiotechnical Engineering School Teaches English During Sleep: and Development of a Method of Teaching During Sleep. Aug., 1964. TT: 64-41166, JPRS: 25895. Clearinghouse for Federal Scientific and Technical Information, Springfield, Va., 22151.

Kulikov, V. N., On the Problem of Hypnopedia. *Soviet Psychol. & Psychiat.* 3: 13-22, 1964.

Levitt, R. A., Sleep as a Conditioned Response. *Psychon. Sci.* 1: 273-274, 1964.

McCulloch, W., *Conference on Cypernetics,* p. 170. Josiah Macy Jr. Foundation, New York, 1949.

Mulholland, T. B., and Runnals, S., The Effect of Voluntarily Directed Attention on Successive Cortical Activation Responses. *J. of Psychol.* 55: 427-436, 1963.

Mulholland, T. B., Occurrence of the Electroencephalographic Alpha Rhythm with Eyes Open. *Nature* 206: 746, May 15, 1965.

Mulholland, T. B., and Evans, C. R., An Unexpected Artefact in the Human Electroencephalogram Concerning the Alpha Rhythm and the Orientation of the Eyes. *Nature* 207, July 3, 1965.

O'Connell, D. N., and Orne, M. T., Bioelectric Correlates of Hypnosis: An Experimental Reevaluation. *Psychiat. Res.* 1: 201-213, 1962.

Oswald, I., Taylor, A. M., and Treisman, M., Discriminative Responses to Stimulation During Human Sleep. *Brain* 82: 440-453, 1960.

Oswald, I., The Experimental Study of Sleep. *Brit. Med. Bull.* 20: 1, 1964.

Rasmussen, T., and Penfield, W., Movement of Head and Eyes from Stimulation of the Human Frontal Cortex. *Ass. Res. Nerv. Dis. Proc.* 27: 346, 1948.

Razran, G., The Observable Unconscious and the Inferrable Conscious in Current Soviet Psychophysiology: Interoceptive Conditioning, Semantic Conditioning, and the Orienting Reflex. *Psychol. Rev.* 68, March, 1961.

Segundo, J. P., A Hypothesis Concerning the Sharp Pitch Discrimination Observed in the Sleeping Cat. *Experientia* 20: 415, 1964.

Simon, C. W., and Emmons, W. H., Responses to Material Presented During Various Levels of Sleep. *J. Exp. Psychol.* 51: 89-97, 1956.

Simon, C. W., Some Immediate Effects of Drowsiness and Sleep on Normal Human Performance. *Human Factors* 3, 1961.

Simon, C. W., and Emmons, W. H., Learning During Sleep. *Psychol. Bull.* 52: 328-342, 1955.

Simon, C. W., and Emmons, W. H., EEG, Consciousness, and Sleep. *Science* 124: 1066-1069, 1956.

Sterman, M. B., and Clemente, C. D., Forebrain Inhibitory Mechanisms: Cortical Synchronization Induced by Basal Forebrain Stimulation. *Exp. Neurol.* 6: 91-102, 1962.

Svyadoshch, A. M., Perception and Memory of Speech During Natural Sleep. *Voprosy Psikhologii,* 1:1, No. 3-9-64, Transl. Unit, NIH., 1962.

Webb, W. B., Antecedents of Sleep. *J. Exp. Psychol.* 53: 162, 1957.

Webb, W. B., and Agnew, H. W., Reaction Time and Social Response Efficiency on Arousal from Sleep. *Percept. Mot. Skills* 18: 783, 1964.

Wenger, M. A., Bagchi, B. K., and Anand, B. K., Experiments in India on "Voluntary" Control of the Heart and Pulse. *Circulation* 24: December, 1961.

Wyrwicka, W., Sterman, M. B., and Clemente, C. D., Conditioning of Induced

Electroencephalographic Sleep Patterns in the Cat. *Science* 137: 616-618, 1962.

Yogananda, P., *Autobiography of a Yogi.* Self-Realization Fellowship, Los Angeles, 1959.

Zung, W. K., and Wilson W. P., Response to Auditory Stimulation During Sleep. *Arch. Gen. Psychiat.* 4: 548-552, 1961.

Zung, W. K., and Wilson, W. P., Auditory Stimuli Discrimination During Sleep. *EEG clin. Neurophysiol.* 13: 313, 1961.

CHAPTER XII

Basic Problems of the Electrophysiology of the Central Nervous System. (Compilation of abstracts surveying Soviet-bloc scientific and technical literature) ATD- P 65, August, 1965, Aerospace Technology Division, Library of Congress, ATD-U-64-76, 17 July, 1964.

Ackner, B., and Pampiglione, G., Some Relationships Between Peripheral Vasomotor and EEG Changes, *J. Neurol. Neurosurg. Psychiat.* 20: 58, 1957.

Bell, C., Sierra, G., Buendia, N., and Segundo, J. P., Sensory Properties of Units in Mesencephalic Reticular Formation. *J. Neurophysiol.* 27, 961, 1964.

Guazzi, M., and Zanchetti, A., Carotid Sinus and Aortic Reflexes in the Regulation of Circulation During Sleep. *Science* 148: 397, 1965.

Kety, S. S., Sleep and the Energy Metabolism of the Brain. In Wolstenholme, G. E. W., and O'Connor, M. (eds.), *The Nature of Sleep.* Little Brown, 1960.

Klosovskii, B. N., and Kosmarskaya, E. N., Changes in the Temperature of the Brain and of the Body During Sleep Inhibition. Structural Alterations in Nerve Cells Characteristic of Sleep-Induced Inhibition During Ontogenesis. Changes in the Vascular Capillary Network of the Cerebral Cortex During Sleep Inhibition. In *Excitatory and Inhibitory States of the Brain.* OTS 63-11176, Office of Technical Services, U. S. Dept. Commerce, 1963.

Moruzzi, G., The Physiology of Sleep. *Endeavour* 22: 31-36, 1963.

Moruzzi, G., Active Processes in the Brain Stem During Sleep. *The Harvey Lecture Series, 58.* Academic Press, 1962.

Rossi, G. F., A Hypothesis on the Neural Basis of Consciousness. *Acta Neurochirurgica,* Vol. 12, Fasc. 2, 1964.

Weinberger, N. M., and Lindsley, D. B., Behavioral and Electroencephalographic Arousal to Contrasting Novel Stimulations. *Science* 144: 1355, 1964.

INDEX